CHINA'S SCIENCE POLICY
IN THE 80s

Tony Saich

Sinologisch Instituit, Leiden

Studies on East Asia

MANCHESTER UNIVERSITY PRESS

First published in 1989 in Great Britain by
Manchester University Press
Oxford Road
Manchester M13 9PL

Not for sale in North America

Editorial responsibility for *Studies on East Asia* rests with the East Asia Centre,
University of Newcastle upon Tyne, England, which promotes publications
on the individual countries and culture of East Asia,
as well as on the region as a whole.

British Library Cataloguing in Publication Data
Saich, Tony
China's science policy in the 8os.
(Studies on East Asia)
1. Science and state — China
I. Title   II. Series
5091'.51
ISBN 0-7190-2986-4

Printed in Great Britain by Billing & Sons Ltd., Worcester

CONTENTS

ABBREVIATIONS

BR – Beijing Review (formerly Peking Review)
CAS – The Chinese Academy of Sciences
CAST – Chinese Association for Science and Technology
CCP – Chinese Communist Party
CD – China Daily
CEN – China Exchange News
FBIS – Foreign Broadcast Information Service
GMRB – Guangming Ribao
JPRS – Joint Publications Research Services
KXX – Kexuexue yu Kexue Jishu Guanli
KYGL – Keyan Guanli
PR – Peking Review (later Beijing Review)
PRC – People's Republic of China
R&D – Research and Development
RMRB – Renmin Ribao
S&T – Science and Technology
SSTC – State Science and Technology Commission
STLG – Science and Technology Leading Group
SWB:FE – Summary of World Broadcasts: the Far East
TDC – Technology Development Centre

INTRODUCTION

Science and Technology (S&T) are seen by China's current leadership as the key to its modernisation programme. Although their modernisation comes last in the list of the 'Four Modernisations' – the modernisation of agriculture, industry, national defence, and science and technology[1] – they are seen by China's rulers as the foundation stones on which the modernisation of the other three sectors will be built. While much attention has been paid to the reforms of the agricultural and industrial sectors,[2] relatively little notice has been taken by Western writers of the reform of the S&T sector.[3] Also, much of what has been written takes as its focus the question of technology transfer. This is assuredly an important topic, but whether China is capable of achieving its ambitious modernisation programme will depend, to a large degree, on the progress made in developing its indigenous S&T sector.

The specific focus of this study is an analysis of the attempted reforms of the civilian S&T research system and the constraints on that system. China's current development strategy means that more than ever before the leadership is dependent on expert advice to make sure that policies devised are the correct ones and that they are properly implemented. Faced with the prospects of feeding a massive and growing population, and presuming that China does not adopt a policy of large-scale food importation, the country must make rapid economic progress simply to stand still. The key role which S&T plays in promoting economic development is now clearly recognised. To help that sector play more fully this role the CCP is granting it more autonomy of operation within broadly defined guidelines. To be sure, as in other countries, the military plays a key role and consumes a large percentage of both funds and personnel within the S&T sector. However, an in-depth analysis of the military S&T system is beyond the scope of this particular study.[4] It will be touched on where relevant to the focus of this study; for example, with respect to the attempts to transfer military technology and personnel to the civilian sector.

The recognition of the major role that improvements in the S&T sector can play in promoting economic growth has led China's leaders to prompt a wholesale re-think about the system. During the eighties, the PRC has embarked on wide-ranging experimentation with reforms culminating in March 1985 with the adoption of the Party Central Committee 'Decision on the Reform of the Science and Technology Management System.'[5] The promulgation of this document is the result of a summing up by the Party of an extended period of experimentation. The 'Decision' provides a good focal point for assessing the Party's view of the reform process to date and how it would like to see it progress further.

Before outlining the structure of the book, it is worth considering briefly why a study of the capability of China's indigenous S&T sector should be so important.

For a developing country, perhaps the most important reason is that a strong indigenous S&T capability not only decreases dependence on the more technologically advanced nations but, even more importantly, it can make sure that imported technology is best suited to the country's needs and that it can be exploited fully. As King and Lemma remark, the successful use of foreign technology is far more than a matter of access to foreign patents and know-how, or even the availability of capital to exploit them.[6]

The policy pursued in 1977 and 1978 entailing the large-scale purchase of whole plants and advanced technology from the West did not provide the hoped-for benefits largely because China's technical capacity for assimilation was inadequate. The hope was that the imports would enable China to catch up with the West, in certain fields, within a relatively short space of time; the failure of the policy made the leadership realise that modernisation would entail a long, up-hill struggle. In fact, the programme of technology importation began in 1972, and as Conroy has observed

> while technology imports during the 1970s did result in significant increases in production capacity of certain sectors, absorption and diffusion activities were neglected. Domestic technological development directly attributable to these imports was marginal, or even negative if the possible returns on alternative uses of the investment are considered.[7]

Thus, China ran into the problem common to most developing countries that the technology being imported was inappropriate to the country's actual needs and situation.[8] The difficulties encountered forced the leadership to recognise that the successful assimilation of foreign technology is dependent on the creation of an effective indigenous network that provides the nation with the ability to analyse the current state of S&T developments throughout the world, enabling the information to be sifted and appropriate processes and products to be selected. Developing countries can profit greatly from the accumulated world scientific knowledge as by tradition most results of basic scientific research are openly published and thus available for those with the necessary skills to determine their significance. With respect to technical knowledge, the situation is somewhat different as this is rarely a 'free commodity' but is usually possessed by corporations or states. Yet, if the price is right, it is invariably for sale, but someone needs to be able to assess whether it is appropriate and whether the price is indeed right. Further, the existence of a good S&T network means that the technology imported can be properly integrated into the local economy and that it can be modified to make use of local raw materials and skills.

Using resources to develop the indigenous S&T system has other advantages, both economic and political.[9] It would enable the necessary knowledge and skills to be developed that would make local scientific discovery and technical innovation easier to achieve. This would reduce the dependence of China on the technologically advanced countries. This would be attractive to China for economic reasons (saving foreign currency earnings), political reasons (reducing the risk of being held to ransom), and cultural reasons (reducing the feeling of being dependent on foreigners who have long been considered inferior).

This is not to deny the fact that 'borrowed technologies' play an important role in promoting economic development in the 'borrowing' country, but suggests that a more carefully co-ordinated approach should be taken to the import of technology. Some writers suggest that Japan's experience in this respect could provide valuable lessons for developing countries. Essentially in Japan, the import of foreign technology has not been used as a substitute for the development of an indigenous capability but as a basis for it.[10] Indeed, such a view has also been put forward in China. For example, in 1978 at the height of the rush to import technology, one writer noted explicitly Japan's experience and suggested that the aim of China's strategy should be to improve and develop imported technologies with the objective of becoming a technology exporter.[11]

Chapter One of this study provides the necessary background for the more specific subsequent chapters by tracing the broad outlines of the development of S&T policy since the death of Mao Zedong. It details the rise and fall of the initial, ambitious post-Mao policies and the adoption of a new strategy for economic development within which S&T would play a key role. By 1981 it was clear that a resurrection of the pre-Cultural Revolution S&T system was not enough and it was recognised that a 'scientific miracle' could not be expected that would overnight transform the economy. The basic criticism levelled at the system was that its work was not sufficiently linked to the needs of the economy and society. Policies were devised to try to forge much closer links between these sectors. This has meant that more emphasis has been placed on applied and developmental research, the results of which can be fed more quickly into production.

Chapters Two and Three look at the question of organisational reform. The former concentrates on the new types of organisations developing as a result of the attempts to link the research to the production sector. The latter examines the impact of the reforms on the already existing organisational structure.

According to Berliner, the main factors that affect the capacity for innovation in any economic system are the organisational structure, prices, incentives and the decision-making system.[12] In a state-socialist society, these are defined by the Party-state apparatus that provides a definition producing a highly rigid bureaucratised structure, the inflexibility of which makes it very difficult for sustained technical innovation to take place. China's reform programme is designed to trim the excesses of this situation by bringing greater flexibility to the organisational framework.

Organisational reform has been clearly identified by Deng Xiaoping and his supporters as a key area. There has been a re-think about organisation in the broadest sense and there has not been one area left untouched by the current reform drive. In the academic sphere, this is reflected in the current obsession with management theory, systems theory and the 'science of science'.[13] In the practical sphere, Deng Xiaoping has called for a 'revolution against the administrative system.' He and his followers clearly feel that the organisational structure as it existed in the late seventies was inadequate for devising and implementing the necessary programmes to realise the 'Four Modernisations.' Technological progress and organisational development are seen as being interrelated and interdependent. Attention will be paid to the ways in which China is trying to ensure that such innovation as does take place in research laboratories finds its way more quickly into production.[14]

Chapters Four and Five look at the two crucial areas of financing S&T and the personnel system. Unlike the Soviet Union and most East European countries which have been able to switch from a basically quantitative approach to S&T development to a qualitative one, China must pursue both. Both the level of financing and the number of qualified personnel are far too low to be able to meet the requirements of China's planned reforms. With respects to finance, attempts have been made to increase state expenditure on S&T development. However, it is recognised that such spending is and will remain too low for the foreseeable future. This means that measures must be introduced to ensure that state allocations are put to the most effective use and that new channels for funding scientific research and development be found.

According to Volti, 'technological advance is precipitated on the diffusion of specialised knowledge' which means that 'no nation can afford to ignore the necessity of continuous capital formation.'[15] Unfortunately, during the Cultural Revolution decade (1966–1976) China did ignore this necessity. This means that at a time when policy requires increased numbers of technically qualified people to manage it the country finds itself faced with a severe shortage of talent. As a result, China is now engaged in an attempt to train sufficiently large numbers of skilled people. Given the numerical shortage, the quality of the existing personnel and their optimal use become of paramount importance. Concern has been expressed about the irrational structure of the personnel system and reforms have been introduced to alter the structure and to encourage greater mobility. The efficacy of such reforms will be considered as well as the measures introduced to improve the political standing and material conditions of intellectuals whose full participation is vital to the success of the current reform programme.

Chapter Six tries to situate the reform of the civilian S&T system within the context of the reform programme as a whole. While the role of S&T is recognised as being crucial to the development of the economy, both internal and external constraints prevent the sector from playing its full role. While Chapters Two to Five look at internal constraints, the final chapter considers external economic and political constraints. The reform of the S&T sector is not taking place in isolation. Whether industry comes in search of new technology will depend not only on innovation within the S&T sector but also on reforms of the economic structure making it financially worthwhile. It also depends on a new breed of manager being appointed to run enterprises who can take full advantage of the increase in enterprise autonomy and the limited experiments with the use of market forces. Whether scientists and research institutes can play their full role will depend largely on the Party being able to create and maintain an atmosphere conducive to research. This requires the Party trying to strike a difficult balance between increasing the autonomy of those engaged in scientific work and maintaining the necessary minimum of central control and guidance.

Notes

1   This programme had been put forward in January 1975 by the then Premier, Zhou Enlai, but fell into disuse during the subsequent succession struggles. Its early revival after Mao Zedong's death and the arrest of the 'Gang of Four' indicated the new leadership's intention to deal with the pressing economic problems. See Zhou Enlai, 'Report on the Work of the Government, January 13 1975' in *Documents of the First Session of the Fourth National People's Congress of the People's Republic of China* (Beijing: Foreign Languages Press, 1975), p 55.

2   Modernisation of the military sector has clearly taken a back seat, a fact that has caused frustrations within the powerful sector.

3   Notable exceptions are the works of Conroy, Orleans, Simon and Suttmeier.

4   For a review of this sector see W T Tow, 'Science and Technology in China's Defense', *Problems of Communism*, July-August 1985, pp 15-31.

5   'Zhongguo zhongyang guanyu kexue jishu tizhi gaige de jueding' ('Decision of the Central Committee of the Communist Party of China on the Reform of the Science and Technology Management System'), *Renmin Ribao*, 20 March 1985, pp 1 and 3.

6   A King and A Lemma, 'Science and Technology for Development', in M Goldsmith and A King (eds), *Issues of Development: Towards a New Role for Science and Technology* (Oxford: Pergamon Press, 1979), p 21.

7   R P Conroy, 'Technological Change and Industrial Development' in G Young (ed), *China: Dilemmas of Modernisation* (London: Croom Helm, 1985), p 134.

8   For a useful summary of what is usually meant by inappropriate technology in this context see C Cooper, 'Science, Technology and Production in the Underdeveloped Countries: an Introduction' in C Cooper (ed), *Science, Technology and Development* (London: Frank Cass, 1973), pp 12-14.

9   For general discussions of the advantages of developing an indigenous S&T system see B Awe, 'Development of an Indigenous Capacity for Science and Technology – Discussion Report' in M Goldsmith and A King, *Issues of Development: Towards a New Role for Science and Technology*, pp 53-56; A King and A Lemma, 'Science and Technology for Development', pp 7-32; F Stewart, 'Arguments for the Generation of Technology by LDCs', *The Annals*, 458, pp 97-109; and the essays in F Stewart and J James (eds), *The Economics of New Technology in Developing Countries* (London: Frances Pinter, 1982).

10   C Cooper, 'Science, Technology and Production in the Underdeveloped Countries: an Introduction', p 17.

11   Yang Min, 'Importing Technology, Maintaining Independence and Keeping the Initiative in Our Own Hands', *GMRB*, 4 October 1978.

12   See J Berliner, *The Innovation Decision in Soviet Industry* (Cambridge, Mass.: MIT Press, 1976).

13   For an interesting Chinese view on activities concerning the 'science of science' and its definition see Yang Peiqing and Liu Ji, 'The Changing Understanding and Management of Science in China', *Science and Public Policy*, vol 12, no 5, pp 241-252.

14   For a review of the organisational reforms in general and their importance see T Saich, 'Party and State Reforms in the People's Republic of China', *Third World Quarterly*, vol 5, no 3, 1983, pp 627-640.

15   R Volti, 'Technology and Polity: the Dynamics of Managed Change', *Studies in Comparative Communism*, vol xv, nos 1 and 2, 1982, p 87.

ACKNOWLEDGEMENTS

This study is a product of a larger project undertaken on behalf of, and financed by, the Netherlands Ministry of Education and Sciences. However, the views expressed here are solely those of the author. The author wishes to thank, in particular, Dr E van Spiegel, the Director-General for Science Policy for the Ministry, and Professor Dr E Zürcher, of the Sinologisch Instituut, for their enthusiasm in starting, and supporting, the project. It is true to say that without their initiatives this particular study would never have seen the light of day.

The Ministry also financed research trips to the People's Republic of China, the United States of America and the United Kingdom. The collection of materials during these trips proved invaluable. During these trips I received much help but I would particularly like to thank the following: Ms G Mulder, of the Netherlands Embassy, Beijing; Mr Zhou Luping, of the Shanghai Municipality Science and Technology Commission; Professor D Simon, MIT: Ms M Brown-Bullock, Director of the Committee on Scholarly Communication with the PRC: Professor G Oldham, the Science Policy Research Unit, Sussex. I would like to thank especially Leo Orleans, formerly of the Library of Congress.

I am grateful for the help of the library and secretarial staff of the Sinologisch Instituut, Leiden. In particular, I would like to thank Mr H W Chan who, although overworked, always found time to handle my requests for materials. Mrs Hamaway-Todd, Mrs Merens and Mrs van Straalen deserve special mention for their patience and perseverance in typing this manuscript.

The manuscript itself benefited from the comments of John Gardner, Dr E B Vermeer and Stefan Landsberger. While they contributed to its improvement, the author, alone, can be held responsible for its shortcomings. Drs S Landsberger also deserves special thanks for his contribution to the larger project of which this forms a part. Without his cheerfulness in adversity matters may well have ground to a halt.

Finally, a special thanks is owed to Mieke Kerkhoven whose friendship and understanding not only helped the author to finish the project but also to keep a sense of perspective by realising that there is certainly more to life than science, technology and China.

A J Saich   February 1986   Leiden

CHAPTER ONE

POLICY EVOLUTION 1975-1985

*Deng Xiaoping, the 'Gang of Four' and
Conflicting Policies for S&T*

Science and Technology (S&T) policy and disagreements concerning the role
S&T could play in the process of economic modernisation were main subjects of
political conflict throughout the seventies. The Cultural Revolution left, in
particular the group later denounced as the 'Gang of Four', clashed with those
Party and States cadres, such as Zhou Enlai and Deng Xiaoping, over the correct
policies to be followed. While the former sought to protect what they saw as the
gains of the Cultural Revolution, the latter sought to give priority to economic
modernisation over the demands of continued class struggle and the accom-
panying political campaigns. Before the 'Gang of Four' were arrested in October
1976, conflict over the role of S&T twice came to the surface: in 1972 and in
1975.[1] Both occasions coincided with attempts by Premier Zhou Enlai and Deng
Xiaoping to concentrate on resolving economic problems, boosting foreign trade
and thereby utilising imported foreign technology to stimulate the S&T sector
and economic growth. The views put forward by this group are worthy of our
consideration as they formed the basis for the policies developed in the period
immediately following the death of Mao Zedong (September 1976) and the
arrest of the 'Gang of Four'.

In January 1975, at the Fourth National People's Congress, it appeared that a
coalition had been put together between the opposing groups within the Chinese
leadership. However, it was a very fragile coalition and it fell apart shortly after
the Congress. Two main reasons speeded up the collapse of this attempt at co-
operation. First, the ill-health of the older generation of China's leaders brought
the question of succession to the forefront of Chinese politics. Secondly,
concrete economic plans had to be drawn up for the new Five Year Plan to be
implemented beginning in 1976. This caused the differing approaches to
development strategy to be brought into sharp focus. While Deng Xiaoping and
his supporters started convening meetings and conferences to draw up
programmes for their growth-oriented policies, their opponents launched a
series of theoretical campaigns directed against those whom they saw 'whittling
away' the gains of the Cultural Revolution.[2]

Deng and his supporters drew up three key documents that were to form the
basis of their policy programme, but its implementation was obstructed by their
opponents. One of the main areas of disagreement concerned S&T policy, and
the contents of these documents, in as far as we know them, and the criticisms of
them after Deng's removal from power in April 1976 enable one to reconstruct

the main points of contention.[3] Essentially views differed on three main issues: the role of theoretical or basic research, the role of the masses in scientific discovery and technological development, and the role of imported technology.

In the late sixties, the Cultural Revolution attacks devastated the institutes of higher education and the research institutes of the Chinese Academy of Sciences (CAS). The guiding principle was that it was only through practice that theory could be advanced and this principle was seen as equally applicable to scientific work. This had the effect of down-grading the role of research laboratories and shifting scientific work out into the fields and the factories. This notion went hand-in-hand with the notion of giving priority to the diffusion of technological knowledge throughout society rather than on the concentration of research facilities in key urban centres. The contribution that China's highly trained scientists could make to the process of discovery was considered of less relevance than the innovative skills of the workforce. Thus, this policy de-emphasised the role of experts and increased that of the masses in the process of scientific discovery. Deng Xiaoping and his followers were worried about the subsequent lack of theoretical research work on China's possibilities for long-term economic development. According to Goldman, even when the universities re-opened in the early seventies, hardly any courses were offered in scientific theory, and thus biology departments did not cover the field of genetics.[4]

In the 'Outline Report on the Work of the Chinese Academy of Sciences' Deng and his followers set out their views on S&T and its role in China's modernisation programme. The report stressed the role of S&T in promoting economic development and indicated that the modernisation of S&T lay at the heart of the whole modernisation programme. Without this, modernisation of industry, agriculture and national defence would be impossible.[5] Implicitly, opponents of an increased role for scientific research were criticised as the report noted that 'some comrades think that doing scientific research is like "distant water that cannot quench an imminent thirst"' whereas in fact 'advancing scientific research' was to avoid 'digging wells only when one is thirsty'.[6]

From this starting-point, the report went on to discuss the correct balance between the role of experts and that of the masses in scientific development. While it called for a combination of the two, the report was clearly concerned with the need to restore the role of the professionals in the system. In fact, according to the report, 'Without a body of technicians, it is difficult to sustain the mass movement. Hence without technicians it will be impossible to raise the mass movement of scientific experimentation to a higher level'.[7] The report also stressed that scientific experiment could not be substituted for by production and that some research had to take place in the laboratory. Criticising the view developed in the Cultural Revolution, it stated that 'we must not demand that all research work "take the factory and the countryside as the base", and indiscriminately shout the slogan: "open the door to conduct scientific research".'[8]

Deng Xiaoping, himself, was concerned about how the lack of theoretical research work was holding back economic progress. In comments on the 'Outline Report' made in September 1975 he stated 'We have to put scientific research to the fore. At the Conference to Learn from Dazhai in Agriculture we said that agriculture is holding back industry. Well, scientific research is holding everything back. You can give applied science the priority, but applied science in turn is based on theory'.[9]

The idea that basic research was important led to demands that the research institutions of the CAS and some higher education institutions be improved along with the conditions of work for China's scientists and technicians. In particular, the report called for the removal of academic debate and discussion from the political realm pointing out that with respect to S&T differing opinions were a good thing, not a bad.[10] In his comments on the report, Deng also made a plea for the scientists' position to be improved and he quoted examples of people having to work secretly or in their spare time to carry on their scientific work. It seems that during the working day they were too busy 'going to the movies and engaging in factional fighting'.[11]

The low level of technological development in China led Deng and his supporters to stress the important role that imported technology could play in China's modernisation programme. The report argued that the prevailing policy of 'self-reliance' should not be interpreted in such a way as to mean that China should develop its S&T system and economy in isolation. It was noted that China's S&T fell considerably short of world standards. In order to catch up it was necessary to 'import some advanced technology and equipment' but such imports were to be used for the 'sake of reference' to stimulate China's creativity and 'not to substitute it'.[12] Deng Xiaoping cited the example of mining to show that the import of foreign technology was necessary to improve productivity.[13] Such technology purchases were to be paid for through long-term credits or by the export of China's oil and coal.[14]

These policies would lead to a greater emphasis on the role of experts and full-time research institutes and a corresponding decrease in the role of the masses as the fount of scientific and technological progress. To make proper use of the imported technology, the document 'Some Problems in Accelerating Industrial Development' suggested that it would be necessary to 'develop the strategic positions of research institutions and research teams, so that they may be closely aligned with the masses in solving and developing major and crucial scientific and technological problems'. One can safely assume that reference to 'the masses' was dictated more by the political climate than by genuine belief. The research institutes themselves were to be brought back under the professional control of the CAS or the relevant production ministry.[15] To strengthen international ties it would be necessary to organise exchanges with the international scientific community.[16]

In a series of articles after Deng Xiaoping was removed from power in April 1976, the 'Gang of Four' and their supporters provided their critique of such a policy programme. They attacked the importance that was attached to S&T as a panacea for all China's problems. They also professed concern about the social consequences of pursuing such a policy. In particular, they were concerned that it would lead to marginalisation of the masses in the process of scientific discovery and technological development and the creation of an élite whose position would be based on their exclusive professional knowledge. Their key position would allow them to assume increasingly more power over the decision-making process.[17] This was precisely the kind of situation that they claimed had been emerging by the mid-sixties and formed, in their view, part of the reason for launching the Cultural Revolution. While it is true that leaders of the pre-Cultural Revolution Party and state apparat relied on expert advice and were willing to accord them both greater freedom and rewards, it was clearly the case that major decisions concerning S&T and scientific priorities in the early sixties were determined by the politicians and not by the scientists themselves. The role of foreign technology and especially the proposed methods of payment provoked a sharp response and tapped the xenophobic vein of the 'Gang of Four'. They criticised Deng for giving the authority to extract Chinese minerals to foreign countries and accused him of being a traitor and turning China into an 'appendage of imperialism'.[18]

As Goldman has pointed out, although in the polemics the 'Gang of Four's' criticisms were overstated, they were not without a certain logic.[19] Indeed, in 1979 when the initial post-Mao policies, policies based on the three documents drawn up under Deng's direction, came in for severe criticism, some of the complaints mirrored the 'Gang of Four's' fears. For example, when the experts were left to their own devices they pursued research topics that were not considered relevant to China's development needs. Also, the faith in S&T as a cure-all was criticised and the policy of technology import, a key part of the initial post-Mao strategy, did not provide the anticipated results. However, it was not Deng Xiaoping who received the blame for the problems that arose but Mao Zedong's hand-picked successor, Hua Guofeng.

Ten Year Plans: an Ambitious New Start [20]

Following the arrest of the 'Gang of Four' in October 1976, a number of important measures were taken to point S&T policy in the direction outlined above. In particular a more positive attitude was adopted towards the role that imported technology could play, scientists were encouraged to air openly their views in the press and through conferences,[21] and, most importantly, top-level political support was given to endorse the importance of developing China's S&T system. Both the then Premier and Party Chairman, Hua Guofeng, and the twice-purged, twice-returned Deng Xiaoping gave their seal of approval to the need for the renewal of the system. A stress on the necessity for expertise in scientific work was revived and while the need to be politically aware was mentioned along with the need to be technically competent, in Chinese political parlance being 'both red and expert', it was evident that the latter was increasingly seen as being more important. Not surprisingly, the 'Outline Report' received praise in the Chinese press and along with the other two documents changed from being a 'poisonous weed' into a 'fragrant flower'. The mention of these 'fragrant flowers' helped prepare public opinion for the second coming of Deng Xiaoping and for a shift in policy direction.[22]

The emerging strands of the new policy were drawn together at the National Science Conference held in March 1978. Careful preparations had been in progress for this Conference for almost a year. On 30 May 1977, the Political Bureau of the Chinese Communist Party (CCP) met specifically to discuss S&T work and it decided to convene the National Conference in the spring of the following year.[23] In September the Central Committee issued a circular on convening a National Science Conference and a number of preparatory meetings were held.[24] For example, in the summer of 1977 the CAS held a national work conference to explore the meaning and implications of the new policy line; in October 1977 a national conference was held in Beijing to prepare an outline of the national programme for the development of the basic sciences; and provincial meetings were held to pave the way for the National Conference.[25]

The new plan for S&T unveiled by Fang Yi, the highest leader in charge of S&T work and later to be Minister-in-charge of the State Science and Technology Commission (SSTC), based itself on the recently released economic plans and shared their ambitious view of China's potential for development. The Ten Year National Economic Plan 1976–1985 was introduced by Hua Guofeng at the Fifth National People's Congress in February–March 1978. Most of the targets set by the plan were unrealistic and it bore resemblances to Mao's Twelve Year Plan of the mid-fifties that had preceded the Great Leap Forward. Indeed the rhetoric surrounding the new plan began to reflect that of the Great Leap: references were made to the Great Leap's general line of 'going all out, aiming high to achieve greater, faster, better and more economical results in building socialism'.[26] The plan accepted a high rate of accumulation that favoured the emphasis on heavy industry. By 1985, 120 large-scale projects were to be completed, steel production was to reach 60 million tons annually and the gross value of industrial output was to increase by over 10% per annum.[27] While this latter goal was achieved it should be noted that it was done by the adoption of a different development strategy. Also, an ambitious programme for importing whole plants and equipment was initiated. Such projections were seriously out of step with China's economic capabilities and did not accord with the noises being made off-stage by China's increasingly powerful economic planners.

Hua Guofeng in his report to the National People's Congress indicated what was expected from the S&T community. S&T was to contribute in 'rapidly transforming the weaker links in our economy, that is, fuel, electricity, raw and semi-finished materials industries, and transport and communications'.[28] To a large extent, Hua also anticipated the research priorities that were to be announced at the National Science Conference. He noted that 'we must strive to develop new scientific techniques, set up nuclear power stations, launch different kinds of satellites and step up research into laser theory and its application, attach importance to the research on genetic engineering and above all to research on integrated circuits and electronic computers and their widespread application. Full attention must be paid to theoretical research in the natural sciences, including such basic subjects as modern mathematics, high energy physics and molecular biology'.[29] Elsewhere, Hua had already stressed the need to perfect the system of agro-scientific research and agro-technical popularisation.[30]

At the National Science Conference, Fang Yi unveiled the 'Outline National Plan for the Development of Science and Technology, 1978-1985 (Draft)'. In keeping with the spirit of the time, the plan proposed ambitious targets emphasising basic research and quickly catching up with advanced world levels in a large number of fields. In broad terms the plan set four objectives to be achieved by the S&T establishment by 1985: to bring the number of professional research workers up to 800,000;[31] to set up a number of up-to-date centres for scientific research; to complete a nationwide system for S&T research; and to reach advanced world levels of the seventies in a number of S&T branches, to narrow the gap with advanced countries to about ten years and to lay the basis for catching up or surpassing advanced world levels in all branches in the ensuing 15 years.

In more detail, the plan called for the development of research in 27 spheres within which 108 items of research were selected as 'key projects'.[32] For special attention eight 'comprehensive scientific and technical spheres, important new technologies and pace-setting disciplines that have a bearing on the overall situation' were nominated. These areas were agriculture, energy, raw materials technology, computer science, laser technology, space technology, high energy physics and genetic engineering.[33]

That high-level political support was given to this new programme is shown by the fact that both Hua Guofeng and Deng Xiaoping addressed the meeting.[34] Deng, speaking on behalf of the Party Central Committee, spoke on two basic questions that were to have a profound effect on the S&T establishment and how its work would be assessed. First, Deng confirmed the view that S&T were a part of the productive forces.[35] This refuted the idea developed by Mao Zedong and promoted by the 'Gang of Four' that S&T were part of the superstructure of society and thus a legitimate arena for political struggle.[36] Having asserted that S&T were a part of the productive forces, Deng used the assertion to claim that the majority of people engaged in S&T work could be considered as belonging to the working class. According to Deng, the difference between 'mental labourers' and manual workers 'lies only in a different role in the social division of labour. Those who labour, whether by hand or by brain, are all working people in a socialist society'.[37] The intended effect of these two pronouncements was to withdraw S&T from the arena of political struggle and to remove the ideological justification for the persecution of intellectuals that had occurred during the Cultural Revolution and indeed even from the mid-fifties onwards. In future, intellectuals who 'made mistakes' would not be treated as 'enemies of the people'. It was further hoped that the removal of the threat of recrimination would stimulate academic debate within the scientific community. The improvement of the situation of intellectuals, as we have seen above, was strongly emphasised in the 'Outline Report' and in Deng Xiaoping's comments on it.

Frustrated Ambitions: the Policies of Re-adjustment

The Ten Year Plan for S&T, although it followed in broad outlines the general economic plan, was 'little more than a statement of intent formulated by the scientific community'.[38] One particular feature it shared with the economic plan was that it bore little resemblance to China's actual situation and had little relevance to China's actual resource capability.

Not long after its promulgation the new Ten Year Economic Plan came under serious and sustained attack. Indeed already in March 1979 the *People's Daily* was warning about 'economic rashness' and the setting of too ambitious plan targets. As the more cautiously minded economic planners, such as Chen Yun and Bo Yibo, extended their powers, the plan came under increasing attack. These two veteran communists who were purged during the Cultural Revolution were rehabilitated at the Third Plenum of the Eleventh Central Committee (December 1978).

This plenum marks the key turning-point in the post-Mao era and is the source for the policy experiments that have led to the formation of the current economic policy. The plenum made what is now regarded by the Chinese press as the historic decision to shift the focus of the Party's work away from political struggle and criticism of the 'Gang of Four' to economic modernisation.[39] This signalled amongst other things a victory for those opposed to the previous ambitious economic plans. Thus, the Second Session of the Fifth National People's Congress (June 1979) postponed the plan and substituted a three-year period of 're-adjusting, restructuring, consolidation and improvement of the national economy' for the years 1979-1981; this was subsequently extended until 1985. The Congress's Third Session was told that the plan had been abandoned altogether. Hua Guofeng stated that preparations were in progress for a new Ten Year Plan for 1981-1990 and that 'it would be meaningless to revise this (the original) ten year outline plan more than four years after it was drafted'.[40]

The re-adjustment of the plans, particularly the return to the emphasis on the agricultural sector rather than the heavy industrial sector and the need to devise plans in line with China's current situation and needs, led to subsequent changes in the S&T sector. However, the reforms in economic policy introduced in 1979 did not find an echo in the S&T sector until 1981. In essence, the new policy direction for the S&T sector was to make it serve the needs of the economy and society by creating numerous links between the research and the production sector.

The Party leadership were clearly not satisfied with the contributions the scientific community were making to economic development. Speaking to the

Second National Congress of the Chinese Association for Science and Technology (23 March 1980), Hu Yaobang, while calling on scientists to be teachers of Party leaders, implied that S&T had not contributed as much to the development that had occurred as had been originally envisaged.[41] The interrelationship between re-adjustment of the national economy and S&T was summed up in the *Journal of the Dialectics of Nature* as follows:

> During the period of re-adjustment of the national economy, scientific research must also be re-adjusted correspondingly. Because national economic development often makes demands upon scientific research and because scientific research must first satisfy the needs of national economic development, therefore, re-adjustment of scientific research work in reality is an important link in the re-adjustment of the national economy. Without such re-adjustment, scientific research will not be able to combine properly with the national economy and it will go against our nation's situation and will hinder the realisation of the Four Modern-isations.[42]

In common with the economic plan, the plan for S&T was accused of being over-ambitious with some people guilty of engaging in 'blind optimism'.[43] According to Tong Dalin and Hu Ping, there were some gains during the initial period but 'in retrospect, there were some attempts at hasty results and unrealistic goals during the science conference with regard to the scale and speed of scientific and technological development and the proposed large-scale research projects'.[44]

In addition to the general criticism that the work of S&T was not sufficiently linked to the needs of the economy, a number of other criticisms were made. The scientists' emphasis on basic research came under attack and this was combined with criticisms of the attempts to catch up with advanced world levels in a number of fields regardless of whether they were relevant to China's needs. It was said that basic research frequently had two tendencies. First, it often separated itself from the nation's technological and economic situation, to pursue some topics that were beyond national economic capabilities. Secondly, that research on technological processes sometimes started without thoroughly doing sufficient work.[45] This imprudent judgment by the nation's scientists when selecting research topics with little regard to facilities available meant that, on occasions, projects had been abandoned because of shortages of labour power, materials and financing.[46] In this respect, the emphasis of research had shifted dramatically from the early seventies when Deng and his supporters had pressed for the recognition of the role of theoretical research and criticised the overconcentration on applied research.

In particular, the predominance of high energy physics came under attack as being a field of 'esoteric' research that China could ill afford at the present stage of its development. The influential voice of the overseas Chinese Nobel Prize winner, Yang Zhenning, was also heard in this debate. He was critical of the development of the high energy physics programme and urged that a more practical and realistic method be adopted. In December 1981 he expounded this view in a letter to Fang Yi and stressed that China's S&T should be geared to the needs of industry and agriculture. In his view a much more profitable area of research for China's physicists was coagulation research as this was closely linked with the production of transistors, calculators and optical fibre communications.[47]

Under attack and fearing that basic research might suffer from stringent cuts, defences were rallied using arguments very familiar to those used in the West to defend basic research from the ravages of governments anxious to see quick returns on their economic investments. Articles argued essentially that attacks ignored the strategic value of most basic research. Using selected historical examples, arguments were constructed to show that over a period of 20 to 30 years seemingly esoteric research in the natural sciences would make a significant contribution to the economy, welfare and defence of the nation. Thus it was argued that long-term benefits should not be sacrificed for short-term gains.[48]

However, while the policy continued that there should be no 'forbidden zones' in scientific research, an increasing number of articles once again began to call on scientists to become more involved in developmental and applied research. This would encourage scientists to address more directly the nation's most pressing problems. The change in emphasis of the economic strategy also led to calls to give priority to those projects that would improve productivity, particularly in the agricultural and light industrial sectors. But the sharp demarcation that existed between research and development activities meant that the majority of institutes working in the formal research sector just did not have the necessary facilities to undertake serious, useful development research.[49]

Applied research, however, was also subject to a number of problems, the major one being that the results were not being put into practice. This was even the case with research institutes that came under the jurisdiction of the production ministries. Lack of planning and inadequate market research meant that products were developed without anyone bothering to find out if they were actually needed. Similarly, little effort was made by researchers and their institutions to popularise the results of their research.[50] This problem has persisted and in 1983 it was reported that few scientific achievements were popularised with the products remaining as a 'sample, display item or gift'. Articles in the Chinese press are fond of pointing out that whereas in the USA 80% to 85% of research can be applied to production only some 10% can be so applied in China. While it is difficult to gauge the accuracy of such figures, it does highlight the concern that not enough of the research work being carried out in China was having direct effect on economic development. The 1983 article mentions a *Guangming Daily* survey on the utilisation of the 245 technical inventions that had won national awards. The survey reported that only 18.5% had been popularised and applied, 36% had not been used while a further 36%

had only been used by the inventor. One result of this was that some of the inventions had become outdated before they had a chance to be used.[51]

The organisational system as it was rebuilt after the Cultural Revolution remained modelled on that of the Soviet Union. The system was organised into vertically separated sectors, and the segmentation of this structure and the poor co-ordination between the sectors have meant that duplication of work has become a major problem. This problem of duplication was compounded by the fact that too few conferences were held, not enough academic journals publicising findings existed and the immobility of personnel meant that the system was extremely rigid. Not only was work within China duplicated but also research work abroad was often repeated. Forty per cent is the figure mentioned for research projects undertaken in China that duplicate work which has already reached fruition in other countries.[52] Such a high percentage represents a waste of scarce resources that could be more fruitfully directed to other projects. It also reflected the low level of contacts between Chinese scientists and the international scientific community and poor dissemination of relevant information within China. The problem within China is in some instances even more serious. *Jiefang Ribao (Liberation Daily)* noted that some 980 units in China were developing haploid seed breeding. In 1978-79, 28 of 69 projects introduced in Shanghai's scientific and higher educational institutions were duplicated and 24 of the projects duplicated ones that were introduced in 1973 and 1974.[53]

Although the scientific plans were drawn up in the optimistic atmosphere whipped up by China's political leaders, the scientists themselves had had a major voice in the process through the conferences held in 1977 and early 1978. The fact that basic research had fared so well in terms of financial and personnel resources indicated that the basic research-oriented CAS had a strong influence over policy formation.[54] In retrospect it seems that many scientists were keen to get their 'pet projects' into the plans regardless of their relevance to China's economic situation. While the political leaders must accept part of the blame, it is clear that they became disillusioned with their scientists and decided to call them more closely to account. A significant number of China's key scientists had been foreign-trained and it seems that they were concerned to get back to the forefront of world research and gain recognition in the international arena. Many of them were working in the fields of basic research and it would appear that they used their positions to boost the position of basic research. Yet this is not surprising given the lack of sufficient demand from the productive sector. In the absence of such demand and without clear central guidance, choice of the research to be undertaken will devolve to the scientists themselves. Not unnaturally they are likely to select the kind of topics that are fascinating the world scientific community.[55]

It has been noted that most, if not all, of the scientists featured in the Chinese press were working in natural sciences such as mathematics and biology. It is claimed that the 'star' treatment that these scientists were receiving meant that youngsters were attracted to these fields rather than to the understaffed and 'less glamorous' applied fields of agriculture, medicine and engineering.[56] China's premier institution for basic research is the CAS. It has been implied that the dominance of natural scientists within the leading body of the CAS has hindered the development of the technological sciences. For example, some 80% of the members of the leading policy-making body of the CAS, the Academic Affairs Committee, are natural scientists.

It seems that during the re-assessment phase, with the criticisms of over-emphasis on basic sciences, some people called into question the existence of the CAS in its current form. In June 1981 an article was dedicated to a spirited defence of the CAS and the importance of its role in the S&T network. The article remarked that some people believe that basic scientific research should be concentrated in institutes for higher learning while technical scientific research should be closely related to production departments and should, therefore, be combined into industrial research organisations. This would mean that the CAS would no longer be a research entity but an honorary and consulting organisation.[57] While this idea never came to fruition it does indicate the level of discontent that existed with China's research system. Although the position of CAS is 'safe', to some extent these suggestions are now being implemented. Research in institutes of higher education is now being expanded and it is proposed that where it would be advantageous research institutes under the CAS should combine with production units and then move out from under the jurisdiction of the CAS. However, this is seen as a long-term development.[58]

Making Science and Technology Serve the Economy and Society

While re-adjustment clearly had implications for S&T policy it was some time before new policy directions were agreed upon and publicised. In fact, it was not until 1981 that the lines of the new policy became clear to outside observers. As is implied in the criticisms noted above, the new policy would call for the forging of much tighter links between S&T and the economy in particular and society in general. Clearly more attention was to be paid to problems of application and development. However, basic research was not to be closed down altogether but was to take greater care in ensuring that its work was relevant to China's needs. The SSTC summarised the situation as follows: 'For a long time science and technology has been out of line with economic and social development in our country. There are many reasons for this. Science and technology has not solved enough vital problems of economic development, economic development has not relied enough on science and technology.'[59]

The main thrust of the reforms for the S&T sector, like those for the agricultural and industrial sectors, concentrates on the need to promote the use of economic levers, rather than administrative mechanisms, to regulate and stimulate activity. At the core of the reforms lies the promotion of the contract and job responsibility system.

The new policy towards S&T had its origins in a national science and technology conference convened by the SSTC at the end of December 1980.[60]

As a result of discussions at this conference, in February 1981 the SSTC drew up and then circulated for discussion the 'Outline Report on Policy Concerning the Development of our National Science and Technology'.[61] This 'Outline Report 1981' is a key document for helping to understand recent policy developments in S&T. It anticipates most of the reforms that have taken place, all of its recommendations have been implemented to varying degrees and were incorporated in the 1985 Central Committee Decision on the Reform of the S&T Management System. Because of its importance it is worth summarising at some length.

On the basis of the evolution of policy to date, the 'Outline Report 1981' summarised policy for future development in five main points. First, S&T was to be developed in co-ordination with the economy and society and the promotion of economic development was to be undertaken as the primary task.[62] In elaborating on the interrelationship between the various sectors of the economy the 'Outline Report 1981' suggested that 'as far as security considerations allow, even the results of military scientific research should be actively transferred to civilian application'.[63] Second, research on production techniques was to be strengthened. It was pointed out that the objective of industrial and agricultural production technology should be to promote the development of low-priced and well made goods that are required by the people. Third, research in production enterprises was to be stepped up. This was highlighted as a 'weak link' in the S&T sector and it was noted that several hundreds of thousands of enterprises and the vast number of villages could not possibly rely only upon a few research institutes.[64] Fourth, despite the criticisms, basic research was to be guaranteed a place and to be expanded steadily and gradually. In particular, basic research affecting national economic development was to be encouraged.[65] Fifth, the previous policy for the import of technology was criticised. In future, technology was to be imported on the basis of national economic requirements rather than simply chasing after the newest and most advanced items. An exception was made for theoretical scientific research as it was deemed that this area needed the most recent knowledge and results to make progress. In the future, the introduction of technology was to comprise the buying of techniques, software and samples of machinery.

On the basis of the above points the 'Outline Report 1981' went on to suggest six tasks to be observed to ensure that the new policy would be properly implemented. Following from the points above, these tasks outlined ways to link together S&T and economic work and suggested a variety of reforms touching on financing, personnel problems and the organisation of research institutes. When formulating S&T policy and plans, the 'Outline Report' called on all bodies involved such as the State Economic and Planning Commissions to work closely with the SSTC. To dovetail work with the priorities of the Sixth Five Year Plan it suggested that ten items in seven fields be concentrated on.[66] The most conspicuous casualty of the new priorities was high energy physics which was excluded from the list. To promote the application of S&T achievements it was proposed that the system of transfer by payment be strengthened. This would be done through the use of contracts to pay for research done and by allowing institutes to retain money derived from such sources. To ensure more efficient use of imported technology the SSTC and related bodies were to be given an overseeing role to make sure that what was imported was suitable to China's conditions and of obvious economic benefit. Further reforms related to the necessity of organisational reform, the need to find more flexible forms of financing scientific research as well as to finding better mechanisms for exchange of information and the popularisation of research results.

In sum this amounted to a major new policy package for the S&T establishment to digest. In its scope it went far beyond the simple recreation of the S&T system as it had operated prior to the Cultural Revolution. In essence, it sought to overcome the limitations of the Soviet-style research system with its rigid segmentation and, through a system of rewards and related reforms, integrate the S&T system both internally and externally with the broader demands of the economy and society. Despite the promotion of this new policy throughout 1981 and 1982, it is clear that the impact was not as great as had been intended. In part the slow introduction of the reforms was linked to the slowdown of the reform programme in the industrial and urban sectors during a period of re-assessment and to a reluctance or an inability on the part of the S&T sector to push ahead with their own specific reforms.

A series of meetings towards the end of 1982 and in the early part of 1983 gave further impetus to the reform programme. On 24 October 1982, Premier Zhao Ziyang addressed the National Science Awards Conference in an attempt to define more precisely the relationship between science, technology and economic development. This was the first time that these issues had been publicly addressed in detail by such a key political figure. Zhao's speech did not flounder around in high-sounding banalities normally uttered by a leading state representative but adopted a strikingly pragmatic tone and took a fairly concrete approach. That Zhao should deliver the speech was symbolically important since as head of the government he was in overall charge of the drawing up of China's new economic plans. Indeed, in December of the same year Zhao unveiled China's new Five Year Plan.

Zhao took as his starting point the economic objective of quadrupling the gross annual value of industrial and agricultural production by the year 2000. This had been put forward by Party Secretary Hu Yaobang, at the Twelfth Party Congress (September 1982).[67] Zhao then proceeded to outline two major policy directives - one for economic and one for S&T work - before going on to more specific matters. According to Zhao, shortages in energy, material and financial resources were holding back the potential for economic growth. As a result, the desired expansion could only be achieved through additional S&T inputs. Thus 'it is necessary to activate the economy by relying on scientific and technological progress. This principle must be taken as the basic guiding ideology for our future economic construction' and 'scientific and technological work should be oriented to serving economic construction.'[68]

Cataloguing the familiar ills of duplication, waste, etc., Zhao acknowledged that, to date, the reforms had not been very successful and he stated openly that the present scientific research system could not effectively serve economic construction.[69] To improve this system he suggested a number of practical measures such as setting up 'technical development centres' for some trades, perfecting the reward system and making sure that research and development that bring good economic results were evaluated suitably. To integrate S&T planning with general economic planning, Zhao suggested that scientists and technicians be brought more directly into the planning process. In the final part of his speech, Zhao indicated that in the future, as with other sectors of the economy, S&T would be increasingly governed by economic rather than administrative measures. According to Zhao, 'When only a few factories are not eager for technical progress, this can be tackled without much effort. But if many are not enthusiastic, then we should locate the causes in our economic system and economic policies.'[70] As a result, Zhao proposed that new policies be introduced to deal with product pricing, taxation, and the protection of intellectual property.

In December 1982, Zhao Ziyang introduced the Sixth Five Year Plan to cover the years 1981-1985. The original draft, drawn up in 1980, was a casualty of the economic retrenchment and because of differences of opinion during the re-adjustment phase, 1981 and 1982 were guided by annual plans. The new plan, not surprisingly, reflected the more sober atmosphere then prevailing and it was more realistic than its immediate predecessor had been. It predicted a modest industrial and agricultural growth rate of 4% to 5% per annum. It also emphasised the need to curtail capital construction and to tackle the bottlenecked energy and transport sectors.

More specifically, the plan laid down guidelines for the development of scientific research. During the five years, the state was to lay emphasis on 38 major scientific and technological projects in eight fields. Table 1 indicates the shift in research priorities since the ambitious Ten Year Plan was introduced in 1978. The major casualties were in the costly areas of research which, while attracting international attention, may not be immediately applicable to production. Thus, high energy physics was removed from the list. Conversely, the beneficiaries were those areas where the economic benefit would be more quickly felt. The drive to improve living standards caused the area of light industry to receive a high priority. Similarly, transport and communications was designated a key area and research into energy saving techniques as well as energy development was to be stepped up. The category of new technologies indicated that by focusing on certain 'sunrise technologies' China did not intend to let itself fall behind in new areas such as biotechnology while racing to catch up in more established areas of technology. However, it should be pointed out that, with the exception of those included in the Ten Year Plan, the areas noted are rather more a list of economic sectors than priorities for S&T research.

Table 1: **Priority areas in China's Science and Technology**

10 Year Plan *1978-1985*	*Outline Report* *1981*	*Sixth Five-Year* *Plan 1981-1985*
Agriculture	Agriculture	Agriculture
Energy	Light Industry	Light Industry: Foodstuffs and Textiles
Raw Materials	Energy and Energy Saving	Energy and Energy Saving
Computer Science	Communications & Transport	Raw Materials
Lasers	Machine Building	Machine Building & Electronics
Space	Raw Materials	Transport & Communications
High Energy Physics	New Technologies	New Technologies[1]
Genetic Engineering		Other Technologies[2]
8 Areas,	7 Areas,	8 Areas,
108 Key Projects	Over 10 Items	38 Key Projects

[1]   This includes optical fibre communications, lasers, superconductors and biological technology.
[2]   This includes contraception, cures for various diseases and environmental protection and pollution treatment.

According to the plan three-quarters of the items listed for S&T research were aimed at providing key equipment and solving technological problems for the major construction projects to be built during both the Sixth and the Seventh Five Year Plans (i.e., up to 1990).[71]

Following Zhao's speech in October, a number of major organisations in the S&T network made serious attempts to implement the new guidelines and to integrate their research programmes more closely with the objectives laid out in the Sixth Five Year Plan. In early November 1982, the Party group of the SSTC held a meeting at which it was decided to develop a 15 year S&T development plan emphasising the economic results of research and development and to make decisions on priorities in accordance with economic needs; to establish on a trial basis several 'technical development centres'; to improve the system of evaluation and reward for S&T personnel; and to improve guidance for local efforts, particularly in small and medium-sized cities and rural areas.[72]

In January 1983, the CAS held a major work conference to discuss ways of implementing Zhao's guidelines. These included making scientific inputs into the national plans, establishing research and development centres in high technology fields and promoting technical consultancy work for factories and agriculture. The Vice-President of the CAS, Yan Dongsheng, announced that the Academy had chosen 26 research projects for attention, 16 of which were listed in the national research programme. These included work on technologies to increase output in selected agricultural areas, energy exploitation and energy conservation technologies, electronic technology and new materials and technology.[73]

In March 1983, following Zhao's direction the Chinese Association for Science and Technology (CAST) established an S&T Consultancy Service that formalised a network of more than 500 S&T organisations. The objective of this was to facilitate the application of technical expertise to economic and production problems.

To give more political muscle to S&T, an important new body was created in January 1983 to preside over the system. It would appear that the SSTC by itself was not powerful enough to break down the compartmentalisation of the system and push through effectively the implementation of the policies. As a result a Science and Technology Leading Group (STLG) was set up directly under the State Council. The group is headed by Premier Zhao Ziyang and draws its membership from key bodies involved in S&T work such as the SSTC, the State Planning and Economic Commissions, the military commission and the Ministry of Education.[74]

Further indication of political support is shown by the references to S&T incorporated into the new Party and State Constitutions adopted in September and December 1982 respectively. In fact the importance of S&T also found expression in the State Constitution adopted in March 1978. Differences in the formulation of the relevant article in the two constitutions show the change in emphasis in the intervening period. Article 12 of the 1978 Constitution notes the state's commitment to the development of S&T and retains the Cultural Revolution emphasis on the role of the masses in combination with professionals. By contrast the 1982 Constitution makes no mention of the role of the masses. Article 20 reads 'the state develops the natural and social sciences, disseminates scientific and technical knowledge, and encourages and rewards achievements in scientific research and technological discoveries and inventions.'[75] This concern for science is also reflected in the newest Party Constitution. Article 3 lists the duties expected of a Party member. The study of science, general education and professional matters are listed first just after the need to study Marxism-Leninism, and Mao Zedong Thought and essential knowledge about the Party.[76] This also reflects the Party's concern that its members are better educated and more technically competent than in the past. The duty to study science and the rest is not mentioned in the 1956, 1973 or 1977 Party Constitutions.

Despite such clear indications of commitment to the importance of S&T and the reform programme, on the whole progress remained rather slow. Such progress as was being made got bogged down when the question of the role of scientists and intellectuals got caught up in the political campaign to clean up 'Spiritual Pollution' which was launched with a vengeance in October 1983. Although the precise origins of the campaign remain uncertain, it is clear that it became a rallying cry for all those opposed to the changes ushered in as part of the reform programme.[77] The lack of a precise definition of what comprised 'Spiritual Pollution' meant that a whole range of activities legitimised by the new policies came under attack. Many intellectuals feared a new round of persecution for their participation in debates on formerly taboo subjects. Scientists and technicians also seem to have come under attack from those opposed to the reform programme. Their increased freedom to investigate scientific problems without interference from the Party, their exposure to 'foreign ideas' and contacts with foreigners made them an obvious target for those wishing to stop the spread of 'foreign contamination'.

Starting from the second half of November 1983 a series of meetings was held to define more precisely the targets of the campaign thereby limiting its scope and ultimately bringing it to an end. In this respect, in mid-December, a National Science and Technology Work Conference was held largely to assure China's scientists that the 'Spiritual Pollution' campaign was not intended to interfere with their work. When addressing the conference, Fang Yi explicitly gave this assurance and said that to ensure it, the State Council had approved a six-point policy guideline for S&T. The guideline was read to the conference and it gives a good impression of which activities came under attack during the campaign.

First, scientists were told that they could study new achievements in their fields from anywhere in the world. The class-free nature of S&T was re-affirmed and scientists were not to fear that their new discoveries would be labelled 'heresies' or 'bourgeois sugar-coated bullets'. Secondly, scientists were encouraged to study the new 'peripheral sciences' bridging the natural and social sciences. Thirdly, during feasibility studies of major projects, scientists were encouraged to speak out freely on scientific and economic questions. When challenging the leaders' views, scientists should not be accused of 'failing to keep in step with the Party'. Fourthly, undertaking comparative studies of scientific and manpower policies of countries with different social systems was adjudged a perfectly acceptable business. Fifthly, there should be free academic discussion in natural sciences. Scientists should be allowed to choose some of their own research topics and trials should be carried out to promote labour mobility. Such practices were not to be labelled 'bourgeois individualism'. Sixthly, it was made clear that the drive against ideological contamination should not be extended to the natural sciences and the technological fields. Differences of opinion, partial successes and even failures were acknowledged as inevitable in the process of scientific experimentation.[78] The continued existence of these problems shows just how widespread and ingrained is suspicion of intellectuals in China. Indeed the Chinese press in late 1985 was still frequently carrying articles on the need to implement correctly the Party policy on intellectuals – a clear sign that problems remained.

However, the defeat of those who wished to turn the 'Spiritual Pollution' campaign into a wide-ranging attack on the reform programme led to another spurt of development in the reform programme. Once again wide-ranging experimentation took place in the S&T sector in an attempt to find suitable policies and organisational reforms that would bring S&T work into line with the demands of the economy and society. This phase of experimentation came to an end in March 1985 when the Party decided to sum up the experiences to date. This was part of a general trend of re-centralisation by the Party as it prepared to launch the next Five Year Plan. This has resulted in the promulgation of a series of key documents summing up the reforms and laying down guiding principles for the subsequent phase.[79]

From the point of view of reform of the S&T system the most important developments were the convening of a National Science and Technology Work Conference in Beijing from 2-7 March 1985[80] and the publication on 13 March of the 'Decision of the Central Committee of the Chinese Communist Party on Reform of the Science and Technology Management System'.[81]

The Work Conference had two major tasks on its agenda. The most important was to discuss a draft of the 'Decision' and to try to 'perfect it' and secondly the Work Conference was expected to 'unify knowledge about the basic direction of the reforms'.[82] The importance of the Work Conference was attested to by the fact that once again China's top political leaders chose to address it. Thus, in addition to Fang Yi and his successor as Minister-in-charge of the SSTC, Song Jian, Premier Zhao Ziyang, Party Secretary Hu Yaobang and Deng Xiaoping all spoke to the Work Conference.

As in 1982, Premier Zhao made a speech that did not flounder around in banalities but touched on key questions concerning the reform programme.[83] Zhao noted that, in common with many other countries, China was seeking to adapt to the new technological revolution by dovetailing S&T with production in an attempt to achieve the co-ordinated development of S&T and economy and society. A major problem was the fact that the organisational system tended to 'isolate S&T from production'. As a result it was necessary to change the way in which both S&T and the economy were managed. According to Zhao, 'scientific research should have been linked organically with production, and such ties should be crosswise, frequent and multi-faceted and should link each other in a thousand and one ways'. One of the keys to this reform was, according to Zhao, to recognise that one can get nowhere in a commodity economy 'if the relations of commodities to currency, the law of value and the economic levers are ignored'. Thus, the value of brain work should be given proper recognition and 'most scientific and technical achievements' should be allowed to be sold as commodities if research institutes were to be able to produce what was needed.

After outlining a number of reforms relating to the question of financing, Zhao claimed that the 'most urgent task' was to enable scientists and technicians to play as full a role as possible in economic development. Zhao asked the question 'What is the biggest difficulty in achieving the four modernisations and rejuvenating China?' He answered his own question thus: 'Our biggest problem lies in the lack of talent'.

Finally, Zhao indicated that China should not be obsessed with just 'sophisticated technology'. He stressed the role of small enterprises in China's development which he referred to as 'a vigorous force in our drive for the four modernisations'. Thus, according to Zhao, China also needed inconspicuous applied technologies and he commented favourably on the World Bank Report on China which mentioned that 'the massive, constant use of inconspicuous technology is more important than using sophisticated technology: the work to narrow the gap in technology between advanced and backward factories within a trade is more important than building a few very advanced factories'.

The 'Decision', the first of its kind in the People's Republic of China (PRC), lays down the kind of reforms that the Party feels are necessary to create the organisational structure capable of ensuring that the S&T system can make the contributions expected of it to the modernisation programme. Given that the 'Decision' is based on the summing up of a period of reform, it is not surprising that it contains nothing startlingly new. It does, however, give one a good idea of which reforms are considered successful and what is considered necessary for the next phase of the reform programme. The 'Decision' will not be dealt with in detail here as its various aspects will be taken up in subsequent chapters. In essence, it covers three interrelated sets of problems. First, it points out the need for the reform of the funding system in order to make use of the technology market thus breaking up the old system of relying on administrative measures to regulate S&T work. Secondly, it calls for the overhaul of the organisational structure to create the 'organic links' between research and production. Thirdly, it deals with the problems of personnel and calls for the easing of restrictions on S&T personnel and enabling them to put their skills to optimum use.[84]

Apart from drawing on the experiences of nearly five years of reforms, the 'Decision' itself went through a careful process of drafting that drew in a number of experts from relevant fields. The drafting process is worth outlining in some detail to give an idea of those organisations involved and to provide a good example of the interaction between the Party and experts characteristic of policy formation in recent years. The published version of the 'Decision' was the eleventh draft and was the culmination of a process begun at the end of October 1984 just after the Third Plenum of the Twelfth Central Committee was held.[85]

Shortly after the Plenum had been convened, a leading group was established by the Central Committee to organise the drafting of documents for the reform of the S&T education systems. The group comprised ten members including Hu Yaobang and Zhao Ziyang. At the same time as the drafting work began, people from relevant organisations were asked to carry out investigative work into the reforms. This initial process drew in some 20 people for the drafting and over 170 people from the various ministries and commissions in the 'special investigations'.[86]

By early January 1985, the fifth draft was ready and the STLG of the State Council and the SSTC convened several meetings with administrative cadres and experts, including 25 American overseas Chinese. Opinions on the draft were also received at this stage from the Standing Committee of the National People's Congress; the Committee for Education, Science, Culture and Public Health; the S&T group of the Chinese People's Political Consultative Conference; and the Central Committees of the China Democratic League and the Jiusan Society. On 26 January, the sixth draft was considered by the Central Committee Leading Group and the STLG of the State Council and in early February they issued the seventh draft to each ministry and commission for their consideration. During this phase, 38 ministries offered written suggestions about the draft. On the morning of 28 February, the Secretariat of the Central Committee was able to consider the ninth draft. Finally, in the first week of March, the tenth draft was sent to the National Work Conference for the last round of discussions before the Central Committee issued the 'Decision' in its final form.[87]

While the measures outlined in the 'Decision', if properly implemented, will go much of the way towards dealing with the problems of China's S&T sector, the reforms themselves have created a new set of problems that will also have to be dealt with. Many of these problems stem from the diminishing of central control giving research institutes greater decision-making powers, and the uncertainty of many during the period of rapid change about what exactly constitutes legitimate activity. To help clarify the situation in June 1985, the SSTC issued a 'Circular on Eight Lines of Distinction for Determining the Direction of Reform and Against Unhealthy Tendencies'.[88] Among other things, the circular called for rewards only to be given to those who had properly deserved them and criticised the 'abrupt preferential promotion of cadres, indiscriminate issuing of bonuses and the arbitrary raising of wages'. While S&T personnel are encouraged to take on extra work outside their unit, 'moonlighting' that causes them to 'unscrupulously neglect their principal work' is not to be allowed. To help with the flow of personnel, units are allowed to release personnel for temporary work in other enterprises or villages but researchers are not to use this as an excuse for making more money elsewhere. Similarly, units are to be stopped from 'poaching' personnel. Given the increasing sensitivity about corruption and, particularly, about cadres abusing their positions of power, it is not surprising to find that the circular forbids party and state officials to exploit their positions to their own benefit.

Notes

1   For a detailed analysis of these debates, particularly those of 1975, see M Goldman, 'Teng Hsiao-p'ing and the Debate over Science and Technology', in *Contemporary China*, vol 2, no 4, Winter 1978, pp 46–69. In 1972 opponents of Cultural Revolution reforms that had sought to downgrade the importance of basic research work launched a counter-attack claiming the support of then Premier Zhou Enlai.

According to Zhou Peiyuan, the main proponent of the need for strengthening basic research, Zhou Enlai, made some ten instructions in 1972 alone in support of scientific experimentation. Zhou Peiyuan set forth his ideas in an October 1972 article in the *Guangming Ribao*. As a result he became the focus of a sharp attack by those who favoured the Cultural Revolution reforms. In 1977, Zhou claimed that Zhang Chunqiao had declared that he, Zhou, was a 'behind-the-scenes boss' and should be criticised no matter how 'big and formidable a boss he was'. The attacks on Zhou's ideas mirror those made again in 1975–1976 when the debate over the role of S&T and also of basic research was revived. Zhou Peiyuan's original article was entitled 'Some Options on the Revolution in Science Education in Universities' and appeared in *GMRB*, 6 October 1972. For Zhou's comments made after the arrest of the 'Gang of Four' see 'Peking University Professor Exposes Crimes of "Gang of Four" in Obstructing Research on Basic Theories of Natural Sciences', *Xinhua* in English, 15 July 1977.

2 See T Saich, *China: Politics and Government* (Houndsmill: Macmillan Press, 1981), pp 56–62.

3 The three documents are 'Lun quandang quanguo gexiang gongzuo de zonggang' ('On the General Programme of Work for the Whole Party and the Whole Nation'), 'Guanyu jiakuai gongye fazhan de ruogan wenti' ('Some Problems in Accelerating Industrial Development'), and 'Kexueyuan gongzuo huibao tigang' ('Outline Report on the Work of the Academy of Sciences'). These three documents denounced by the 'Gang of Four' as 'poisonous weeds' and hailed after their arrest as 'fragrant flowers' have never been published in full. In July/August 1976 parts were included as appendices in pamphlets distributed by the 'Gang of Four' as material for criticism. The whole of the 'General Programme', one of the drafts of 'Some Problems' and the third section of the 'Outline Report' were distributed in this fashion. See Xiang Qun, 'Dazhuo fan fubi de qihao gao fubi - pipan "sirenbang" dui "lun zonggang" de "pipan" ' ('Flaunting the Banner of Opposing Restoration to Engage in Restoration – Criticise the "Gang of Four" 's Criticism of "On the General Programme" '), *RMRB*, 7 July 1977. Fragments that tally with these versions appear in articles published in 1976 attacking their contents. See, for example, Kang Li and Yan Feng, ' "Huibao tigang" chulong de qianqian houhou' ('The ins and outs of the Appearance of the "Outline Report" '), *Xuexi yu Pipan (Study and Criticism)*, no 4, 1976, pp 20–27; ' "Guanyu jiakuai gongye fazhan de ruogan wenti" xuanpi') ('Selected Criticisms of "Some Problems in Accelerating Industrial Development" '), *Xuexi yu Pipan*, no 4, 1976, pp 28–35; the articles in the section 'Shenru pipan deng xiaoping de xinzheng zhuyi luxian' ('Thoroughly Criticise the Revisionist Road of Deng Xiaoping'), *Hongqi (Red Flag)*, no 5, 1976, pp 35–65; the Workers' Theoretical Group of the Shanghai Watch Components Factory, 'Yige fubi daotubi de tiaoli - "guanyu jiakuai gongye fazhan de ruogan wenti" pipan' ('A Restorationist Retrogressive Regulation - Criticism of "Some Problems in Accelerating Industrial Development" ') *Hongqi*, no 7, 1976, pp 31–35; the Mass Criticism Group of Beijing and Qinghua Universities, 'A Confession of Attempts of Reversal of Verdicts and Restoration - Criticising an Article Concocted at Teng Hsiao-p'ing's Bidding', *PR*, no 28, 9 July 1976, pp 9–12; and the Fudan University Science Department Mass Criticism Group, Yifen fangeming de xiuzheng zhuyi tigang ping "kexueyuan gonzuo huibao tigang" de "pipan" ') ('A Counterrevolutionary Revisionist Outline, Reviewing the "Outline Report on the Work of the Academy of Sciences' 'Criticisms' " '), *RMRB*, 19 July 1976. An English translation of what is available of the three documents can be found in Chi Hsin, *The Case of the Gang of Four* (Hong Kong: Cosmos Books, 1977), pp 201–295.

4 M Goldman, 'Teng Hsiao-p'ing and the Debate over Science and Technology', p 48.

5   'Outline Report' in Chi Hsin, *The Case of the Gang of Four*, p 279.
6   Ibid.
7   Ibid, p 280.
8   Ibid, p 281.
9   'Comments by Deng Xiaoping on the Presentation of Hu Yaobang's Report', 26 September 1975, in Chi Hsin, *The Case of the Gang of Four*, p 290. These were comments on the 'Outline Report'. This document had been drawn up by two of Deng's supporters, Hu Yaobang, the current Party Secretary, and Hu Qiaomu, later a Politburo member, on the basis of visits to the CAS in July/August 1977.
10   'Outline Report', in Chi Hsin, *The Case of the Gang of Four*, pp 285-286.
11   'Comments by Deng Xiaoping', ibid, pp 290-291.
12   'Outline Report', ibid, pp 282-283.
13   'Talk Given by Deng Xiaoping on Industrial Development', 18 August 1975, ibid, p 275.
14   'Some Problems', ibid, p 264. 'Talk Given by Deng Xiaoping', ibid, pp 274-275.
15   'Some Problems', ibid, pp 262-263.
16   'Outline Report', ibid, pp 283.
17   Tan Wen, 'Deng Xiaoping xuanyang "bai zhuan" juxin hezai' ('What is Deng Xiaoping up to in Propagating "White Expertise"?'), *RMRB*, 6 June 1976. For a defence of the role of the masses in promoting scientific discovery see Xiang Qun, 'Zhongshi kexue puji gongzuo' ('Attach Importance to Popularising Science'), *Hongqi*, no 11, 1975, pp 68-72.
18   See Liang Xiao, 'Yangwu yundong yu yangnu zhixue' ('The Yangwu Movement and Slavish Comprador Philosophy'), *Lishi Yanjiu (Historical Research)*, no 5, 1975, pp 68-74 and Kao Lu and Cheng Ko (Gao Lu and Zheng Ge), 'Comments on Teng Hsiao-p'ing's Economic Ideas of the Compradore Bourgeoisie', *PR*, no 35, 27 August 1976, pp 6-9.
19   M Goldman, 'Teng Hsiao-p'ing and the Debate over Science and Technology', pp 59-65.
20   The following three sections are based on T Saich, *The Evolution of Science and Technology Policy in the People's Republic of China since the Death of Mao Zedong*, Amsterdam Asia Studies no 55 (Amsterdam: University of Amsterdam, 1985), pp 1-74 and T Saich, 'Linking Research to the Productive Sector: Reforms of the Civilian Science and Technology System in Post-Mao China', *Development and Change*, vol 17, no 1, 1986, pp 3-33.
21   For example, in the first year after the arrest of the 'Gang of Four' some 16 or more academic conferences were held for specialists in the field of S&T.
22   The Third Plenum of the Tenth Central Committee (July 1977) restored Deng to his posts and also expelled the 'Gang of Four' from the Party forever and confirmed Hua Guofeng as Party Chairman.
23   Li Chang, 'Developing Science and Technology in a Big Way is an Urgent Task of Building a Modern and Strong Socialist Nation', *Ziran Bianzhengfa Tongxun (The Journal of the Dialectics of Nature)*, vol 4, no 1, February 1982, p 30.
24   'Communist Party of China Central Committee Circular on Holding National Science Conference', 18 September 1977, *PR*, no 40, 30 September 1977, pp 6-11. The Circular stated the tasks of the Conference as being: hold high the great banner of Mao Zedong Thought and implement the line of the Eleventh National Congress of the Party; make in-depth exposure and criticism of the 'Gang of Four'; exchange experiences; draw up plans; commend advanced personnel, especially scientists, technicians, workers, peasants and soldiers who have made investigations and innovations; and mobilise the whole Party, the whole army and the people of all nationalities in the country as well as all scientists and technicians to work for modernisation of S&T. Despite the political nature of the first two tasks, the

Conference spent most of its time dealing with the detailed questions of planning and organisation.

25 For details see G Dean and T Fingar, *Developments in PRC Science and Technology Policy October–December 1977 United States–China Relations*. S&T Summary no 5 (Stanford) pp 2–10. It is interesting to note how many of the academic conferences dealt with topics such as high energy physics, thus clearly emphasising the need for theoretical research that had no immediate relevance for application.

26 Hua Guofeng, 'Unite and Strive to Build a Modern Powerful Socialist Country!', 25 February 1978, in *Documents of the First Session of the Fifth National People's Congress of the People's Republic of China* (Beijing: Foreign Languages Press, 1978), p 41.

27 Ibid, p 39.

28 Ibid, p 70.

29 Ibid.

30 Ibid, p 45.

31 From what base is unclear. However, Fang Yi said that it would be an increase of several times. Suttmeier suggests a figure of 225,000 for 1978 as being possible. R P Suttmeier, *Science, Technology and China's Drive for Modernisation* (Stanford: Hoover Institution Press, 1980), pp 52–53. Suttmeier shows how difficult it would have been for China to meet this figure and indeed the Chinese soon rejected it as impractical.

32 These 27 spheres included: agriculture, industry, natural resources, national defence, transport and communications, oceanography, environmental protection, medicine, finance and trade, culture and education as well as the two major departments of basic and technical sciences. A project selected as a key project is given a priority by the central government for funds and material allocations.

33 ' "Abridgement" of Fang Yi's Report to National Science Conference', *New China News Agency*, 28 March 1978 in *FBIS*, 29 March 1978. See also, R P Suttmeier, *Science, Technology and China's Drive for Modernisation*, pp 2–6 and 'China's New Priorities for Technology Development' in *The China Business Review*, May–June 1978, pp 3–8.

34 Hua Guofeng, 'Raise the Scientific and Cultural Level of the Entire Chinese Nation', 24 March 1978, *PR*, no 13, 31 March 1978, pp 6–14.

35 This point had been made in the 'Outline Report' which stated that 'Science and technology are also productive forces. Scientific research takes the lead in furthering production. The great advances in oil industry have proven this.' 'Outline Report' in Chi Hsin, *The Case of the Gang of Four*, p 279.

36 It is interesting to note that Hua Guofeng in his speech to the Conference dealt not only with the question of productive forces but also spent time dealing with the relations of production themselves.

37 Deng Xiaoping, 'Speech at Opening Ceremony of National Science Conference', *PR*, no 12, 24 March 1978, p 11.

38 R Conroy, 'Recent Issues and Trends in Chinese Policy Towards Science and Technology', *The Australian Journal of Chinese Affairs*, no 6, 1981, p 173.

39 For a translation of the Communiqué adopted by the Plenum see *PR*, no 52, 29 December 1978, pp 6–16. For a discussion of the decisions of the Plenum and their initial impact on political life in China see T Saich, 'New Directions in Politics and Government' in J Gray and G White (eds), *China's New Development Strategy* (London: Academic Press, 1982), pp 19–36.

40 Hua Guofeng, 'Speech at the Third Session of the Fifth National People's Congress', 7 September 1980, in *Main Documents of the Third Session of the Fifth National People's Congress of the People's Republic of China* (Beijing: Foreign Languages Press, 1980), p 156.

41 Hu Yaobang, 'Speech at the Second National Congress of the Chinese Scientific and Technical Association', *BR*, no 15, 14 April 1980, pp 13-16.

42 Yang Yike, 'Efficiency of Scientific Research Must be Improved', in *Ziran Bianzhengfa Tongxun* vol 3, no 2, 10 April 1981, p 3.

43 'Outline Report on Policy Concerning the Development of our National Science and Technology by the State Science and Technology Commission', 23 February 1981 (Outline Report 1981), *Issues and Studies*, vol xviii, no 5, May 1982, p 89.

44 Tong Dalin and Hu Ping, 'Science and Technology' in Yu Guangyuan (ed), *China's Socialist Modernisation* (Beijing: Foreign Languages Press, 1981), p 626.

45 Na Baokui, 'Guanyu keyan tixi de jidian yijian' ('Some Opinions on the Scientific Research System'), *KYGL*, no 4, 1982, pp 50-53.

46 Xia Yulong and Liu Ji, 'It is also Necessary to Eliminate Erroneous "Leftist" Influence on the Science and Technology Front' in *Jiefang Ribao (Liberation Daily)* 2 June 1981, p 4. Translated in *FBIS* China-81-112, 11 June 1981, K8-K12.

47 'Yang Zhenning Talks to this Paper on the State of Science and Technology in China' in *Da Gongbao* (Hong Kong), 23 February 1983, p 1.

48 Such arguments are familiar to scientists the world over as they seek to protect projects against the swing of the government's financial axe. Professor Sir Hans Kornberg, President of the British Association for the Advancement of Science, in August 1985 bemoaned the British government policy of directing funds away from pure science to applied research. He pointed out that the major steps that had changed the world were not merely improvements of existing practices but represented 'quantum jumps to entirely novel procedures that are rooted in basic research, the outcome of which was totally unpredicted and unpredictable and the application of which was not foreseen until virtually all the work had been done'. 'BA Head Attacks Science Research Cuts', *The Guardian*, 27 August 1985. For a defence of the role of basic research see P M Bhargave, 'Penetration of Science and Technology into Society: the role of basic research', in M Gibbons and B M Udgaonkar (eds), *Science and Technology Policy in the 1980s and Beyond* (London: Longman, 1984), pp 51-66.

49 On this point see R Conroy, 'Technological Innovation in China's Recent Industrialisation', *The China Quarterly*, no 97, 1984, p 8.

50 Xia Yulong and Liu Ji, 'It is also Necessary to Eliminate Erroneous "Leftist" Influence on Science and Technology', p 4.

51 Hu Jinxiang, 'Preliminary Explorations of the Economic Results of Scientific and Technological Progress', *KXX*, no 12, 10 December 1983, pp 2-5.

52 Xia Yulong and Liu Ji, 'It is also Necessary to Eliminate Erroneous "Leftist" Influence on Science and Technology', p 4. Wang Huangong, 'Woguo keyan tizhi shang de jige wenti' ('Some Problems Concerning our Nation's Scientific Research System'), *GMRB*, 22 August 1980, p 4.

53 Xia Yulong and Liu Ji, 'It is also Necessary to Eliminate Erroneous "Leftist" Influence on Science and Technology'.

54 This idea was suggested to the author by Professor D F Simon, MIT.

55 See C Cooper, 'Science, Technology and Production in the Underdeveloped Countries: An Introduction', in C Cooper (ed), *Science, Technology and Development* (London: Frank Cass, 1973), pp 5-6.

56 Liu Ying, 'Fazhan woguo kexue jishu gongzuo de jige wenti' ('Some Questions Concerning Developing our Nation's Scientific and Technological Work'), *RMRB*, 6 June 1982, p 3. Liu uses his argument to suggest that in addition to the CAS, an Academy of Science and Engineering should be set up.

57 Luo Wei, 'The Position and the Role of the Academy of Sciences in the Chinese Scientific Research System', *Ziran Bianzhengfa Tongxun*, vol 3, no 3, 10 June 1981, p 25.

58 Interview with Luo Wei, Deputy Director of the Science Policy Study Office of the CAS, 16 January 1985.
59 'Outline Report 1981', *Issues and Studies*, vol xviii, no 5, p 93.
60 See 'Scientists Urged to Contribute to Production', *Xinhua*, 26 February 1981, translated in *FBIS – PRC*, 27 February 1981, p 1-10.
61 A full translation of the 'Outline Report 1981' can be found in *Issues and Studies*, vol xviii, no 5, pp 88-101.
62 This became popularised as the 'Triple Combination' policy.
63 This was adopted as one of the 'Four Transfers'. The 'Four Transfers' were from the research sector to the production sector, from urban centres to the rest of the country, from the military sector to the civilian sector and from overseas to China. For a fuller description of these see T Saich, '*The Evolution of Science and Technology Policy in the People's Republic of China*', pp 22-34.
64 To encourage this a system of rewards was to be introduced for innovations and closer links were to be forged between research enterprises and production units.
65 The 'Outline Report' noted that while academic theses and research work reports were important yardsticks for gauging achievements, their ability to solve practical problems was also to be emphasised. It also seemed to imply that a degree of dishonesty had been taking place for it stated that 'academic theses must be strictly scientific and have precise proofs and data'. Expenditure for national basic research was only about 5% of the fund for civilian scientific research.
66 These fields were: agriculture, light industry, energy development and energy saving techniques, communications and transport, machine manufacturing, material industry and new techniques. For a comparison with the priorities of the Sixth Five Year Plan see below.
67 This would mean raising the value from 710,000 million *yuan* in 1980 to 2,800,000 *yuan* by the year 2000. Hu Yaobang, 'Create a New Situation in All Fields of Socialist Modernisation' in *The Twelfth National Congress of the CPC* (Beijing: Foreign Languages Press, 1982), p 19.
68 Zhao Ziyang, 'A Strategic Question on Invigorating the Economy', *BR*, no 46, 15 November 1982, p 15.
69 Ibid, p 16.
70 Ibid, p 19.
71 *The Sixth Five Year Plan of the People's Republic of China for Economic and Social Development (1981-1985)* (Beijing: Foreign Languages Press, 1984), p 194.
72 In October 1982 a conference was held on scientific work in small and medium-sized cities and in January 1983 one was held on such work in the rural areas. The objective of these two conferences was to underscore the idea that research and development should not be confined, as in the past, to a small number of scientific centres such as Shanghai and Beijing. Instead, to bring research results to bear on economic production, it (research) must be carried out on a national scale. It was particularly important to transfer technology from advanced urban centres to the rest of the country.
73 For details see *Xinhua* in English, 2 February 1983, *JPRS* 83145 *S&T* 192, pp 1-2. Also see Yan Dongsheng, 'The Chinese Academy of Sciences and Key Problem-Solving Efforts in Scientific Research', *Ziran Bianzhengfa Tongxun*, vol 5, no 1, 10 February 1983, pp 1-3. In January 1984, the CAS announced that it was now concentrating on 29 key research projects, 15 of which involved the 38 major national problems to be solved before 1985. These included eight projects relating to agriculture, including research on the comprehensive development and exploitation of the north China and north east China plains, seven to energy, including key technical problems in constructing a national base for energy and the chemical industry in Shanxi Province and solving the energy shortage in the rural areas, four

on developing new materials such as special alloys, high-molecular compounds and inorganic structural materials and seven on new technologies such as computers, large-scale integrated circuits, biotechnology, superconductors, laser and remote sensing and radiation. *Xinhua* in English, 4 January 1984 in *JPRS - CST* - 84-011, p 210.

74 The S&T Leading Group will be discussed in more detail in Chapter Three.

75 'Constitution of the People's Republic of China', translated and annotated by T Saich in *Review of Socialist Law*, vol 9, no 2, 1983, pp 183-208. Article 13 of the Constitution reads, 'The state devotes major efforts to developing science, expands scientific research, promotes technical innovation and technical revolution, and adopts advanced techniques wherever possible in all departments of the national economy. In scientific and technological work, we must follow the practice of combining professional contingents with the masses, and combining learning from others with their own creative efforts.' By contrast the 1954 Constitution contained no such article while Article 12 of the more 'radical' Constitution of 1975 simply stated that 'culture and education, literature and art, physical education, health work and scientific research work must all serve proletarian politics, serve the workers, peasants and soldiers, and be combined with productive labour'. The 1975 Constitution is translated in *Documents of the First Session of the Fourth National People's Congress of the People's Republic of China* (Beijing: Foreign Languages Press, 1975), pp 4-29.

76 'The Constitution (Statutes) of the Communist Party of China', translated and with an introduction by T Saich in W B Simons and S White (eds), *The Party Statutes of the Communist World* (The Hague: Martinus Nijhoff, 1984), pp 85-113.

77 For an account of the campaign see T Saich, 'Party Consolidation and Spiritual Pollution in the People's Republic of China', in *Communist Affairs: Documents and Analysis*, vol 3, no 3, pp 283-290.

78 For an English summary of the six-point guideline see *BR*, no 3, 16 January 1984, pp 10-11.

79 Thus in addition to the Decision on S&T, in October 1984 the Central Committee issued its decision on the reform of the economic system and in May 1985 the decision on the reform of the education systems. For the texts of these two decisions see *RMRB*, 21 October 1984, pp 1-3 and 29 May 1985, pp 1 and 3 respectively.

80 The Conference was attended by over 460 people of whom 428 were present as representatives of provinces and relevant ministries and commissions or were experts in natural science research, education or production. See 'Quanguo keji gongzuo huiyi jianbao' ('Bulletin of the National Science and Technology Work Conference'), 2 March 1985, p 1 and Fang Yi, 'Zai quanguo kexue jishu gongzuo huiyi shang de kaimuci' ('Opening Address to the National Science and Technology Work Conference'), 2 March 1985, p 1.

81 'Zhonggong zhongyang guanyu kexue jishu tizhi gaige de jueding' ('Decision of the Central Committee of the Communist Party of China on Reform of the Science and Technology Management System'), *RMRB*, 20 March 1985, pp 1 and 3.

82 'Quanguo keji gongzuo huiyi jianbao', p 1.

83 Zhao Ziyang, 'Speech to the National Science and Technology Conference', 6 March 1985 translated in *SWB:FE* 7908. Excerpts from Zhao's speech are in *BR*, no 14, 8 April 1985, pp 15-19.

84 'Zhonggong zhongyang guanyu kexue jishu tizhi gaige de jueding', p 1.

85 It was the Third Plenum that had promulgated the Decision on the reform of the economy.

86 Those involved in the drafting of the Decision were drawn from the State Science and Technology, State Planning, State Economic Commissions; the State Commission for Reconstructing the Economic System; the Commission of Science,

Technology and Industry for National Defence; the office of the Science and Technology Leading Group; the Chinese Academy of Sciences; the Ministries of Education, Finance, Agriculture, Animal Husbandry and Fisheries, Machine-Building Industry, Public Health; the research department of the Secretariat, the General Office of the Central Committee, the Chinese Association for Science and Technology; and the Science and Technology Commissions of, among others, Shanghai and Hunan. The investigations were carried out in 14 provinces and involved several hundred units and discussions with over 3,000 experts and administrative cadres.

87   The process of the drafting of the Decision is drawn mainly from Fang Yi, 'Zai quanguo kexue jishu gongzuo huiyi shang de kaimu ci', pp 1-3.

88   Staff Reporter, 'The State Science and Technology Commission Issues a Circular on Eight Lines of Distinction for Determining the Direction of Reform and Against Unhealthy Tendencies', *Jishu Shichang (Technology Market)*, 25 June 1985, p 1, translated in *JPRS-CST-85-034*, pp 9-11.

CHAPTER TWO

SCIENCE, TECHNOLOGY AND THE MARKET

The current leadership see organisational reform as a necessary prerequisite for attaining their policy objectives. The fact that a simple resurrection of the pre-Cultural Revolution system is seen as taking China into a cul-de-sac means that new organisational forms and mechanisms for regulating economic activity are deemed as necessary in order to provide the institutional flexibility and responsiveness to the demands of a society that is undergoing the often unpredictable process of modernisation. In China, technological progress and organisational development are now viewed as being interrelated and inter-dependent. Heavy-handed administrative fiat is to be replaced by a blend of administrative guidance and regulation via economic levers. This chapter looks first at the problems of the organisational structure of the civilian S&T system and then at the implications of the introduction of a 'market for S&T' in terms principally of the emergence of new organisational forms. Finally, the major problems in the way of this reform attempt will be considered.

Problems in the Civilian S&T Organisational Structure

The virtually unreformed Soviet system of the S&T structure as it operated in China in the late seventies, while useful for mobilising scarce resources to focus on the solution of designated problems, was singularly unsuccessful in providing a sufficient, consistent link between the research and productive sectors. Indeed there were even problems in co-ordinating work within the research sector itself. The organisation of the system into vertically distinct sectors and the poor co-ordination between them have meant that strong barriers are placed in the way of co-operation, and wasteful duplication of work and effort occurs.

The key problem identified by China's Party and state leaders for quick solution is the inability to turn research results into production. Consequently, the major reforms of the S&T system are designed to bring about closer links between these two sectors. According to Premier Zhao Ziyang, 'there should be countless organic links between scientific research and production units on a regular basis and in different forms. However, the past management system cut off direct links between them.'[1] Zhao attributed this problem precisely to the vertical structure of the S&T system with research institutes being responsible to higher authorities in their own command structure and not developing horizontal links with society and individual production units.

Problems have existed on both sides that have contributed to this divide between the two sectors. From the side of the production units, there was little incentive for them to adopt new technology before the reform programme started in 1979. Correspondingly, with the lack of demand there was very little incentive for China's scientific research institutes to focus on projects that could be swiftly applied to the production process.[2]

Lack of planning and inadequate market research in the past have meant that in many instances products were developed without sufficient guarantees that they were actually needed. These problems have been exaggerated by the lack of knowledge about the production system. Thus complaints by industrial departments about research institutes noted that they did not adequately consider product competitiveness in the market when planning research on new products nor the special features of the trade in order to take full advantage of them.[3] Such complaints about the isolation of the research and development (R&D) sector are common to all systems, not just China's. However, in China industrial organisation tended, on the whole, to inhibit the development of new technologies. There was not much finance available for such development within the enterprises themselves and very little incentive for them to seek out new technology from the research institutes.

Even where relevant, little effort was made by researchers and their institutions to popularise the results of their research.[4] This tendency was exacerbated by the fact that no system existed for a fair, paid transfer of research results. Scientific research results were treated as common property that could be used and adopted without any form of recompense. The free use of invention is said to have had a disincentive effect on the conduct of research and led to the hoarding of information for fear of research results being pirated by other institutions. One writer has referred to this graphically as thinking that 'our manure shall not fertilise other people's land'. Thus even when institutes or researchers themselves could not make use of results, these were not passed on to those who could.[5] In turn this attitude has led to the duplication of research. The *Jiefang Ribao* reported that some 980 units in China were developing haploid seed-breeding. In 1978-1979, 28 of 69 projects introduced in Shanghai's scientific and higher educational institutions were duplicated and 24 of the projects duplicated ones that were introduced in 1973 and 1974.[6] The duplication of research work was not helped by the fact that insufficient funds and channels existed for the dissemination of research results. The mushrooming, during the eighties, of scientific journals and conferences has provided an extensive system of communication and dissemination of information for the scientific community that should lead to the eradication of the worst instances of duplication. While problems of duplication may be declining, the question of application was still far from being resolved. A survey of the situation in 1984 implied that little progress had been made in this respect.[7] The survey covered over 3,500 scientific institutes throughout the country and showed that less than 10% of what the state termed scientific achievements had been applied to production.

Science and Technology as Commodities: the Contract System and the System of Payment for the Transfer of Scientific Results

To improve the situation as it existed in the late seventies, and as it persisted to some degree into the eighties, wide-ranging experimentation with some reforms has taken place. The current leadership is trying to give the market a greater role in deciding what kind of R&D it is necessary for scientific research institutes to undertake. Science, technology and knowledge are all now defined as commodities that have a price and that can be exchanged in the market place. Although it should be noted that the market place in China is a far from perfect one which is capable of distorting the kind of research undertaken. The justification for the definition of technology as a commodity is derived from Marx's assertion in *Capital* that a thing is a commodity when, apart from its having use value, its production consumes human labour, with an accumulation of human labour involved. It is argued that this applies not only to material products but is applicable also in the form of knowledge (scientific and technological). Technology can be defined as a commodity because it has 'use value and also has consumed people's labour.'[8] Further, given the current official definition that China operates a socialist commodity economy, transfer of technology and its popularisation are said to take the form of compensation or the form of commodity exchange.[9] Thus, the 'Decision on the Reform of the S&T Management System' states that 'the technology market constitutes an essential part of our country's socialist market'.[10] Prices are to be decided by the buyers in consultation with the sellers with no restrictions imposed by the state unless one of the parties involved is deemed to be acting unreasonably. Given the large number of virtual monopolies that exist in China such brokerage may well be necessary. The State Council's 'Temporary Regulations on Technology Transfers' state explicitly that 'units and individuals may all conduct technological transfers without local, organisational and economic forms of restrictions'.[11] This naturally requires that there is a demand for research and that there are guarantees for both buyers and sellers.

Successful reforms in the agricultural and industrial sectors have certainly led, in the last few years, to the demand for relevant technology. The introduction of the production responsibility system in agriculture has led to a rapid rise in income for many peasant households, particularly those in the vicinity of large and medium-sized cities. It is hoped that this new-found wealth and the tapping of latent potential in the rural areas will lead the peasants to seek out necessary technology. Certainly, the initial impact of the effective dismantling of the commune structure was the destruction of the S&T organisational structure in the rural areas. In Henan province, the agricultural scientific network at the basic levels was shattered with 80% of the organisations losing their functions.[12] In four counties in Anyang prefecture, the original scientific research team was reduced from 1,224 people to only 106.[13] However, the real impact was not as great as these figures would suggest. While the organisational structure was done away with, the personnel and their skills remained. Thus, it is not unusual that a former member of a commune or brigade office for scientific popularisation becomes the head of a specialised, or scientific, household. He or she then continues to peddle his or her skills on an individual, fee-paying, basis.

Despite the initial disruption, the current leadership clearly see the production responsibility system as the best method for updating agriculture with relevant modern science and technology. As peasants get richer they will acquire the necessary technology and, in turn, it is hoped that the system will impel machinery factories to organise production according to the peasants' need and to 'put farm mechanisation on to a solid mass foundation'.[14] However, increased agricultural mechanisation will be held up somewhat by the decrease in the size of the units of land caused by the adoption of the production responsibility system. Yet there is evidence to suggest that a comprehensive S&T system is re-emerging. By the end of 1984, 2,277 counties, about 93% of the total, had established associations for S&T. Also, over 41,000 township-level popularisation associations and 60,000 technical service organisations have been set up.[15] The key element in this new system is the agricultural technology contract that links the peasants to the agro-technicians and rewards the experts in relation to the increase in production.[16]

In the industrial sector, two major decisions have been taken that have had an impact on increasing the demand for S&T knowledge. The first was the extension of the responsibility system into the industrial sector, thus making enterprises responsible for their own profits and losses. Enterprises were also given the autonomy, within general guidelines, to decide how profits would be used. Consequently, enterprises would be able to purchase relevant new technology when necessary. The second important decision was to focus policy on the technological upgrading of existing plant rather than on the building of new factories and the reliance on the importing of modern technology. It was decided that the former represented the best route to increased industrial productivity and it would also force enterprises to seek primarily domestic sources for the necessary technology; although it should be pointed out that, in part, the upgrading of existing plant is to be achieved by using imported technology. In addition to these two major factors other related policies also had the effect of increasing demand. For example, the emphasis on energy conservation has led in many instances to enterprises searching for energy-saving technology. However, the subsidy system for the provision of energy supplies has in some cases distorted this policy.[17]

Summarising the situation, Tong Dalin and Hu Ping claim that two major problems stood in the way of successful application and popularisation of S&T achievements. The first was the absence of proper protection of an investor's interest by law. The second was the lack of normal channels for the transfer of achievements.[18] A major step towards solving the first of these problems was taken with the adoption of a Patent Law in March 1984 which came into force on 1 April 1985.[19] On 1 April, a total of 3,546 applications were filed and by 9 September the Patent Bureau had received 9,967 applications of which 3,235 had been filed by foreign businesses and individuals. Most of the applications were for new inventions with some for improvements and new designs.[20] By December 1985 China was beginning to grant its first patents.

The process of drafting the Patent Law began in 1979, while China joined the United National World Intellectual Property Organisation in March 1980.[21] It is expected that the Patent Law will 'give incentive to scientific and technical members to invent new devices and techniques and will play an active role in accelerating the imports of technology, the utilisation of foreign funds and the development of international economic and technical exchanges.'[22]

The law incorporates bold measures and should help with the import of technology. It effectively revives the patent right system after a hiatus of more than 20 years[23] and provides legal protection for patented foreign technologies that have hitherto been protected only by individual contracts. However, it should be noted that under the provisions of Article 6, the inventions of foreign businesses made in China will revert to China should the foreign business withdraw from the country. For a number of areas no patents will be granted, for example foodstuffs, beverages, flavourings, pharmaceutical products, chemical substances and animal and plant varieties. However, patents can be granted for the processes used in producing such products.

To handle the new work the China Council for the Promotion of International Trade – a non-governmental organisation – has become China's patent agency. Since 1957 the Council had been the sole trademark agency in China. Now it is to assist foreign individuals and companies in applying for patents in China and Chinese organisations in applying for patents abroad. It will draw up and translate patent applications, advise on how to apply for a patent and provide legal services dealing with patent lawsuits, patent transfer and licensing negotiations.[24] To support the new patent system a crash training programme had to be undertaken in order to provide the necessary personnel. By mid-1985, some 4,400 patent agents had been trained to staff the patent offices scattered across China while another 1,500 were undergoing training. In the head office in Beijing there were 207 patent examiners and an archive containing 30 million patent documents.[25] Given the speed with which many of these people must have been trained a question mark must hang over their capacity to deal with complicated legal problems. This is compounded by the fact that there is virtually no precedent for them to refer to.

Setting up the patent system is only part of the solution. Funds must also be provided to create conditions so that patents serve their purpose and a system capable of absorbing new inventions swiftly and fruitfully is created. In the words of one writer, when China 'can afford to buy the horse' it must also be able to 'fit the saddle'.[26]

It is not surprising that the attempts to reform the S&T system to encourage the transfer of technology have followed those in the Soviet Union and Eastern Europe. Faced with the same problems of the lack of integration between research institutes and the production sector, the Soviet Union introduced, in 1961, 'Decisions Relating to the Transformation of the Economic Accounting System in Scientific Research Units and Design Institutes'. This made it necessary for research institutes to derive part of their funds from economic agreements signed with enterprises. Similar reforms were introduced somewhat later in the East European nations. In Hungary, after the economic reforms were implemented in 1968, this system became common. For example, after the reform the Budapest Steel Research Institute derived 80% of its annual research expenses from contracts concluded factories and only 20% from government organisations. Clearly the with Chinese made careful study of these reforms while introducing the contract system.[27]

Experimentation with the system in China has been underway for a number of years, but it was only in mid-1984 that the system became the central component of national policy. After 1979, when it was decided to broaden the decision-making powers of enterprises, experiments were also introduced to give greater powers to research institutes. This experimentation began in some 15 or 16 provinces and municipalities including Sichuan, Shanghai and Hebei and in the Ministries of Machine-Building Industry, Chemical Industry, Aeronautics and Astronautics.[28] On the basis of experimentation, in April 1984, the SSTC and the State Commission for Reform of the Economic System formulated 'Suggestions on the Experiment of Changing Research and Development Units from the System under which Operating Expenses are Paid Directly by the State to the System under which they are Paid for by Fulfilling a Contract with the Enterprises they Serve.' This document formed the basis for extending the use of contracts throughout the system.[29]

The State Council announced that it had approved a remunerative contract system for all China's developmental research institutes to be implemented within three to five years. By the end of 1984, 535 such institutes were experimenting with the paid contract system and they were expected to become financially independent within two or three years. This represents some 12% of China's 4,450 independent research institutes. In early 1985, 187 scientific research institutes were said to be providing their own expenses and were thus no longer relying on government appropriations.[30] Evidence from provincial sources suggests that local leaders are trying to meet the earlier rather than the later of these time-scales. In Shanxi province, in April 1985, it was proposed that all relevant institutes at and above prefectural and city levels should adopt the system before the end of 1986 and become financially independent within two to three years. Beijing municipality announced in August 1984 that the contract system had been extended to all areas and it was required that all such institutes should eliminate all operating expenses by 1986.[31]

The contract system then is seen as the key to revitalising the S&T research sector and linking it to the production sector. Praise such as the following is quite common in the Chinese press: 'In economic reform, the implementation of the paid contract system has revitalised every cell of many research institutes, activated the whole body of S&T research systems and spurred on reforms related to the system of planning, investment, personnel, wages and leadership. Therefore, in the reform of S&T research systems, the implementation of the paid contract system is a big issue of great significance.'[32]

To press this claim and to encourage a wider adoption of the paid contract system many reports have been publicised about its success in those institutes that have experimented with the reform. For example, in the first two years of experimenting with the new system introduced in 1980, the Shanghai Textile Research Institute and the Research Institute of Machine-Building Technology managed to apply 70% to 80% of their laboratory achievements to production.[33] According to the *Guangming Ribao*, the utilisation ratio by the second half of 1984 of scientific results of units that practised the paid contract system was generally over 80-90%. The same article refers to the experience of, among others, the Precision Machinery Research Institute of the Ministry of Aeronautics since it adopted the new system in 1980. In 1983, the institute yielded 24 achievements, 22 of which were popularised (91.7%).[34] When the system was introduced in the last quarter of 1981 in the research institutes of 20 industrial units in Beijing they showed a 20% increase in their results while institutes not included in the trial showed a 6.2% decrease. Application of results increased by 21% in the trial institutes compared with 12.7% for the other institutes.[35]

A second advantage, obviously related to the first, is that the contract system, and also consultancy work, etc., opens up new channels for funding and thus reduces dependence on state allocations for operating expenses. As was noted above, 187 institutes were said to be capable of ensuring their own financing. In 1983, according to incomplete statistics on 3,536 research institutes under provincial control, the income received from contracts was 36.6% of the state-granted operating expenses.[36] A 1985 survey of 20 institutes implementing the contract system in Hubei province also indicated the progress made. The survey found that nine institutes were no longer dependent on state funds while the other 11 derived more revenue from contracts, etc., than from state appropriations and they were said to be 'basically economically independent'.[37]

A third perceived advantage of the system is that it will 'bring out the initiative of S&T personnel'.[38] The contract system is intended to regulate relations not only between the research institute and other organisations but also within the institute itself. In the institute, research projects and other forms of job economic responsibility systems are to be used in dealing with its laboratories, shops and individuals. It is expected that this system will enable the extra income generated by the institute to be used to reward people in terms of wages, bonuses, etc., according to the quantity and quality of work done. This would bring research workers into line with the reward system already operating in the countryside and being extended throughout the industrial sector.[39]

One final advantage is that it is seen as a way of overcoming the uneven and unequal distribution of research institutes within China. It is hoped that organisational barriers that previously hindered the transfer of technology will be broken down and that technology will flow not only into the production sector and across the different organisational systems but also across different regional systems. Thus paid contracts, consultancies, and also increased mobility of personnel are seen as mechanisms to encourage the transfer of research results and expertise from advanced centres within China to the 'more backward regions'. The previous dominant method for the dissemination of advanced technology relied heavily on enterprises adopting experiences of 'advanced units' through promotion and emulation of models. While this method is good for highlighting a particular experience, it is, on the whole, a very hit and miss, inefficient approach in terms of ensuring that individual enterprises acquire the correct technology for their particular needs.

At the forefront of technology transfer within China has been the municipality of Shanghai. During the years 1977-1981, incomplete statistics show that 48 scientific research institutes and institutes of higher learning in Shanghai supplied 342 items of technical know-how to the rest of China. In the same period of time, province-level authorities entrusted 1,385 research and trial production tasks to 56 Shanghai research institutes, colleges and universities. This earned Shanghai's 44 municipal research units and institutes of higher education under the central authorities a total of 20 million *yuan* from the supply of technical help, undertaking experiments entrusted to them and the provision of technical services and advice.[40] On the basis of Shanghai's experience, a conference was held to 'exchange experiences' on co-operative scientific research in Shanghai.[41] This has led to a further increase in this work. For example, in 1983, Shanghai signed agreements on 517 technological co-operation projects with regions inhabited by minority nationalities including Yunnan, Ningxia, Xinjiang, Tibet and Qinghai. This was more than twice the number of agreements signed between 1978 and 1982. To help promote these 'transfers', Shanghai municipality has adopted a number of measures including tax concessions and the provision of loans to encourage local research institutes and colleges to establish direct links with these 'resource-rich and economically underdeveloped regions'.[42]

Clearly, where possible other less well-endowed provinces have been taking advantage of these new possibilities. The Shanxi Provincial People's Government has signed a protocol with the CAS to help build up its energy and chemical industry bases.[43] Between 1980 and October 1982, Yunnan province signed contracts of co-operation with other provinces and municipalities for 178 technical projects.[44] Contracts for technical co-operation have also been agreed between production units themselves. Thus, with help from the Shanghai No 3 Sewing Machine Plant, the Luoyang Sewing Machine Plant in Henan province was able to improve its technological capabilities. After the agreement had been in operation for a year the Luoyang plant had tripled its monthly output, converting an annual loss of 4-500,000 *yuan* into an annual profit of roughly the same amount.[45]

Interrelated and also of importance is the promotion of consultancy work. Consultancy work has been developing slowly since 1979/80 but is now being promoted more vigorously. According to *Wenhui Bao* the 'provision of science and technology consulting services is an implementation of the policy that science and technology must serve economic construction and is an important way of stimulating the development of science and technology in co-ordination with the economy and society'.[46] As a result of the new emphasis, a number of technical consultancy agencies have been set up. The first of its kind was the China Science and Technology Consultancy Service set up by the CAST in March 1983.[47] Shortly afterwards, the CAS announced that it had set up its own Science and Technology Consultancy and Development Service Department. It also stated that the branches and research institutes of the CAS were to establish corresponding S&T consultancy and development service departments.[48]

An ambitious development in Wuhan in July 1984 saw the setting up of the Yellow Crane (*Huanghe*) Associated Development Centre for Education, Science and Technology. The centre has under it 25 units in the Wuhan area, 23 of which are institutions of higher learning. The objective of the centre is to promote the activities of its component units and to facilitate the commercialisation of R&D for the units organised under it. The centre has no facilities of its own but will contract out work to the relevant institutions. It intends not only to work within China but also to 'carry out extensive co-operations with the units of the same trade in other parts of the world, and will undertake domestic and foreign business concerning cultural, educational and scientific research'.[49]

New Organisational Forms: Scientific Research and Production Bodies and Technology Development Centres

Where longer-term co-operation between research institutions and production units is desirable and profitable a variety of new organisational forms are emerging. Important in this respect are the formation of integrated systems of scientific research and production or, where a teaching unit is also involved, integrated systems of teaching, scientific research and production. The Decision on the Reform of the S&T Management System called on developmental research institutes to 'set up various forms of partnership with enterprises and design units on a voluntary and mutually beneficial basis'. Some of these partnerships may 'develop themselves into research and production-type enterprises, or associated technology development organs of medium and small-sized enterprises'. Units that come under this classification are permitted to set aside a certain percentage of the 'newly-increased portion of profits' as technology development funds.[50] In fact, Zhao Ziyang had given his seal of approval to this type of organisation as early as May 1982 when he stated:

> If in the future, based on its own actual teaching circumstances and the direction of its scientific research, a college can combine with a factory, there will be formed a regular joint body for teaching, scientific research, and production, or what is called a community.[51]

These research and production bodies, or communities, have two main defining organisational characteristics. First, their main component is a scientific research organisation that also exercises a certain degree of leadership at various levels. This distinguishes them from large-scale trust companies as the main components of those are large key enterprises and not scientific research institutes. The second organisational characteristic is that they include organisations needed for each step from theoretical research to application in production. This sets them apart from technology development centres as those centres do not include all the steps in the research-production process.

Depending on the degree of integration, three types of research and production bodies, or teaching, research and production bodies, exist. The first type is the 'loosely-structured type' which, to date, is the most common. They are established where steady, long-term, and comprehensive S&T co-operation already exists. In general, they are not regulated by any special administrative arrangements. They do not constitute a legal entity and the member units remain independent. The second type is the semi-entity research production body. This body has some permanent organisational features and some member units remain legally independent while some do not. It has special administrative organs to support it and the permanent organisations have their own, independent properties that are separate from the member units and thus qualify as legal corporations. The most integrated form is the entity-type scientific production body. This integrated enterprise is formed by several scientific research organs, enterprises and production units or universities and forms a separate legal entity.[52]

Two examples of the scientific research and production body are the China Gas and Turbine Research and Development Company and the Dalian Textile Printing and Dyeing Complex. The former was set up in late 1982/early 1983 by one of the institutes under the CAS and a machinery plant under the Ministry of Aviation Industry. Its objective is to develop turbines for use in a number of fields and its venture capital of 3 million *yuan* was supplied by the State Planning Commission. At the time of its establishment the venture was heralded as a way of developing an advanced technological sector and as a method that would become more common in the future.[53]

The Dalian venture was established by four research institutes, two universities and 16 textile enterprises. By the end of 1983, the venture had undertaken 46 major scientific research projects and developed more than 250 new varieties and designs. In 1983 it created over 100 million *yuan* of output value and turned over to the state 19.25 million *yuan* in the form of taxes and profits.[54]

An example of a venture that combines teaching, scientific research and production is the Huadong Chemical Engineering College. The college has signed nine agreements for teaching, research and production joint bodies with Changzhou City (Jiangsu province), Jiading county (Shanghai municipality) and Zaozhuang City (Shandong province) and has undertaken 55 projects which was 24.1% of the total of the college's research projects. One of the staff members divided the types of teaching, scientific research and production joint bodies into three: large enterprises, medium-sized enterprises and small and rural commune-brigade enterprises or border area enterprises. Work for the first type entails devising projects of a technical development exploitation nature and providing on-the-job training of engineering technicians or class study. The second type calls for transferring scientific and technological results, mainly new products, energy-saving techniques and also for the running of short-term training classes. The last type also entails the transfer of S&T results and helping to put them into production and the training of technical workers.

More recently, the college began to move beyond the idea of a loose coalition to forming a jointly run factory geared to rural commune-brigade industry. It is said that 'compared with a joint body, it is further developed organisationally, economically and technologically'. One such factory is jointly run with the Songyin Resin Factory in Jinshan. The factory is run by a management committee in which both sides have a quota or representation. Financially, both parties jointly make investments with the college mainly making the technological investment. Profits are distributed according to the proportion of investment. Technologically, the college takes an overall responsibility, including the training of technical workers in-house. It is expected that the college will be able to gather around it a series of 'jointly run factories that will be its own teaching, scientific research, and production bases'.[55]

Naturally enough, these organisations are seen as a major step forward in the process of linking scientific research to production. In particular, they are said to speed up the process of transfer of research results. Thus, in the Dalian Textile Printing and Dyeing Complex the development of new products now only takes six months to a year instead of the previous two years.[56] Secondly, it is said that they can not only shorten the development time for a new product but also improve the quality of the products. It is argued that since the bodies have all the links in the research-production cycle, it is possible for them to organise 'a strict and effective quality control system and create good-quality products'.[57] A third key advantage is that they can serve as 'modern science and technology training schools'. Because the technicians and workers in the production unit are, in theory at least, continually exposed to new advances it is said that the work-force will diversify their skills and will also step-by-step upgrade their knowledge.[58] Where such bodies are linked with teaching institutions this can provide advantages for the students. The students, especially those completing their studies, can be introduced to concrete examples of problems to be solved in the production process.[59]

One further possibility of metamorphosis for a developmental research institute is to turn itself into a Technology Development Centre (TDC). TDCs have also been given Premier Zhao Ziyang's seal of approval. In October 1982, when speaking at the National Science Awards Conference, he commented on them favourably and stated that the number of centres should be small and that they should be well-managed and function properly. Clearly Zhao was not in favour of setting up TDCs just for the sake of it. Once established, according to Zhao, they should be oriented to serving their own trades and in particular small and medium-sized enterprises.[60]

Two main methods exist for developing a TDC from a scientific research institution. The first method is simply to base the centre on an existing institution and carry out such adjustments and replenishments as are necessary. A second possibility is to use an existing institution as the skeleton on to which other relevant research laboratories would be attached to form a joint TDC. In the former case, the research institute advises the business of various laboratories in the trade forming a technical development network using the institute as a development centre. In the latter, the research institute leads the work of various industrial laboratories in the trade to form jointly a TDC.[61] However, as Premier Zhao has warned, in this case 'one particular department should undertake primary responsibility'.[62]

This can lead to a variety of forms for TDCs, but they can be broadly categorised in three main groups. A generalised TDC is in a highly specialised trade with a wide technical coverage such as may be formed from institutes of welding, laser and technical physics. A specialised TDC is formed in a highly specialised trade with a concentrated technical coverage. This would be based on a research institute in paper-making, timing devices, glass, leather, synthetic fibre, knitting or furniture. A comprehensive TDC combines many disciplines across a number of trades and would be based on a research institute of chemical, textile or biomedical engineering.[63]

Despite Zhao's call that the number of centres should be small, they have been mushrooming and more recently individuals and collectives have been able to set up TDCs. By July 1984, 11 such centres had been set up in Beijing. The first to be established, in April 1983, was the Huaxia TDC. The centre was opened by Chen Chunxian, a research fellow at the Institute of Physics of the CAS, with a 100,000 *yuan* loan from a local industrial company. In mid-1984, it had a staff of 70, including two engineers from the Institute of Physics and 'dozens of spare-time technicians'. Its main achievements to date have been to supply technology for making ground cable power leakage monitors to the Liaoyuan Radio Factory in north-east China and it drew an agreed commission on the factory's profits of 600,000 *yuan* during its first year.[64]

The primary task of a TDC is to concentrate on technical transformation of the industries within their own specific trade. They are seen as a vital cog in the wheel of replacing the 'five olds' with the 'five news'.[65] In addition, such centres are expected to work on the development of new technology in the trade and to assist medium and small-scale enterprises in the development of new technology and products. They are also expected to help absorb the import of new technology and make sure that what is imported is relevant to the needs of the particular trades and can be fitted smoothly into China's production sector.[66]

Matchmakers: S&T Service Centres and S&T Fairs

To play the role of matchmaker between those looking for technical knowledge and those who wish to sell their research results, a variety of organisations have grown up and a series of S&T fairs have been sponsored to bring the relevant partners into contact.

There has been a rapid growth in organs promoting the development of exchange of S&T information and services. Essentially, they are S&T Development and Service Centres but they operate under a variety of names such as a S&T Development Exchange Corporation (*Keji kaifa jiaoliu gongsi*) or a Technology Service Corporation (*Jishu fuwu gongsi*).

The first initiative in this direction was taken by the Shenyang Scientific and Technology Committee which set up the 'Shenyang Scientific and Technical Services Corporation' in 1980.[67] The following year in Wuhan the first National Technical Exchange and Trade Symposium was held to discuss experiences to date and to expand the system.[68] By early 1985, at and above the level of district and city (*Dishi*) there were approximately 1,400 of these centres,[69] a rapid increase from the 1,000 that existed in August 1984.[70]

Of the existing service organisations at the end of 1984 more than 140 belonged to the various state ministries and commissions.[71] In 1983, a nationwide co-ordinating network was set up for all these organisations called the 'National Liaison Net for Scientific and Technological Service Co-operation Among Large and Medium Cities'. This move was supported by the SSTC and in 1985 it set up a National Market Development Centre to promote the circulation of scientific research findings and technology.[72] One of the main activities of these organisations is to arrange for 'technology fairs' to exchange technology and skilled personnel. These fairs may also be sponsored by other government organisations, industries or even individuals.[73]

Tianjin municipality is said to have been the first to open the technology market by starting a S&T store and it was quickly followed by a number of others.[74] Many cities have been active in promoting exchanges via the 'technology fairs'. For example, in Beijing, the Centre for the Exchange of S&T Developments has co-ordinated the activities of a variety of organisations since it was set up in 1981 and held four fairly large-scale trade fairs.[75] The last of these was primarily intended to serve small-town enterprises and it brought some 10,000 of them into contact with over 250 Beijing institutions of higher education and scientific research units.[76]

Clearly, the scope and the scale of these fairs are expanding. For example, in March 1985, the first national fair for the transfer of military industrial technologies to civilian use was held in Hangzhou while in the city of Liaoyang,

Liaoning province, a special fair is held every five days providing consultancy and technical services for the local peasants.[77] According to statistics released by eight technical development and exchange organisations in Beijing, Wuhan, Shenyang, Dalian, Chongqing, Hangzhou, Xian and Chengdu, 34 large-scale scientific and technical exchange fairs have been held since 1981, featuring a total of 19,000 scientific achievements and services. At the fairs, 5,300 contracts on technical transfers and technical co-operation have been signed and the total volume of business conducted has amounted to 130 million *yuan*. Over one million people have participated. Also, the technical fairs have organised 123 scientific research-production complexes and concluded 9,320 scientific research agreements with a total value of 160 million *yuan*. This has contributed two billion *yuan* to the state in output value and enriched the coffers of the treasury by 320 million *yuan* in profits taxes. Moreover, they have organised 512 technical training classes which have provided training for 42,000 people.[78]

The success of these latter fairs led to the convening of China's 'First National Technical Products Fair' held in the Beijing Exhibition Hall from 14 May to 10 June 1985. The fair concentrated on areas such as negotiating technology transfer, technical consulting, bidding for projects, technical training, joint ventures, and product design and contracting.[79] The fair had powerful co-sponsors: the SSTC, the State Economic Commission, the defence sector commission and the Beijing municipality government. Over 10,000 contracts were signed and agreements reached on about 3 million *yuan* worth of technology transfers.[80]

Serving the Civilian Sector: the Transfer of Military Technology

As in the USA and the USSR, much of the most advanced research and many of the most talented personnel are working in the military research sector with much better financial backing and invariably with more sophisticated and up-to-date equipment and facilities. The breakdown of the barrier between the military and the civilian S&T sectors is seen as a key mechanism for the advancement of the civilian S&T capabilities. This policy objective was taken up in the Decision on the Reform of the S&T Management System. The 'Decision' calls on defence research institutes to establish a 'new system of army-people co-operation'. As long as national defence assignments are fulfilled, these institutes are to accelerate technology transfer between the two sectors and to 'engage enthusiastically in the research and development of civilian products'.[81] The appointment of Song Jian as the head of the SSTC is seen as important in this respect as his previous experience has been in the military sector. Before assuming the post of minister, Song had been a vice-minister of the Astronautics Industry, chief and vice-minister of the Seventh Ministry of Machine Building and director of a research office under the Ministry of National Defence. Both the Astronautics Ministry and the Seventh Ministry of Machine Building work predominantly for the military sector. Song's appointment is seen as conducive to encouraging other personnel to transfer from the military to the civilian sector and military research institutes to re-focus their work.

The attempt to redirect some of the work of the military research institutes towards civilian production is compounded by the fact that underuse of both the research potential and the production capacity of the military sector is a widespread phenomenon. Despite the proclamation of this policy, considerable opposition exists within the military to redirecting its work towards the civilian sector.[82] It has been said that 'some comrades believed that developing civilian products was an "extra burden" and was "not doing proper work". Some scientific and technical personnel worried that developing civilian products would "waste technology", "affect specialisation" and "be a blow to the military industry".'[83]

Such complaints notwithstanding, it has been made clear that the new policy is a long-term one. Lest military units saw the policy as a temporary measure until military spending picked up again, the *Liaoning Daily* warned that such technology transfer is 'definitely not just an expedient to solve the military industry's "lack of enough to eat" problem during the period of re-adjustment' but is an 'important peacetime measure and a basic and long-term national scientific and technological policy through which military industrial departments can contribute to and serve economic construction'.[84]

The problem of effective transfer is hampered by a number of other factors such as confidentiality, lack of information and mechanisms for the transfer of technology. Confidentiality of military industrial technology clearly provides a problem for those wishing to find out if it may be suitable for civilian use. To deal with this problem, it was made known in May 1985 that China was formulating measures to revoke this confidentiality in order to 'liberate the technology from its frozen state so as to make the technological achievements in this field promptly become the means of large-scale commodity production'.[85] To help with the flow of information, a newspaper was launched, on 15 March 1985, sponsored by the national defence technology information committee. The newspaper covers the question of transferring military industrial technology to the civilian sector.[86]

Many of the methods outlined above in this chapter are seen as being applicable to promoting co-operation between the military and civilian sectors. An article in 1982 suggested four main methods should be used through which the transfer could be effected. First, the military and civilian sectors are to be joined together, with enterprises producing for both sectors as demands arise. Secondly, technical services are to be provided to the civilian sector. Thirdly, scientific and technological knowledge and experience are to be transferred. This extends beyond exchange of information in so far as the national security is protected to the exchange of personnel. Fourthly, joint ventures in scientific research and production are to be set up.[87] The use of 'technology fairs' can also now be added to this list. The March 1985 national trade fair carried out business transactions to the tune of 1,120 million *yuan* and concluded transactions on more than 3,200 projects, 44.3% of all the projects offered at the fair.[88]

Despite the problems that exist some notable successes have been made in linking the military and the civilian sectors. A number of ministries and research institutes that had previously done most of their work for the military sector have begun to redirect substantial resources to production for civilian use. In January 1985, Vice-Premier Li Peng told a work conference of the Ministry of Nuclear Industry to focus its work on civilian rather than military needs. The work conference in fact decided to increase the output value of civilian goods produced by the nuclear industry in 1985 by 25% over that of 1984.[89] In May 1985 an official of the industry stated that whereas in the past 80% of the work had been directed towards military production, in the future 80% would be used for civilian production.[90] An example of a research institute that has similarly redirected the focus of its work is the Inorganic Coating Research Laboratory of the CAS, which originally did over 90% of its work on the study of new materials for the national defence industry. However, by mid-1982 some 54% of its work was involved in scientific research for civilian use.[91] Longer-term co-operation between the military and provinces and municipalities has also been developing. In May 1983, the National Defence Commission and Tianjin municipality agreed on a long-term economic and technical co-operation agreement. Under the agreement 296 co-operation projects have been established. The main emphasis was on 83 of these projects of which 34 were to be completed by the end of 1984.[92]

To promote closer co-operation, 16 provinces have set up 'Integrated Military-Civilian Leadership Organs' under the leadership of a local government official and drawing members from among the leaders of the local economic, planning, and S&T commissions and the national S&T and industry office. The organs' administrative office is set up within the scientific work office.[93] To promote technology markets and the circulation of commodities, 13 provinces have set up National Defence S&T and Industrial Technology Development or Consultancy Companies.[94] As a consequence of such measures, the amount of technology transfer work has been increasing. In 1983, economic and technological contracts between military and civilian units totalled 416, while in 1984, according to incomplete statistics from 14 provinces, the number of contracts agreed was over 8,000. The volume of business was around 430 million *yuan*.[95]

Certainly, production for the civilian sector can be very profitable and it has turned the accounts of some institutes from being in the red to being in the black. Cut-backs in military expenditure have forced some enterprises to look elsewhere for work to keep them going. One such case was the Nanhua Power Machinery Research Institute which in 1979 through lack of work found itself in a 'half-starving state'. As a result it decided to branch out into civilian research. Its most noteworthy success was the development of an automatic bread production line for the Zhuzhou Bread Factory, the first such system to be developed in China.[96] Also, at the provincial and the national level civilian production is playing an increased economic role for the military. In Jiangsu province, the defence industry has assigned 130 production lines to produce 1,145 varieties of some 100 categories of civilian products such as televisions, electric fans and refrigerators. The output value of these products accounted for over 60% of the total output value of the provincial defence industry.[97] For the defence industry as a whole, in 1983 the output value of civilian products had risen to 22% of the total value from 10% in 1978.[98]

Market Reforms in an Imperfect Market

The basic problem with an increased use of the market to regulate both economic and S&T activity is quite simply that the market at present is an imperfect one. Both Chinese and foreign observers have noted that the whole programme of economic reform has been taking place within an irrational price structure. The Chinese government has now committed itself to dealing with the thorny issue of price reform and the potentially explosive problem of the subsidy system. However, it is recognised that this will be a slow, complicated and, for some, possibly painful business; the example of Poland has been carefully studied and digested by China's leaders. The inconsistencies in the pricing system may mean that some developmental research institutes find it impossible to become profitable through no fault of their own. At present, the true market value of research that is being done by a particular institute may not necessarily be reflected in the price it can charge to the enterprises which need it. In some instances it can even be uneconomic for an enterprise to chase after new technology. In May 1984, the *Guangming Daily* carried a report on an investigation carried out in Shanghai. The Shanghai Joint Section for the Development of New Products investigated the situation in 472 factories and found that the average profit rate of the costs of new products was generally lower than that of old products. For example, the average profit rate of the pressurised vacuum flasks was said to be only 10%, compared to rates of 25% for older products. This had the effect that the higher the output of new products, the lower the average profit.[99] Not surprisingly, many enterprises see it as too risky to open a new venture and often find it not worthwhile to adopt new technology.

The problem of encouraging the development of new products has led to calls for and the introduction of measures for them to be accorded preferential treatment in terms of loans, reduction of taxes and trial sale prices, and for merging funding for S&T achievements and technical transformation into production costs. The crippling effect of industrial and commercial taxes on new product development is illustrated by the following example that occurred in Tianjin. In 1982, a research institute found itself facing industrial and commercial taxes of 2.06 million *yuan* covering 1981 and 1982 for the new eddy spinning technology that it had developed. Originally, in 1981, the new technology had been exempted from tax. After mediation by officials in the Tianjin government the bill was reduced to 980,000 *yuan* but in 1983 a further bill of 1.2 million *yuan* was presented. Not surprisingly, this seriously hampered the development of the technology and finally after numerous appeals it was agreed that no taxes would be levied, beginning in 1984.[100]

At present profitability is no guide to efficiency as statistics compiled by Ishihara on profit-funds ratios make very clear.[101] High ratios exist for wristwatches (61.1%), bicycles (39.8) and domestic appliances (30.0) as well as for rubber processing (44.9), petroleum (37.7) and pharmaceuticals (33.1). At the bottom end of the scale, low ratios are found for raw materials such as chemical fertilisers (1.4), iron ore (1.6), coal (2.1) and cement (4.4), and for activities such as shipbuilding (2.1).[102] Problems exist with respect to military products. Here prices are also said not to reflect true value. In 1985, prices for military products were established according to costs added to profits, the latter being fixed at 5% of costs. This leads to the phenomenon of higher total profits deriving from higher costs.[103]

Price reform is recognised in the 'Decision on the Reform of the Economic Structure' (October 1984) as the 'key to the reform of the whole economic structure'.[104] In particular three major irrationalities within the price system are identified: insufficient or no price differentials for a product with diverse quality; price ratios between different commodities are skewed, this is especially the case with the relatively low prices for some mineral products and raw and semi-finished materials in comparison with manufactured goods; and the retail prices of major farm products are lower than the price the state pays for them.[105] Thus the reforms aim at eliminating these particular problems although an extremely cautious approach to the problem is suggested.

Sharp price rises for staple and consumer goods have caused unrest in a number of state-socialist societies and it is not surprising that China has chosen to proceed carefully. This caution is increased because of China's own experience with trying to raise low prices in 1979 and 1980. These attempts caused unrest, for not only did the *Renmin Ribao* in January 1981 devote an editorial to discussing the problem of why price rises could not be lowered,[106] but appeals were made to protect commodity price workers against retaliation from angry citizens.[107] This and the alarm at the rise in the retail price index caused experimentation to be called to a halt along with the general slowdown in the urban economic reform programme that took place in 1981. In November 1982, when Premier Zhao Ziyang announced a new phase in experimentation, it was notable that he indicated that during the subsequent three years priority would be given to the reform of the tax system rather than the price system.[108] By late 1984, it was recognised that reform could be delayed no longer. The destabilising effect and the fears of the population have been noted and the 'Decision' promises that the price rises should not result in a fall in the real income of urban and rural inhabitants. However, the proviso is added that productivity will have to go up to bring about the necessary pay rises.[109] Despite these promises, it is clear that by the end of 1985 concern did exist about price rises, particularly in those groups on fixed incomes such as students. In December 1985, the *Beijing Review* noted that the economic reforms had sent food prices up, sometimes to alarming levels,[110] and as China entered 1986 the whole question of price reform appeared once again to be becoming bogged down.

The introduction of production units becoming responsible for their own profits and losses does not automatically mean that profit-making units will go in search of new technology to upgrade their technological capacity. Adoption of new technology and processes disrupt production for a time, and some factory directors have clearly opted for a certain short-term gain rather than gambling on a potentially larger gain over the long term. Probably in the earlier years of the reform programme, this tendency was reinforced by uncertainty about how long it would last. Despite constant reassurances by the leadership about the continuity of policy even after Deng Xiaoping's death, China's population have seen too many abrupt policy changes over the last 25 years for no niggling doubts to remain in the back of their minds. While this fear may be less in the mid-eighties, it was certainly widespread in the early eighties and strengthened tendencies to look for short-term returns rather than to plan long-term investments. Some directors who do decide to upgrade the technological level of their enterprises may decide to do so by relying not on domestically produced technology but on imports from abroad. This is because in many instances where technology is imported the cost is borne in some form by the state. By contrast the factory must foot the bill if it uses domestically produced technology. Finally, whether an enterprise takes advantage of the new technology on offer depends on the calibre of its leadership personnel. In this respect, the policy of appointing those with technical skills to leadership positions has been important as have the corresponding policies to increase enterprise autonomy and to increase the independence of the enterprise director from the interference of the enterprise's Party committee.

Despite success in promoting the paid contract system for developmental research institutes, problems need to be solved before it can be extended fully throughout the system. To date adoption of the system has not been mandatory; only those institutes that have actually applied operate the system. Presumably those institutes that have adopted the contract system already are those which have most to gain from such a system. In part, this helps to explain the high percentage of success stories that have been reported. If, however, the system is to be extended to all developmental research institutes within three to five years, a number of problems will arise and some difficult decisions will have to be made. Many institutes have neither the facilities nor the personnel necessary to make a success of the contract system. For example, a survey of research institutes in Tianjin municipality showed that only 28.2% were in reasonable shape, 50% were said to be mediocre while 21.4% were described as being relatively poor.[111] While it is impossible to know what the categories really mean, they indicate that problems are widespread. According to a member of the municipality's science committee, although the contract system had brought undoubted benefits 'generally speaking, current research work still cannot satisfy the urgent need of economic development'. He claimed that in Tianjin some of the institutes still could not conduct scientific research five years after their foundation.[112]

Do the authorities have the power or the political will to make those institutes that prefer the status quo adopt the new system? It remains to be seen whether those institutes that are not financially viable will be closed down. Chinese officials answer enquiries about this by saying that such institutes will be amalgamated with other research institutes or industrial enterprises or that their personnel will be redeployed. It seems unlikely, however, that successful institutes or enterprises will willingly take in unprofitable institutes if it would damage their new-found economic success. Also, if institutes are really to be given greater powers over the employment of personnel, it is difficult to see how extra staff can be forced on them if they do not have a positive contribution to offer.

With the introduction of the contract system there is no reason why the barriers between research institutes should be broken down. Certainly, if there is money to be made it should be the case that various research institutes will pool their knowledge and facilities for particular projects. On the other hand, institutes may jealously guard their innovations in order to maximise their own gains and to prevent others from profiting from their work. In this respect the degree of efficacy of the new Patent Law will be of great importance in regulating the process of sufficient rewards for innovation.

The contract system etc. are seen as important methods for ensuring the transfer of research results from China's advanced centres to its more backward regions. Yet the need to pay for technology and knowledge may well hamper the development of China's backward and relatively poorer regions. Increasingly, a region's access to necessary technology will be defined by its ability to pay for it. While examples of internal technology transfer are publicised in the press, it is unclear how extensive and consistent they are. If the poorer regions are unable to develop their own S&T research force, their level of development and development strategy will become increasingly dependent on that area's relationship with advanced centres such as Shanghai. Already examples exist of poorer regions becoming suppliers of raw materials to China's developed coastal regions in return for the necessary technology to exploit their raw materials. However, it can equally be argued that such dependence is more rational than notions of provincial 'self-reliance' and purchase of technology may prove cheaper than the development of a large number of provincial S&T research networks.

Notes

1 Zhao Ziyang, 'Gaige keiji tizhi, tuidong keji he jingji, shehui xietiao' ('Reform the Science and Technology System, Promote the Co-ordination of Science and Technology with the Economy'), *RMRB*, 21 March 1985, pp 1 and 3.

2 According to Luo Wei, Deputy Director of the Science Policy Study Office of the CAS, while both sides had to accept the blame, he felt that industry should bear the greater responsibility. Interview 16 January 1985.

3 See Chen Xianhua, 'Zhuajin jianli hangye jishu kaifa zhongxin' ('Pay Close Attention to the Establishment of Technology Development Centres'), *KYGL*, no 1, 1984, pp 35-36.

4 Xia Yulong and Liu Ji, 'It is also Necessary to Eliminate Erroneous "Leftist" Influence on the Science and Technology Front', *Jiefang Ribao*, 2 June 1981, p 4, translated in *FBIS* China - 81-112, 11 June 1981, K8-K12.

5 Xie Shaoming, 'Shixing you chang hetong zhi' ('Implement the Paid Contract System'), *GMRB*, 22 October 1984, p 2.

6 Xia Yulong and Liu Ji, 'It is also Necessary to Eliminate Erroneous "Leftist" Influence on the Science and Technology Front'.

7 'Combine Research with Production', *BR*, no 11, 18 March 1985, p.4.

8 For examples of this kind of reasoning see Xiao Liang, 'Lun jishu shangpinhua de jige lilun wenti' ('On Several Theoretical Problems Concerning the Commercialism of Technology'), *GMRB*, 7 April 1984, p.4; and 'Technical Markets are the Key to the Reform of the Science and Technology System', *Jingji Ribao (Economic Daily)*, 27 December 1984, p.1. The relevant passage in *Capital* reads as follows: 'all these things now tell us that human labour power has been expended to produce them, human labour is accumulated in them. As crystals of this social substance, which is common to them all, they are values - commodity values' (Waren Werte). K Marx, *Capital*, vol 1 (Harmondsworth: Penguin Books, 1976), p 128.

9 See, for example, 'Technical Markets are the Key to the Reform of the Science and Technology System', *Jingji Ribao*, 27 December 1984, p 1.

10 'Zhonggong zhongyang guanyu kexue jishu tizhi gaige de jueding' ('Decision of the Central Committee of the Chinese Communist Party on Reform of the Science and Technology Management System'), *RMRB*, 20 March 1985, pp 1 and 3.

11 The only restrictions noted are that transfers contrary to the state's law and regulations must not be carried out and that those technologies that involve 'national security or important economic benefits requiring secrecy should be processed first'. 'Temporary Regulations on Technology Transfers Issued by the State Council (10 January 1985)', *JPRS - CST - 85 - 012*, pp 11-13.

12 Zhang Penghui and Xiao Zuliang, 'Shixing rongye shengchan zerenzhi hou keji gongzuo shang de jige wenti' ('Several Problems in Scientific and Technical Work after Implementation of the Responsibility System in Agricultural Production'), *KYGL*, no 4, 1982, pp 59-62.

13 Ibid.

14 'China's Countryside under Reform', *BR*, no 33, 13 August 1984, pp 16-20.

15 'Scientific Knowledge Spreads in the Countryside', *Xinhua* in English, 14 January 1985 in *JPRS - CST - 85 - 004*, pp 40-41.

16 See, for example, 'Peasants Seek Science Ardently', *BR*, no 9, 28 February 1983, p 5.

17 The problem of prices is discussed further in the concluding section of this chapter.

18 Tong Dalin and Hu Ping, 'Science and Technology' in Yu Guangyuan (ed), *China's Socialist Modernisation* (Beijing: Foreign Languages Press, 1984). pp 656-657.

19 The Patent Law was adopted by the Standing Committee of the National People's Congress on 12 March 1985. For an English translation of the Patent Law see *BR*, no 15, 9 April 1984, Supplement, pp i-viii.

20 *Xinhua* in English, 10 September 1985, in *JPRS - CST* - 85 - 034, p 34 and *Xinhua* in English, 15 May 1985 in *JPRS - CST* - 85 -019, p 37.
21 Tong Dalin and Hu Ping, 'Science and Technology', p 657.
22 Hu Mingzheng, 'Patent Law Encourages Chinese and Foreign Investors', *BR*, no 15, 9 April 1984, p 23.
23 The two previous codes governing this field were abolished on 3 November 1963.
24 See Hu Mingzheng, 'Patent Law Encourages Chinese and Foreign Investors', p 24 and 'China Launches Patent Agency', *BR*, no 32, 6 August 1984, p 5.
25 *Xinhua* in English, 15 May 1985 in *JPRS - CST* - 85 - 019, p 37 and *Xinhua* in English, 16 August 1985 in *JPRS - CST* - 85 - 035, p 26.
26 Li Chang, 'Developing Science and Technology in a Big Way is an Urgent Task of Building a Modern and Strong Socialist Nation', *Ziran Bianzhengfa Tongxun*, vol 4, no 1, *JPRS* - 81620, p 111.
27 See Du Shunxing, 'Kexue yanjiu danwei de jingji guanli' ('The Economic Management of Scientific Research Units'), *Keyan Guanli*, no 4, 1984, pp 73-76 and Li Guoguang and Fan Qiongying, 'Shixing you chang keyan hetong shi dashi suoqu' ('Implementing Paid Contracts for Scientific Research is the Irresistible General Trend'), *RMRB*, 13 December 1984, p.3.
28 Xie Shaoming, 'Shixing you chang hetongzhi'.
29 Ibid.
30 Interview with Mr Liu Jidong, Deputy Head of the Scientific Management Department of the SSTC, 14 January 1985. See also Ji Dong, 'Keyan tizhi gaige de guanjian he tupo kou chuyi' ('My Humble Opinion on the Key to and Breakthrough in the Reform of the Scientific and Technological Research System'), *KXX*, no 3, 1985, pp 19-22.
31 Xing Changming, 'Major Reforms to Take Place in Shanxi's Science and Technology System', *Shanxi Ribao (Shanxi Daily)*, 3 May 1985, p 1, translated in *JPRS - CST* - 85 - 019, p 25.
32 Ji Dong, 'Keyan tizhi gaige de guanjian he tupo kou chuyi'.
33 'Transform Science and Technology into Productive Forces', *BR*, no 16, 19 April 1982, p 26.
34 Xie Shaoming, 'Shixing you chang hetongzhi'.
35 Li Guoguang and Fan Qiongying, 'Shixing you chang keyan hetong shi dashi suoqu'.
36 Xie Shaoming, 'Shixing you chang hetongzhi'.
37 This is out of a total of 85 scientific research institutes directly responsible to the provincial authorities. See *JPRS - CST* - 85 - 019, p 22.
38 Interview with Mr Liu Jidong, 14 January 1985. See also Ji Dong, 'Keyan tizhi gaige de guanjian he tupo kouchuyi'.
39 For a discussion of the management contracting system see Wu Lantian and Zhang Guangren, 'A Model for Reforming the Economic Management of Scientific Research Units', *KXX*, no 5, 1983, pp 19-23.
40 These earnings were to be used for expanding further research work and improving the welfare of workers and staff.
41 'Transferring Technology', *BR*, no 39, 27 September 1982, p 7.
42 Interview with Mr Yan Chengzhun, Deputy Secretary-General, and Mr Zheng Qibiao, Deputy Chief of the Planning Division of the Science and Technology Commission of Shanghai Municipality, 21 January 1985. See also *SWB:FE* W 1319, and Shen Shiwei and He Zijia, 'Shanghai Successfully Transmits Advanced Technology to the Interior; Over 500 Co-operative Projects with Several Remote Border Regions during the Last Two Years', *RMRB* (Overseas Edition), 10 July 1985, p 3, translated in *JPRS - CST* - 85 - 034, pp 22-23.
43 'Making Science Serve Economy', *BR*, no 10, 5 March 1984, p 11.

44 Men Jinru, 'Gaohao diqu jishu xiezuo, tuidong jishu yanjiu' ('Do a Good Job in Technical Co-operation between Localities'), *RMRB*, 15 October 1982, p 2.

45 Ibid.

46 'Organisation and Leadership in Science and Technology Consulting Services', *Wenhui Bao*, 3 December 1981, p 2.

47 'CAST Advisory Group Established', *CEN*, vol 11, no 2, 1983, p 38. The service provides help for both Chinese and foreign clients. It gives advice on construction projects, technology transfer, foreign investment and environmental protection and conducts feasibility studies.

48 'Zhongguo kexueyuan chengli keji zixun kaifa fuwubu' ('The Chinese Academy of Sciences Establishes a Scientific and Technological Consultancy and Development Service Department'), *RMRB*, 8 May 1983, p 3. The department provides services in over 20 fields such as agriculture, energy resources, the study and development of natural resources, computers, semi conductors and optics.

49 *A Brief Introduction to China's Yellow Crane Associated Development Centre for Education, Science and Technology*, p 1.

50 'Zhonggong zhongyang guanyu kexue jishu tizhi gaige de jueding'.

51 Zhao Ziyang quoted in Yu Ren, 'Yitiao xinluzi' ('A New Approach'), *KXX*, no 2, 1984, pp 7-9.

52 Chen Chuansheng and Ma Aiye, 'Shilun woguo de kexue shengchan lianheti'.

53 *SWB:FE* W1221, 8 January 1983.

54 'Woguo keji tizhi gaige chuangzaole jiaogao de jingji xiaoyi' ('The Reform of our Nation's Science and Technology System has Produced Better Economic Results'), *GMRB*, 24 January 1984, p 1.

55 Yu Ren, 'Yitiao xinluzi'.

56 'Woguo keji tizhi gaige chuangzaole jiaogao de jingji xiaoyi'.

57 Chen Chuansheng and Ma Aiye, 'Shilun woguo de kexue shengchan lianheti' ('A Preliminary Discussion of our Nation's Scientific Production Body'), *KXX*, no 3, 1984, pp 2-5.

58 Ibid.

59 Yu Ren, 'Yitiao xinluzi'.

60 Zhao Ziyang, 'A Strategic Question on Invigorating the Economy', *BR*, no 46, 15 November 1982, pp 16-17.

61 Chen Xianhua, 'Zhuajin jianli hangye jishu kaifu zhongxin'.

62 Zhao Ziyang, 'A Strategic Question on Invigorating the Economy', *BR*, no 46, 15 November 1982, pp 16-17.

63 Chen Xianhua, 'Zhuajin jianli hangye jishu kaifu zhongxin'.

64 The TDC has also supplied a steady flow power source, a combustible gas meter, and an automatic digital rainfall counter. The other ten centres all offer services in computing technology. *Xinhua* in English 26 July 1984.

65 The 'five olds' and the 'five news' refer to technology, equipment, material techniques and products.

66 See, for example, Chen Xianhua, 'Zhuajin jianli hangye jishu kaifa zhongxin', Wu Shimin, 'Lüelun hangye jishu kaifa zhongxin' ('A Brief Discussion of Technology Development Centres for Various Trades'), *KYGL*, no 1, 1984, pp 40-41, 39; and Li Minquan, 'Shilun hangye yanjiusuo tiaozheng chongshi wei hangye jishu kaifa zhongxin' ('A Discussion on Transforming Research Institutes of Various Trades into Technology Development Centres through Readjustment and Improvement'), *KYGL*, no 1, 1984, pp 42-46, 50.

67 Meng Xiangjie, 'Qiaoliang yu niudai' ('Bridges and Links'), *Liaowang (Outlook Weekly)*, no 4, 1985, pp 32-33.

68 'Technical Markets are the Key to the Reform of the Science and Technology System'.

69 Interview with Mr Liu Jidong, 14 January 1985. A September 1985 *Xinhua* report suggested continued rapid growth with over 2,000 in existence, although the report does not indicate at what level. *Xinhua* in English, 10 September 1985, in *JPRS - CST* - 85 - 034, p 31.

70 'Technical Markets are the Key to the Reform of the Science and Technology System'.

71 Meng Xiangyie, 'Qiaoliang yu niudai'.

72 *Xinhua* in English, 10 September 1985, in *JPRS - CST* - 85 - 034, p 31.

73 For an overview of the development and functions of technology markets see Ma Xiliang, 'Lun keji shichang de xingqi he fazhan' ('Discussion of the Rise and Development of Science and Technology Markets'), *KXX*, no 1, 1985, pp 2-5.

74 Ji Dong, 'Keyan tizhi gaige de guanjian he tupo kou chuyi'. In the first ten days the S&T store is said to have clinched 495 deals with a total value of 3.48 million *yuan*. Ma Xiliang, 'Lun keji shichang de xingqi he fazhan', p.2.

75 Seven organisations were involved including the Beijing Corporation for Co-ordinated Scientific and Technological Development of Small Town Enterprises, the Beijing Navigation Scientific and Technological Development Corporation and the Beijing Centre for the Development of Construction Technology.

76 Meng Xiangjie, 'Qiaoliang yu niudai'. In a little over a year, the Shanghai Centre for Scientific and Technological Developments held eight fairs to exchange achievements in lasers, matrices, energy conservation, etc.

77 These fairs began in mid-January 1985 and some 70 experts provide advice on agriculture, forestry, livestock and poultry.

78 Interview with Mr Liu Jidong, 14 January 1985 and 'Technical Markets are the Key to the Reform of the Science and Technology System'.

79 'Spring Fair Debuts to Swap Technology', *CD*, 26 March 1985, p 2.

80 The fair also helped in the promotion of the transfer of military technology. For example, a delegation from the Ministry of the Aeronautics Industry signed more than 2,000 technology transfer contracts worth 300 million *yuan*. 'Technology Fair Gets Results', *BR*, no 25, 24 June 1985, p 9. See also *Xinhua* in Chinese, 23 May 1985 translated in *JPRS - CST* - 85 - 019, p 13 and *Xinhua* in English, 15 May 1985 in *JPRS - CST* - 85 - 019, p 12.

81 'Zhonggong zhongyang guanyu kexue jishu tizhi gaige de jueding'.

82 Indeed the military has been the major institution that has provided a stumbling block to the reform programme.

83 The Nanhua Power Machinery Research Department, 'Nuli zuohao "sange zhuanyi", dali cujin minpin keyan de fazhan', ('Strenuously Carry out the "Three Transitions" Well and Promote the Development of Scientific Research on Civilian Products in a Big Way'), *KYGL*, no 3, 1982, p 61.

84 Yang Jianzheng, 'We Must Pay Better Attention to the Transfer of Military Technology', *Liaoning Ribao (Liaoning Daily)*, 16 September 1983, p 2.

85 *Xinhua* in Chinese, 7 May 1985, translated in *SWB:FE* 7946.

86 The newspaper is *Jungong Jishu Zhuan Minyong Xinxi Bao (Information News on Transferring Military Industrial Technology to Civilian Use)*.

87 See Sun Guangyun, 'Shitan danchun junyong jishu xiang junmin jianyong de zhuanyi' ('Preliminary Discussion of Transferring Military Technology to Both Military and Civilian Use'), *KYGL*, 1982, pp 14-19.

88 *Xinhua* in Chinese, 24 March 1985, translated in *JPRS - CST* - 85 - 010, p 1 and *Xinhua* in Chinese 7 May 1985, translated in *SWB:FE* 7946.

89 *SWB:FE* 7847, 12 January 1985.

90 *Xinhua* in Chinese, 3 May 1985, translated in *SWB:FE* 7946. A similar shift in focus of work has taken place within the Ministry of Astronautics. In 1984, the output value of civilian products surpassed that of military products, see *SWB:FE W1339*.

91   Wu Tingman and Jin Xiaoyin, 'Jiehe bensuo tedian nuli wei difang de jingji jianshe fuwu' ('Serve Local Economic Construction by Linking up our Institutes' Characteristics'), *KYGL*, no 3, 1982, pp 35-37, 55. For details of other co-operative projects see 'Jungong jishu xiang minyong zhuanyi shi woguo jishu shichang de zhongyao zucheng bufen' ('The Transfer of Military Technology to Civilian Use is an Important Part of Organising our Nation's Technology Market'), National Science and Technology Work Conference Exchange Material Number 6, pp 4-9.

92   'Jungong jishu xiang minyong zhuanyi shi woguo jishu shichang de zhongyao zucheng bufen', p 1. See also Xie Zi, 'Cujin jishu jinbu de yitiao zhongyao tujing - guofang kegong wei yu tianjinshi jingji jishu hezuo de qishi' ('An Important Channel for Accelerating Technological Advance - Learn from the Economic and Technological Co-operation between the National Defence Science, Technology and Industrial Commission and Tianjin Municipality'), *KXX*, no 7, 1984, pp 14-17.

93   The provinces include Liaoning, Jiangsu, Shaanxi, Hunan, Henan and Guizhou.

94   The provinces include Liaoning, Hunan, Jiangsu, Shanghai, Henan, Sichuan and Shaanxi.

95   'Jungong jishu xiang minyong zhuanyi shi woguo jishu shichang de zhongyao zucheng bufen', pp 2 and 6.

96   This system is said to have involved the 'massive use of a military scientific research achievement, the electrical eddy sensor, in measuring fluid materials, cutting, canning and in the main synchronous transmission for the automatic production line. See The Nanhua Power Machinery Research Department, 'Nuli zuohao 'sange zhuanyi', dali cujin minpin keyan de fazhan', p 61.

97   *Xinhua* in English, 16 April 1985 in *SWB:FE* 7929.

98   'Our Great Wall of Iron' translated in *JPRS - CST - 84 - 034*, p 17.

99   Mu Gongqian, Wang Lin and Huang Shengli, 'Gaige guojia dui yanjiusuo guanli de sanxiang cuoshi' ('Three Measures to Reform State Management of Research Institutes'), *GMRB*, 7 May 1984, p 1.

100   Zheng Ruizeng and Zhang Fuming, 'Yao "yang ji chan dan" bu yao "sha ji qu luan" ' ('We should "Raise a Chicken to Lay Eggs", not "Kill a Chicken to get Eggs" '), *GMRB*, 21 May 1984, p 2.

101   The profit-fund ratio is calculated through the division of the total amount of profits by the total amount of fixed and circulating funds. The total amount of profit is the total of sales minus costs and taxes. The depreciation costs are subtracted from fixed funds. K Ishihara, 'The Price Problem and Economic Reform', *China Newsletter*, no 46, 1983, p 2.

102   Ibid, p 3.

103   'Guofang kegongwei tizhi gaige bangongshi bai junde, zhu mingjin tongzhi shuo: junshi jishu de keyan ye yao jinxing tizhi gaige' ('Comrades Bai Junde and Zhu Mingjin of the System Reform Office of the National Defence Science and Industry Commission Say: Scientific Research for Military Technology Must also Undergo Reform of the System'), *KXX*, no 5, 1985, pp 11-12.

104   See 'Decision of the Central Committee of the Communist Party of China on Reform of the Economic Structure', *BR*, no 44, 29 October 1984, pp i-xvi. The original Chinese version can be found in *RMRB*, 21 October 1984, pp 1-3.

105   Ibid, p viii.

106   Editorial, 'Tongxin tongde, zaijie zaili, wending wujia' ('With One Heart and Mind, Make Persistent Efforts, Stabilise Commodity Prices'), *RMRB*, 10 January 1981, p 1.

107   *SWB:FE* 6623.

108 See Zhao Ziyang, 'Report on the Sixth Five Year Plan', 30 November 1982, *BR*, no 51, 20 December 1982, pp 10-20.

109 'Decision of the Central Committee of the Communist Party of China on Reform of the Economic Structure', p ix.

110 'Price Reform: Six Months Later', *BR*, no 49, 9 December 1985, p 6. This report notes, for example, that the price of meat in Beijing had increased by 30% since the reforms were introduced on 1 June 1985.

111 Xu Qianwei, 'Tan keyan jigou de zhengdun yu gaige' ('Discussion of the Re-adjustment and Reform of Scientific Research Organs'), *KXX*, no 7, 1984, p 27.

112 Xu Qianwei, 'Shitan keyan tizhi gaige' ('A Preliminary Discussion of the Reform of the Scientific Research System'), *KYGL*, no 1, 1984, p 30.

CHAPTER THREE

THE ORGANISATIONAL STRUCTURE OF CHINA'S CIVILIAN S&T SECTOR

This chapter outlines the role of the key organisations in the civilian S&T sector, first looking at the governmental commission system and then outlining China's research and development system. At the end of 1983 there were 4,450 specialised research institutes above the level of county administration and there were 5,000 early in 1985,[1] and 328,000 people engaged in scientific research in state owned enterprises.[2] The majority of these research institutes are small-scale, as can be seen from the following figures. Research institutes with a staff of over 1,000 comprise 3.6% of the total number; a staff of between 500 and 999 comprise 6.5%; a staff of between 100 and 499 comprise 31.2%; and those with a staff of fewer than 100 make up 58.7% of the total.[3] The research institutes are divided between five different sectors referred to as the 'five front armies', the 'five ranks' or the 'five legs'. The five are the institutes under the Chinese Academy of Sciences (CAS), the institutions of higher education, the institutes and departments of the ministries under the State Council, the provincial and municipality-run institutes and those at lower administrative levels, and those institutes and departments that come under the wing of the national defence system. This chapter will concentrate on the first two of these sectors. An analysis of the military research and development system is beyond the scope of this study. Most of China's developmental research is carried out in the institutes that come under the authority of the ministries or the provincial authorities. As the previous chapter dealt in some detail with the impact of the reforms in developmental research institutes it is not necessary to repeat such information here. However, policies to link the research with the production sector are also affecting the work of the CAS and the institutions of higher education and this will be considered in this chapter. Finally, the functions of the non-governmental organisation, the Chinese Association for Science and Technology (CAST), will be outlined.

Science and Technology Leading Group, and the State Science and Technology Commission

The Science and Technology Leading Group (STLG) and the State Science and Technology Commission (SSTC) are the two key bodies at the heart of China's civilian S&T organisational system. (See Figure 1.) They are responsible for devising, co-ordinating and implementing China's S&T policy, with the

Figure 1: The Organisation of China's Civilian S&T System (Simplified), January 1986

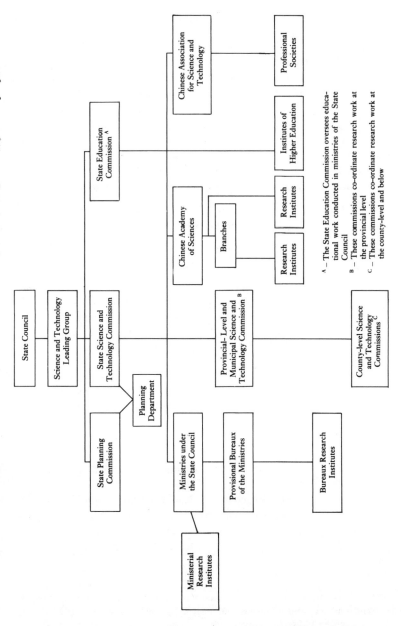

A – The State Education Commission oversees educational work conducted in ministries of the State Council

B – These commissions co-ordinate research work at the provincial level

C – These commissions co-ordinate research work at the county-level and below

STLG dealing with broader, long-term strategic issues and ensuring that civilian S&T policy is properly integrated with that of the military sector.[4] Indeed the need for better integration between the two sectors may well have been one of the major reasons for its establishment.

The STLG was formed in January 1983 with the objective of giving more political muscle to S&T within China's governmental framework. It would appear that the SSTC itself was not sufficiently powerful to break down the barriers between the different vertical hierarchies that make up the S&T system.[5] The STLG comes directly under the authority of the State Council, the highest organ of the state administration, and is headed by Premier Zhao Ziyang. Membership of the group has a functional basis rather than being tied to particular individuals, thus its members are drawn from the key organisations involved in work directly, or indirectly, relevant to S&T development. This includes the SSTC, the State Planning and the State Economic Commissions, the National Defence Science, Technology and Industrial Commission and the Education Commission. (See Figure 2 for the composition of the STLG.) The

Figure 2: Membership of the Science and Technology Leading Group[(a)]

Position in STLG	Name	Other Relevant Functions
Head	Zhao Ziyang	Premier, Minister of State Commission for Readjustment of the Economic System
Deputy Heads	Fang Yi	Former Minister-in-charge of SSTC
	Song Ping	Minister-in-charge of State Planning Commission
Members	Lu Dong	Minister of the State Economic Commission and Deputy Head of the Leading Group for the Development of Computers and Large-Scale Integrated Circuits
	Ding Henggao[b]	Minister of the Commission of Science, Technology and Industry for National Defence
	Zhao Shouyi	Minister of Labour and Personnel
	Li Peng[c]	Minister-in-charge of the Education Commission
	Yan Dongsheng	Vice-President of the CAS
	Zhao Dongwan	Vice-Minister of the SSTC and the Planning Commission
Member and Director of General Office	Song Jian	Minister-in-charge of SSTC

a) China has recently undergone a number of changes in key personnel and thus this list represents the author's estimation of the composition as of January 1986.
b) Ding replaced Chen Bin in June 1985.
c) Li Peng was appointed Minister of the newly formed Education Commission in June 1985.

functional structure of the STLG emphasises the intention that it should act to break down the compartmentalisation of the system by bringing together key figures in one body. The group is described as 'authoritative, efficient, small and powerful' and it is expected to provide 'unified leadership over economic planning, research and development and scientific and technical manpower training and allocation'. Whether, in the long term, it will succeed in its objective or whether it simply becomes another link in the hierarchical chain remains to be seen.

The establishment of leading groups to focus on key problem areas that require co-ordination has become a feature of recent organisational developments. In addition to the STLG, for example, a Leading Group for the Development of Computers and Large-Scale Integrated Circuits was set up in September 1985 (subsequently renamed as the Leading Group for Development of the Electronics Industry) with Vice-Premier Li Peng as its head, and in July 1985 a Leading Group for Major Technical Equipment was established.

The need for better direction and co-ordination at the provincial level has led to the establishment of provincial S&T leading groups. Such groups were set up in most provinces during late 1983 and 1984. Thus a S&T leading group was formed in Hunan in December 1983, in Guangdong in April 1984, in Henan and Hubei in July 1984.[6] As with the national leading group, members are drawn from the related departments in the province that are engaged in S&T work such as the science and education department of the provincial Party central committee and the science and technology, planning and economic commissions.[7] The groups are established on a joint decision by the provincial Party committee and the local government and are usually headed by the governor of the province.[8] The day-to-day running of the group appears to be placed in the hands of the provincial level S&T commission as the office for the leading group is situated within the commission. Generally the Director and deputy Director of the commission act as the Director and deputy Director of the office of the leading group. The groups are expected to devise specific policies for the province in line with the directions and policies of the Central Committee concerning S&T work. This entails working out long-term plans for the provinces' S&T development and specific programmes for reform such as the transformation of key enterprises and the importation and circulation of skilled personnel, and deciding on the important technological items to be imported and on technical transformation projects.

Before the STLG was established, the most important body in the civilian S&T system was the SSTC. Although this has clearly led to a decline in its preeminent role in the process of policy formulation, it still remains important. It is the principal body for gathering information on the S&T system and this fact alone gives it considerable influence over policy formulation. Also, it remains the most important body for co-ordinating policy once formulated and seeing that it is properly implemented. The resurrection of the SSTC began in the last quarter of 1977 when China's leaders sought to solve the problems of the Cultural

Revolution by simply reviving the organisational structure as it had existed in the early sixties.[9]

According to its first post-Cultural Revolution Minister, Fang Yi, the SSTC was expected to 'take charge of overall planning, co-ordination, organisation and administration of the country's scientific and technological work'.[10] Although, as was noted above, it was not entirely successful in this role, the SSTC is still described as being 'charged with co-ordinating S&T affairs for the whole country'.[11] More specifically its principal tasks are described as being: to implement the programmes and policies of the Central Committee that are concerned with S&T; to draw up long- and short-term S&T plans; to monitor the implementation of these plans, including establishing important research academies and institutes, and judging the importance of research projects; co-ordinating work on key state S&T projects[12]; organising the application and popularisation of S&T results in production; and representing the government in S&T relations and exchanges with foreign countries.[13]

The staff of the SSTC are divided between ten major departments and its functional offices.[14] A brief description of these various departments gives a further idea of the scope of the work of the SSTC. The major departments are:

1 The Science and Technology Policy Department (*Kejizhengce ju*) is concerned with the development of the nation's S&T, devising policy and drafting relevant S&T regulations.

2 The Forecasting Department (*Yushi ju*) is concerned with the analysis of data for the projection of future developments.

3 The Planning Department (*Jihua ju*) is a joint department with the State Planning Commission. The sharing of this department is seen as being conducive to promoting co-ordination of the work of the two commissions particularly with respect to promoting the policy of linking S&T policy more closely to the needs of the economy and society.

4 The Work Management Department (*Gongguan ju*) co-ordinates the work of all China's industrial ministries. It also co-ordinates work of the CAS that relates to specific state projects. This especially concerns the 38 key projects defined in the Sixth Five Year Plan.

5 The Department of New Technologies (*Xinxing jishu ju*) investigates basic research work into new fields such as lasers, informatics and new materials.

6 The Science and Technology Management Department (*Keji guanli ju*) deals with the problems of organisational reform insofar as they relate to the various institutions in the S&T system. It also organises work to do with the results of inventions.

7 The Financial Facilities Department (*Caiwu tiaojian ju*) organises financial affairs, particularly with respect to capital construction.

8 The Scientific and Technical Cadres Department (*Keji ganbu ju*) is responsible for organising the nation's S&T cadre force and devising policies to improve the standard of their work and to promote labour mobility.

9 The Information and Data Department (*Qingbao ju*) is responsible for data collection and analysis.

10 The Department of International Scientific and Technical Co-operation (*Guoji keji hezuo ju*) is responsible for deciding on joint projects and research programmes with foreign countries as well as formal S&T exchange agreements.[15]

The commission system spreads down China's administrative hierarchy to the provincial and the county levels. The commissions operate as a department of the local government and are thus subject to horizontal control, by the local authorities, and vertical control as they are subordinate to the commission at the next higher level. As with the national body, these commissions are engaged in the work of planning, co-ordinating and implementing S&T work within the area under their jurisdiction. Thus, the Shanghai Municipal Science and Technology Commission defines its most important tasks as being the development of S&T policies in line with those of the state; the planning and development of the S&T sector within the Shanghai Municipality; the arranging of financing for S&T projects undertaken by research institutes within the Municipality; and organising the relevant institutes under the authority of the commission to work on certain selected research topics.[16] In late 1984/early 1985, for example, to help guide its work, the Shanghai commission drafted a Five Year Plan covering the period from 1986 to 1990 outlining the current development priorities[17] and a long-term S&T development plan covering the period 1986-2000.[18]

The county-level commissions form the link between the governmental system, of which they are the base, and the system of S&T bodies in the townships and the countryside. In 1985 there were some 2,700 county-level S&T commissions overseeing work in a variety of urban and rural environments. In theory, these commissions could play a key role co-ordinating policy and carrying out popularisation work, particularly with respect to agriculture. However, it seems that, for a number of years, these commissions have suffered an identity crisis. The rapid pace of reforms has, presumably, led to an increase in the feeling of uncertainty about their proper role. As a result, attempts have been made to define their role more clearly. An article published in February 1984 stated that for a long time their duties had not been understood, responsibilities and rights were not clearly defined, personnel were slack, and people felt that they were 'not essential' and 'felt weak in power and as if they were nothing'.[19] The article notes, however, that these commissions play a role that neither the SSTC nor the provincial commissions could replace. While these latter commissions are engaged primarily in the development of principles and policies, and engage in organising theoretical research and applied research on 'sophisticated projects', county-level commissions are expected to 'integrate these principles and policies with the local situation and thoroughly implement them'. Thus, these commissions engage in organising developmental research for technical transformation and conduct projects of a 'decidedly applicable nature'.[20]

The increasing complexity of economic life at the basic level means that county-level S&T commissions will have to deal with problems not just related to the promotion and dissemination of agricultural technology but also with small-scale industrial development, energy, transport and communications. Given the extreme shortage of skilled S&T personnel, and the increasing demand for such personnel from all sectors, finding sufficiently qualified staff for these commissions, particularly those in remote rural areas, is a major problem. It has been proposed that these commissions should have a staff of some 15 to 20 people. This would require a workforce of around 50,000 to make sure that they are properly staffed. A lack of people with sufficient qualifications in the right subjects further compounds the problem. It is proposed that the ratio of those with college and technical secondary school education should be 3:2, preferably with their specialities in agriculture, biology, physics and machinery. Finding the necessary graduates will be difficult and will be dependent on the success of the policy to expand technical and vocational education rapidly in the second half of the eighties.[21]

The Chinese Academy of Sciences

As in the Soviet Union, the Academy is the most prestigious research organisation and the place on which China's ambitious young scientists set their sights.[22] The CAS is a nationwide comprehensive research unit with its work mainly devoted to the natural sciences. It is also China's premier institution for basic research. The CAS organises annually some 4,000 to 5,000 research projects. In terms of expenditure, around 15% is devoted to basic research, a little under 50% to applied research topics and about 35% to developmental research. This research work is carried out in 120 research institutes under the sole or, in some cases, joint jurisdiction of the CAS. The CAS has a total staff of 80,000 of whom 35,000 are said to be scientific and technical personnel.[23] The CAS comprises the greatest concentration of China's scientific workforce with about 10% of the nation's researchers and consuming 10% of the research funds.[24]

The CAS, unlike many other scientific organisations, survived the Cultural Revolution but its authority and scope of control were very much reduced. Before the Cultural Revolution, the CAS had under its jurisdiction over 100 research institutes with over 22,000 research workers and technical personnel.[25] During the Cultural Revolution authority over all but 36 or 37 of these institutes was transferred out of the CAS.[26] In line with the general policy of the Cultural Revolution, particularly those institutes engaged in developmental or applied research had authority over them transferred from the CAS to a production ministry or to the local provincial government. Of those institutes that remained under CAS control, 17 also came under the control of provincial or municipal authorities. From the late seventies onwards, authority over its 'lost' institutes has been returned to the CAS in a process of recentralisation.

Despite this recentralisation of control, two policies suggested moves in the opposite direction. First, 'branch academies' have been set up as a form of decentralisation within the CAS structure. These 'branch academies' had previously been experimented with as a part of the decentralisation programme of the Great Leap Forward (1958-1960).[27] Most of these were abolished in the early sixties and, as we have seen, the form of decentralisation favoured in the Cultural Revolution was one that placed the institutes under dual control or moved them out of the Academy structure entirely. Outside the central authorities in Beijing, there are now 12 CAS branches.[28] The fact that not all decisions have to be referred to Beijing considerably simplifies the bureaucratic chain. With the drive to try to link research work to production, this decentralisation enables the 'branch academies' to become more flexible in directing the work of their research institutes towards projects that would be of local use. While the main research projects, especially in basic research, are handed down to the 'Shanghai branch' from Beijing, it does have the autonomy to make decisions concerning projects proposed by the Shanghai government and local industry.[29] However, the institutes in Shanghai, Beijing and in the other 'open cities' are expected to have an international orientation as well. A member of the Management Science Group of the CAS has stated that they should be capable of competing on an international level in all aspects of their work. By contrast, research institutes in frontier regions and the interior are expected to gear their work totally towards the needs of the particular area. Over the long term, it is hoped that these institutes will also bring their research work up to international standards.[30]

Secondly, the idea of transferring institutes out of the control of the CAS has been revived during the eighties. The Party decision to reform S&T suggested that those institutes under the CAS that are mainly engaged in developmental research and have developed extensive contact with production ministries' enterprises, should move out of the CAS sector into a different administrative system, thus taking them off the CAS payroll.[31] While this is seen as a policy option, it has not occurred as yet and is seen by those within the CAS as only a very long-term development.[32]

It seems that the autonomy that research institutes enjoy has led to problems of co-ordination and direction of research. Within the CAS, directive scientific plans account for some 20% of the total, meaning that research institutes enjoy considerable freedom as far as selecting scientific research plan topics is concerned. The introduction of the contract system has not entirely solved the problem of making sure that individual institutes are conducting the right research. Two problems have exacerbated this situation. First, the centre's leadership is said to have been too weak with respect to directive scientific research plans. Work has not been properly co-ordinated and examination and supervision of projects have been too slow. Secondly, the centre has given no guidance over the selection of an institute's remaining research plans. This has contributed to the familiar problems of waste and repetition in research projects.[33] The solution to both these problems would seem to be increased central control, thus moving in the opposite direction to the current drive to give the research institutes greater decision-making powers.

In theory, the work of the CAS is governed by the plenary meeting of the scientific council but, as with so many organisations in China, real power lies elsewhere within the structure, in this case with the presidium and the Academy's President and Vice-Presidents. The scientific council was first formed in 1955 with the 'aim of rallying scientists of various fields throughout the country to participate in the leadership over academic work and keeping in close touch with the scientists of the whole nation'.[34] Originally it had 233 members of whom 123 were drawn from the natural sciences. What happened to the council during the Cultural Revolution is unclear but by Spring 1979 only 117 of the original members remained alive, and in March 1981 the State Council authorised the addition of a further 283 members, thus bringing its strength up to 400. Of these 400 noted scientists, 79 were mathematicians and physicists, 67 chemists, 89 biologists, 75 geoscientists and 90 engineers. They represented 27 ministries and departments, 43 universities and colleges and 114 research institutes.[35]

However, given the infrequency of its meetings and the fact that many of the members of the scientific council are drawn from outside the Academy's ranks, it is clear that through its plenary sessions it cannot exert a genuine leadership role. Fang Yi, addressing the fifth session of the scientific council in January 1984, suggested a different emphasis for the council's and its members' role. Fang pointed out that because most council members came from outside units 'at ordinary times' they could not 'deeply understand the state of work' carried out by the Academy. Consequently, he noted, it was difficult for the scientific council session to function as the Academy's highest policy-making organ. Council members, in order to let them concentrate on their academic work, were to do as little administrative work as possible. Thus, in future, Fang suggested, the council sessions should function as 'an organ for academic assessment and consultation' and the council and the presidium should organise their members to study China's S&T development and questions concerning S&T in the modernisation programme, to take an active part in formulating the state's major S&T policy decisions and economic policy decisions and to assess and guide major academic work carried out by the Academy and its research institutes.[37]

When the council is not in plenary session, its work is carried out by the 29-member presidium which it elects. The presidium meets three or four times a year, thus giving it a continuity. The members are elected for a four-year term with the possibility of extension for a second term. Two-thirds of the members are drawn from the divisions of the Academy while the remaining one-third are 'nominated through consultation between the ministries and commissions concerned under the State Council and the Party organisation of the Academy'.[38] Its more important areas of work are supervising the Academy's research programmes and development plans, the election of the President,

Vice-Presidents and the appointment of a Secretary General, the nomination of branch academy presidents and directors of institutes, the establishment and reorganisation of institutes and international co-operation.[39]

Fang Yi's comments would indicate that effective power in the Academy now lies with the President and the full-time administrators. According to the Academy's Constitution, the President carries out the presidium and council decisions, submits scientific research plans and the budgets of the Academy, oversees research work, nominates and removes vice-presidents of branch academies, deputy directors of institutes and principal leading members of the various functional departments of the Academy, and handles important affairs concerning international scientific co-operation and exchanges.[40] The power of the President has been increased by application of the policy whereby the Party is to adopt a lower profile in institutions and enterprises and to allow them to be run by professionals who have a greater say in decision-making. This, of course, can lead to a problem for the Party should it wish to 'guide' or oversee work in a particular unit. Thus, the Party has tried to recruit more professionals and appoint more suitably qualified Party members to leadership positions. The current President of the CAS is Lu Jiaxi who, not surprisingly, is a highly qualified scientist and a Party member. This linking in one person of professional skills and Party membership avoids the problem of having to co-ordinate the work of a Party leadership running parallel with that of the institute's scientific leadership. In May 1982, it was announced that the leading Party group within the CAS had been reformed with Lu Jiaxi as its Secretary. This move was approved by the Party's Central Committee and was said to be a 'realisation of the policy of the Party that management of the Academy of Sciences should be in the hands of scientists'.[41] Kühner points out (with respect to the role of the Party) that according to the Academy's Constitution, the CAS comes under the leadership not only of the State Council but also of the Party Central Committee.[42]

The President is helped in his work by the Vice-Presidents. In a reform designed to cut down the number of administrative positions and to bring younger people into key positions, in mid-1984 the number of Vice-Presidents was cut from six to three and two new faces brought in. Yan Dongsheng retained his position but the others were removed and replaced by Zhou Guangzhao (55), the Director of the Institute of Theoretical Physics, and Sun Honglie (52), a soil scientist and geographer.[43]

To exercise leadership over the scientific activities, the institutes are grouped into six academic divisions. There is one division for each of mathematics and physics, chemistry, biological sciences, and earth sciences, and two divisions for technological sciences.[44] Academic divisions were originally set up in June 1955 and at that time there were only four: mathematics, physics and chemistry; biology and geosciences; technological sciences; and philosophy and the social sciences. In 1957, biology and the geosciences were divided, and in 1961 philosophy and the social sciences were placed under the jurisdiction of the Party

Central Committee.[45] Academic divisions were another casualty of the Cultural Revolution and, in January 1967, they were forced to suspend their activities. They were not revived until Spring 1979; since that time in 1981 chemistry has been set up as a separate division[46] and technological sciences has been split into two divisions.

Apart from these organisational reforms of the CAS structure, the emphasis on scientific work serving economic construction has also had an impact on the Academy's research institutes. This has resulted in the signing of a number of contracts with outside organisations for the paid transfer of research results. In fact the Party decision on the reform of the S&T system expressly states that institutes under the CAS engaged in developmental research are being encouraged to set up various forms of partnership with enterprises and design units on a 'voluntary and mutually beneficial basis'.[47]

As a result of the new policies, by early 1985 the CAS had signed 17 long-term co-operation agreements with localities and ministries.[48] For example, in March 1984 the CAS reached an agreement with the Tianjin municipal authorities to supply new research results to Tianjin industry. In terms of the agreement, the CAS is to give Tianjin access to new research results and deal with technical problems that occur in Tianjin industry. The Tianjin Municipal Government is to organise the application of research results and to pay for the transfer of technology. To co-ordinate the agreement, the two parties are expected to meet annually to draft new plans and examine the previous year's implementation and problems.[49] The CAS has also signed an agreement with the Ministry of the Petroleum Industry on long-term co-operation in such fields as petroleum processing, geological surveys and oilfield development. In May 1982, it established co-operative relations with the Beijing Yanshan General Petro-chemical Corporation.[50]

In addition, the CAS and institutes under its jurisdiction are engaging in a number of joint research production ventures. The example of the China Gas and Turbine Research and Development Company has already been mentioned in Chapter Two and there are a number of others. One further success story has been the co-operation between two extremely improbable sounding bedfellows: the Shanghai-based Institute of Nuclear Research and the Shanghai Municipal Vegetable Corporation. They have established a factory with an annual processing capacity of 35,000 tons of vegetables using radiation technology to keep them fresh.[51]

If institutes are to be able to take proper advantage of the opportunities presented by such co-operation, it is necessary to ensure that they are given a greater degree of autonomy. Also, administration must be made less cumbersome and more power must be placed in the hands of experts in the institutes rather than Party officials.[52] However, Party officials who are not technically qualified may prove unwilling to accept limits to their former authority and provide a stumbling block to the implementation of reforms. Press reports still frequently give examples of Party officials who have blocked reforms because they were said not to recognise the value of scientists' opinions.

This need was recognised at the annual meeting of the CAS in January 1985. A number of reforms were proposed to give institutes greater autonomy. In particular, it was suggested that daily administration of institutes be transferred from the CAS headquarters to institute personnel with the Academy continuing to manage long-term research and development strategy. Also, it was proposed that institutes be given the authority to accept research contracts from industrial and other institutions, be allowed to send people abroad for further study, and be permitted independently to import necessary research equipment.[53]

The introduction of the job responsibility system and new mechanisms for financing research within the CAS have led to changes in the internal organisation of the institutes as they seek to find the organisational form best suited to taking advantage of these new possibilities. The system of the director taking full responsibility is to be introduced and within the institutes a variety of job responsibility systems will be brought in to ensure greater accountability than in the past. It is stressed that a variety of forms will emerge best suited to the individual institute concerned and that no one model will be bureaucratically imposed on unwilling institutes.[54] However, there is a trial institute in the CAS for the reforms – the Institute of Theoretical Physics. Given its success to date others may well choose to copy its example.

The Institute of Theoretical Physics has abolished the previous research laboratories and groups and now only has project teams that are drawn together for specific projects. Under this new system, the project teamleader is in an extremely powerful position. He or she is invested with five powers. First, once the leadership has decided on the general direction, the teamleader decides on which specific project should be investigated first. Secondly, once the project money has been allocated, the leader has the say in how it should be used and in its distribution. Thirdly, he or she has the power to invite the specific researchers needed for the project. The reform started in mid-1984 but as of January 1985 no researchers from outside the institute had been recruited for the project teams although one or two 'overseas Chinese' had helped with the projects. Fourthly, he or she exerts leadership over the actual project. Finally, the leader decides on the promotion of the researchers and the division of the rewards for the work done.[55] The degree of power that this gives teamleaders will depend, of course, on what comes under the notion of the leadership deciding the 'general direction'. Given the criticism noted above that the central leadership had been too weak in its guidance, one might expect this notion to become more pervasive. It must mean the setting of research topics and their priority, at least. Also, before the funds can be distributed, they must first be obtained and a budget approved. However, the ability of the teamleader to invite specific researchers and to decide on promotions would lead to the emergence of strong research groups, if implemented.

Institutions of Higher Education

The institutions of higher education are the weakest of the sectors in terms of their contribution to scientific research. In the 1950s when China opted for the Soviet model of development, it naturally enough adopted a system that de-emphasised university-based research and emphasised its concentration within the academy structure. This similarly led to the management of education being based in the Ministry of Education and to a lesser extent in the trade committees of the various industrial ministries.[56] The adoption of this model reinforced China's pre-liberation experience when it was common practice for research on specific problems to be based in special institutes outside the formal education sector.

In 1985 there were 902 institutions of higher education, a rapid increase over the figure of 715 for the end of 1982 and 805 at the end of 1983.[57] These institutions comprise various types, such as comprehensive universities offering a full range of disciplines, polytechnical universities that specialise in the sciences and engineering and specialised institutes for particular areas of technology.[58] Despite some successes, the promotion of research in these institutions has proved difficult and it seems that the thinking of many college administrators is still strongly influenced by having been trained in a Soviet-style system. A member of Xiamen University noted that the leaders in some institutions of higher education are 'not aware of the new situation we are facing. They are not effectively preparing for the new situation of research in institutions of higher education.' In addition, he remarked that 'some responsible school leaders often place scientific research in contrast to teaching. They do not see the role of research in teaching.'[59]

The low level of educational financing has exacerbated the problem of research within the higher education sector as little money remains to finance the purchase of the necessary equipment for advanced scientific research. In 1984 China spent about 14.6 billion *yuan* on education, accounting for 10.35% of the state's budget, an increase of 14.2% over 1983. This spending compares well with 1978 when the state spent 5.49 billion *yuan* on education, making up only 6.26% of the budget.[60] However, most of this extra spending has gone on wage increases and the construction of new buildings and facilities to satisfy the demands of the rapidly increasing student numbers. Also, despite these increased expenditures, China spends only 3.1% of the gross national product on education, a sum that compares badly with other developing countries.[61] Though China's attempts to develop education on the cheap have been remarkably successful in creating a basic framework, this has hindered the development of the more advanced research sector. One account notes that 'only a few ten million *yuan*' in S&T expenditures are allocated by the state to the higher education sector each year. Neither will this sector gain much from the 'several billion *yuan*' to be spent on administrative expenditures for key S&T problems in the Sixth Five Year Plan (1986-1990).[62]

Problems in the education sector have been recognised and it has been given a higher profile in China's policy-making. In mid-May 1985, a National Education Conference was held to draw up a comprehensive education policy, and on 29 May the Party Central Committee published its Decision on the Reform of the Educational System.[63] The fact that the role of education had been previously underestimated was pointed out by Wan Li in his speech to the Education Conference. While acknowledging the problem of 'limited educational investment and a shortage of educational funds' Wan concluded that what was even more important was 'the issue of understanding the importance of education'.[64]

In organisational terms, the importance of education has been recognised by the creation, in June 1985, of a State Commission for Education to replace the former Ministry.[65] The establishment of the Commission not only signals the importance of education in the eyes of China's leadership but also gives the Commission the chance to co-ordinate education work across the various ministries. This, it is hoped, will provide the framework for devising a coherent, consistent policy. As with the SSTC, the desire for better co-ordination across the system is reflected by the fact that the Commission's personnel are drawn from key institutions within the system.[66] When setting up the Commission, it was pointed out that the Ministry of Education had experienced difficulty as a co-ordinator because it only ranked the same as other ministries.[67]

According to the State Council, the new Commission as a comprehensive department will be better placed to 'ensure and improve education, unify strategy and guide reform'.[68] It will be responsible for the setting of educational principles and policies, and formulating regulations for the education sector.[69] The appointment of Li Peng to head the Commission is similarly indicative of the importance attached to education. Li, an energy expert and an engineering graduate, was appointed to the Politburo of the Party Central Committee in September 1985 and is widely seen as an eventual successor to Zhao Ziyang as Premier of the State Council.

Current policy stresses the need to promote scientific research within the higher education sector. Arguments used to support this policy are similar to those the world over. It is pointed out that it would improve the standard of teaching, students would be brought into contact with the most recent scientific developments and the general underuse of people and facilities is criticised.[70] As a result, the Decision on the Reform of Education states that institutions of higher education should be made to contribute more to scientific and technological development.[71] Co-ordination and promotion of research activities should be improved by the establishment of the Commission. Previously such guidance as did exist was fragmented. In the former Ministry of Education, there was a science and technology department that was supposed to take care of the planning of S&T research and its financing. However, other ministries also had an education department that handled S&T work that took place in those institutions under their jurisdiction. Thus, an extremely complicated system existed for co-ordinating scientific research and it was clearly a problem to co-ordinate it.[72] In particular, the co-ordination of work for enrolment, job assignment, teaching, management and development of institutions not directly under the Ministry's jurisdiction was made extremely difficult. The scale of this problem is shown by the fact that just before its abolition only 36 of the institutions of higher education were directly administered by the Ministry of Education; 250 were attached to various other ministries and commissions with the remainder administered by various provincial-level authorities.[73]

In terms of scientific research, those institutions designated as key-points are the most important. These key-points are to serve as an impetus to promote the gradual development of the whole system by relying on the concentration of resources on a few key institutions to maximise returns on limited investments. Therefore, an institution of higher education designated as a key-point receives more funds from the state to provide the best facilities and to pay the best and most experienced teachers. It is allowed to enrol the best students and is, in turn, expected to produce the best results. The system was abolished in the Cultural Revolution because of its élitist nature and when it was resurrected 88 institutions were designated as key-points. Others were gradually added to the list until at the end of 1983 there were approximately 100. Such an expansion in the numbers put a strain on the state's finances and it seems that in 1984 the total of key-points was cut back. The key-points are expected to excel in both teaching and research. To facilitate this second objective, a key-point system within the key-point system exists so that special funds can be directed to particular institutions for selected topics. Thus, in November 1981, when the World Bank loaned China US$200 million it was to be used for purchasing instruments and computers and for training at 26 key universities.[74] In early 1985, it was announced that five key universities had been selected as sites for government-funded laboratories. The choice was based on the track record of the universities and the quality of their staff members.[75]

As with research institutes of the CAS, institutions of higher education are being encouraged to forge links with the local community and the production sector and are being given greater autonomy to facilitate such contacts. This was spelled out in the Decision on the Reform of Education where it was stated that institutions should have 'the power to accept projects from, or co-operate with, other social establishments for scientific research and technological development, as well as setting up combines involving teaching, scientific research and production'.[76] These links have, in fact, been steadily developing and as early as February 1984 it was reported that 25 major universities and colleges had signed over 50 long-term contracts with government and industry and had set up 30 entities to combine research with production.[77]

Clearly institutions with a technical focus such as Qinghua University in Beijing or Jiaotong University in Shanghai will be able to take greater advantage of these opportunities than comprehensive universities such as Beijing and Fudan (Shanghai). However, even the latter have been able to diversify their work to fit in with the new reforms. While the overwhelming amount of Fudan's finances still come from the state, the number of research contracts being signed is expanding. In 1981 and 1982, the university signed approximately 40 or 50 contracts whereas during 1984 it concluded about 150.[78] Universities like Qinghua and Jiaotong have been able to develop a variety of forms of co-operation using the skills possessed by the respective universities. Both universities have signed scientific and technological co-operation agreements with relevant local government organisations and industrial departments. Thus Qinghua undertakes some 50 research topics a year on behalf of Beijing Municipality in the fields of energy resources, materials, computers and their application, urban construction, biomedicine and chemical engineering.[79] Jiaotong University, for example, has a broad ranging co-operation agreement with the Xinjiang Autonomous Region Government. Under this agreement, by early 1984 Jiaotong had undertaken 18 research topics. These ranged from free advice on Xinjiang's long-term development plan to cost compensation for a project to process aerial remote-sensing photographs of the natural resources of the Tali river valley.[80]

Both universities have also formed joint bodies for scientific research and production. An example of this at Qinghua is the Qinghua Electrical Equipment Company formed between the university's Electrical Engineering Department and the Tongxian County Micro-Electrical Machinery Plant. By early 1984, this body had realised 12 technical results and the plant's profit and gross output value increased by 32.3% and 21.3% respectively over the year before the joint body was set up.[81] Where co-operation is not on such a long-term or structured basis it can take the form of simple handover of results on a payment basis, the provision of technical services on an *ad hoc* basis, offering consultancy services or providing technical training.[82]

Despite the various handicaps, scientific research in institutions of higher education has scored some notable successes. According to statistics in the 'Index of Invention Awards' prepared by the SSTC, these institutions accounted for 95 out of the 340 inventions announced publicly from April 1979 to July 1982. In 1982, in the 'Index of Awards in Natural Sciences' out of the 122 natural science accomplishment awards, 57 were authored primarily by institutions of higher education while four out of six of the first-class awards went to people working in this sector.[83]

Research Institutes under the Ministries and the Provincial and Municipal Governments

Research institutes under the jurisdiction of the ministries and the provinces are most important for carrying out applied and developmental research. The division of labour for research work is not entirely clearcut because, as we have seen, institutes under the CAS also conduct this type of research and, when it is deemed necessary, institutes under the production ministries can conduct basic research.[84]

Most production ministries have their own research and training institutions. Indeed, the Ministry of Agriculture, Animal Husbandry and Fishery, and the Ministry of Public Health, among others, have their own academies; namely, the Chinese Academy of Agricultural Sciences, the Chinese Academy of Medical Sciences and the Chinese Academy of Traditional Medicine.[85]

At the end of 1984 there were said to be over 800 research institutions under the jurisdiction of the ministries with a total staff of 500,000, of whom 230,000 were classified as scientific and technical personnel.[86] These institutes deal with problems of application and development within their respective fields. They are either administered directly by the relevant ministry in Beijing or via the ministry bureau at the local level. Each ministry has a department of science and technology that has a responsibility for overseeing the research and development conducted within the ministry's jurisdiction.

Under the administrative control of the provincial and municipal authorities are approximately 3,500 research institutions with a staff of 380,000 of whom 150,000 are classified as scientific and technical personnel.[87] Apart from other tasks these institutes are expected to undertake research projects contributing to the industrial and agricultural development of the local economy. Research institutes under these two sectors are clearly the ones that have the most to gain from the new policies if they have a staff that is sufficiently competent and adequate research facilities. As was shown in Chapter Two, while there has been progress in terms of research institutions financing themselves and the formation of joint research–production bodies, to date this progress has not been as swift and as far-reaching as was hoped. Success stories such as that of the Zhuzhou Electronics Research Institute are the exception rather than the norm. This particular institute, which has been lauded in the Chinese press, carries out research on the development and application of micro–computers and employs 59 scientists and technicians and 96 other workers. Unusually, the institute has operated an independent accounting system since it was founded in 1978. This is portrayed as the secret of the institute's success. By the end of 1983 output value reached 6.27 million *yuan* and by mid-1984 the institute was said to have an estimated 2.52 million *yuan* in accumulated fixed assets and circulating funds.[88] In fact, the institute's innovative methods ran into stiff opposition. During the campaign to combat spiritual pollution in late 1983, the institute was criticised for making 'illegal transactions' and 'illicit deals', and for indiscriminately giving out bonuses. In October 1983, some government departments went so far as to freeze the institute's funds and refused to give it materials, bringing the institute's work to a grinding halt.[89] Although these incidents took place in the unusual atmosphere of the spiritual pollution campaign and the institute was later given a clean bill of health by Premier Zhao,[90] it does show how deep-seated resistance to change, and possibly the envy of success, really is. It does not bode well for the extension of such reforms throughout the system.

Chinese Association for Science and Technology

The Chinese Association for Science and Technology (CAST) is described as a mass organisation that is formed and run by people working in the S&T sector. Although it receives its funds from the state, it is depicted as a non-governmental body having the right to elect its own officers without their appointment having to be ratified by any other state body.[91] Essentially the CAST is a professional association and it performs a vital function in co-ordinating the work of various professional societies and providing various forums in which people from these societies can meet. At the end of 1984, there were 106 societies under the jurisdiction of the CAST, an increase from 87 societies at the time of its Second National Congress in March 1980.[92]

The CAST was originally founded in 1958 at its First National Congress through the merger of the All-China Federation of Scientific Societies and the All-China Federation for the Dissemination of Scientific and Technical Knowledge. As Suttmeier has noted, this was an expression of the leadership's desire to merge together professional and popular science but, as Zhou Peiyuan, President of CAST, has noted, it was also conducive to strengthening Party leadership.[93] Despite this fusion of the professional and the popular, work was disrupted by the Cultural Revolution and it was not until after the arrest of the 'Gang of Four' that the CAST and academic societies were able to resume their work properly.[94]

The CAST's Second National Congress outlined a more active and broader role for the association and its constituent elements.[95] Zhou Peiyuan, confirmed as the head of the association, made it clear that the CAST was seen as playing a role that would cut across the rigid, hierarchical structure of China's research system by providing forums through which people from different parts could be brought together to air and exchange their views. However, the role of CAST was envisaged as going beyond the simple increase of academic exchanges and the popularisation of scientific knowledge. It was also expected to provide a vital link between China's policy-makers and experts in the field of S&T. This is a role common to all China's mass organisations that are expected to pass on decisions of China's leaders to their members while at the same time feeding back information on how such policies are received and implemented as well as providing an input source for professionals into the decision-making process itself. In fact, the CAST had performed this kind of function prior to the Cultural Revolution.[96] Zhou Peiyuan, in his speech to the Congress, called on the organisations attached to the association to act as advisers to the Party and government in modernising science and technology and that they should strive to make proposals by S&T workers succeed in this respect.[97] Hu Yaobang, in his speech to the Congress, warmly embraced this view stating that: 'on behalf of the Secretariat of the Central Committee, I now formally apply to the scientists present today for enrolment. We wish to invite some of you comrades to forums or special study sessions and ask you to act as our teachers'.[98]

To help the CAST fulfil its role, Zhou Peiyuan stated that the association would have the freedom to debate questions concerning S&T without the fear of administrative interference or of having one academic viewpoint coercively imposed on it.[99] Finally, the association was assigned the tasks of discovery and training of S&T personnel and of developing academic contacts with other countries.[100]

These tasks have guided the CAST's work through the eighties and were recognised at a Work Conference held in November 1983 and new functions have been created as a result of more recent S&T policy developments. The attempt to link S&T work to economic development resulted in calls for the CAST to provide information and services for industrial units, particularly for medium- and small-sized enterprises.[101]

In this cadre, the CAST set up the China Science and Technology Consultancy Service in March 1983 – the first of its kind in China.[102] Attempts to decentralise decision-making have also affected the relationship between the CAST and its member organisations. Fang Yi, addressing the CAST in December 1984, said that it should grant the societies under its jurisdiction decision-making power in order to increase their role in academic exchanges both within China and with foreign countries.[103]

Notes

1   The figure for 1983 is from an interview with Mr Xu Zhaoxiang of the Science Policy Department of the SSTC, 15 January 1985. The figure for 1985 is quoted in Li Yongzeng, 'Research System Undergoing Reforms', *BR*, no 12, 25 March 1985, p 20. These figures do not include research units in industrial enterprises or agricultural research organisations at the county level or below. In mid-1985, it was said that since 1982, 10,000 non-governmental research institutes had sprung up. These mainly serve smaller factories in urban and rural areas and undertake projects outside the scope of state-owned institutes. *SWB:FE W*1343.

2   *Zhongguo Tongji Nianjian 1984 (Statistical Yearbook of China 1984)* (Beijing: Zhongguo tongji chubanshe, 1984), pp 497 and 499.

3   Interview with Mr Liu Jidong of the Scientific Management Department of the SSTC, 14 January 1985.

4   The development of S&T for the military sector is presided over by the Commission of Science, Technology and Industry for National Defence. This Commission is under the leadership of Ding Henggao and it was established in August 1982 through the merger of the National Defence Industries Office and the National Defence Science and Technology Commission. The merger clearly represented an attempt to integrate better research and development with industrial development in the military sector.

5   A commission is set up when it is considered necessary to co-ordinate work across different ministries and thus ranks higher than a ministry which is only responsible for work in one particular sphere. In China, apart from the SSTC there are, for example, State Commissions for Planning, the Economy and Education.

6   See, for example, *JPRS - CST - 84 - 031*; *JPRS - CST - 84 - 011*, p 22; *JPRS - CST - 84 - 018*, p 3; and *JPRS - CST - 84 - 034*, pp 2-3.

7   The Hubei Provincial Science and Technology Leading Group draws its members from nine relevant departments. *JPRS - CST - 84 - 034*, p 2.

8   This is the case, for example, in the provinces of Hubei and Henan.

9   A Central Committee Circular of September 1977 stated that it had been decided to set up the Commission and in December Fang Yi noted that the Central Committee had decided to establish a National Science and Technology Commission to take care of unified planning, co-ordination and administration of S&T work. See 'CPC Central Committee Circular on Holding National Science Conference', *PR*, no 40, 30 September 1977, p 9 and Fang Yi, 'Fang yi tongzhi zai sijie zhengxie quanguo weiyuanhui changweihui qici kuoda huiyishang zuo de guanyu kexue he jiaoyu shiye qingkuang de baogao (zhaiyao)' ('Report on the State of Science and Education Delivered by Comrade Fang Yi at the Seventh Enlarged Meeting of the Standing Committee of the Fourth National Committee of the Chinese People's Political Consultative Conference (Excerpts)'), *RMRB*, 30 December 1977.
The SSTC was originally set up in 1958 through the merger of the Science Planning Committee and the State Technology Committee but during the Cultural Revolution it was disbanded. For a short review of its history see R P Suttmeier, *Science, Technology and China's Drive for Modernisation* (Stanford: Hoover Institution Press, 1980), pp 20-22.

10 Fang Yi, 'On the Situation in China's Science and Education', *PR* no.2, 13 January 1978, p 16.

11 Interview with Mr Mei Jinfang, (formerly) Head of the West Europe Department of the State Science and Technology Commission, 14 January 1985.

12 Thus in late 1982, the SSTC jointly with the Planning Commission and the Economic Commission selected 38 key projects to concentrate on during the following three years. These projects came within the broad categories of agriculture, light industry, energy exploration and conservation, machinery and electronics, and transport and communication. See *China Exchange News* (*CEN*) vol 11, no 1, 1983, p 30 and *CEN* vol 10, no 4, 1982, p 24.

13 Interview with Mr Mei Jinfang. See also, Zhou Peiyuan, 'Tantan "san ke" de fengong yu xiezuo' ('On the Division of Labour and Cooperation Between the "Three Scientific Organisations" '), *RMRB*, 28 January 1985, p 3.

14 In late 1979, the SSTC had a staff of over 200. J Sigurdson, *Technology and Science in the People's Republic of China* (Oxford: Pergamon Press, 1980), p 70.

15 Interview with Mr Mei Jinfang.

16 Interview with Mr Yan Chengzhun, Deputy Secretary-General, and Mr Zhang Qibiao, Deputy Chief of the Planning Division, of the Shanghai Municipal Science and Technology Commission, 20 January 1985

17 This plan outlined seven new areas for development, 22 key projects relevant to the current situation, four major problems in urban construction, six medical questions and four concerning rural technology. The seven new areas for development were selected from an original list of 17. Interview with Mr Yan Chengzhun and Mr Zhang Qibiao.

18 Interview with Mr Yan Chengzhun and Mr Zhang Qibiao. See also *Xinhua* in English, 9 May 1984 in *JPRS-CST*-84-031, p 85.

19 Hubei Provincial Science and Technology Commission and the Journal's Editorial Department, 'Woguo keji guanli tixi jianshezhong de yige zhongyao keti' ('An Important Subject in the Construction of our Country's Scientific and Technological Management System'), *KXX*, no 2, 1984, p 29.

20 Ibid. pp 31-32.

21 The problem of personnel is dealt with in detail in Chapter Five.

22 Apart from the CAS there are a number of other academies of which the most important are the Academy of Agricultural Sciences and the Academy of Medical Sciences. These operate independently under the jurisdiction of the Ministry of Agriculture, Animal Husbandry and Fisheries and the Ministry of Public Health

respectively. For further discussion see below Research Institutes Under the
Ministries and Provincial and Municipality Governments.

23   Another source gives a figure of 44,000 for scientists and researchers. *Xinhua* in
      English 13 February 1985 in *JPRS-CST*-85-006, p 8.

24   Interview with Mr Luo Wei, Deputy Director of the Science Policy Study Office of
      the Chinese Academy of Sciences, 16 January 1985.

25   Both Suttmeier and Kühner give a figure of 120 and while Suttmeier gives no
      source, Kühner cites an interview with Luo Wei. See R P Suttmeier, *Science,
      Technology and China's Drive for Modernisation*, p 24 and H Kühner, 'Between
      Autonomy and Planning: The Chinese Academy of Sciences in Transition',
      Minerva vol 22, no 1, 1984, p 29. However, two recent Chinese sources give the
      figure of 106 prior to the Cultural Revolution. See *The Chinese Academy of Sciences:
      A Brief Introduction* (Beijing: Chinese Academy of Sciences, 1981), p 2 and Li
      Chang, 'Problems of Development of the Science of Managing Scientific Research'
      Ziran Bianzhengfa Tongxun, no 6, 1981 translated in *JPRS* 80391 *S&T* 154, p 8.

26   Suttmeier gives a figure of 37, Kühner a figure of 36 for 1974. See R P Suttmeier,
      Science, Technology and China's Drive for Modernisation, p 24 and H Kühner,
      'Between Autonomy and Planning: The Chinese Academy of Sciences', p 19.
      Kühner derives his figure from Max Planck-Gesellschaft zur Förderung der
      Wissenschaften, 'Bericht über die Reise einer Delegation der MPG in die
      Volksrepubliek China' (Munich 1974). The CAS book gives a figure of 53 for 1973.
      The Chinese Academy of Sciences: A Brief Introduction, p 2, and notes that the total of
      research workers and personnel was reduced to 13,000.

27   R P Suttmeier, *Science, Technology and China's Drive for Modernisation*, p 24.

28   These are Shanghai, Hefei, Chengdu, Nanjing, Kunming, Guangzhou, Changchun,
      Shenyang, Wuhan, Lanzhou, Xinjiang and Xi'an.

29   Interview with Mr Huang Weiyuan, President of the Shanghai Branch of the
      Chinese Academy of Sciences, 22 January 1985. The degree of involvement with
      research for the locality depends, of course, on the nature of the particular research
      institute. Of the 14 institutes under the 'Shanghai Branch' of the CAS, seven are
      involved in the biological sciences and 70 per cent of their projects are in the area of
      basic research. Whereas, the Institute of Ceramics derives many of its projects from
      local demand.

30   Wang Minxi, 'Shilun zhongguo kexueyuan de gaige qianjing' ('A Preliminary
      Discussion of the Prospects for Reforms in the Chinese Academy of Sciences'),
      KYGL, no 2, 1985.

31   'Zhonggong zhongyang guanyu kexue jishu tizhi gaige de jueding' ('Decision of the
      Central Committee of the Chinese Communist Party on Reform of the Science and
      Technology Management System'), *RMRB*, 20 March 1985, pp 1 and 3.

32   Interview with Mr Luo Wei.

33   Wang Minxi, 'Shilun zhongguo kexueyuan de gaige qianjing'.

34   'Scientific Council of the Chinese Academy of Sciences', *BR* no 22, 1 June 1981,
      pp 6-7.

35   Ibid. See also, 'Members of Division of Chemistry, Academy of Sciences
      Introduced', *Huaxue Tongbao (Chemistry Bulletin)*, no 9, 1981, pp 40-52 translated
      in *JPRS* 80189 *S&T* 150, p 1.

36   Some 60 per cent of the members are drawn from outside bodies such as universities
      and industrial research departments. Interview with Mr Luo Wei.

37   Fang Yi, 'Address to the Fifth Session of the Scientific Council of the Chinese
      Academy of Sciences', *Xinhua* in Chinese 5 January 1984, translated in *SWB:FE*
      7541.

38   Chapter Two of the Provisional Constitution of the CAS (18 May 1981) in *The
      Chinese Academy of Sciences: A Brief Introduction*, pp 221-222.

39 Ibid.

40 Ibid., p 222.

41 'Expression of the Policy of the Party Central Committee on Relying on Scientists to Manage the Academy of Sciences – Formation of New Leading Party Group in the Chinese Academy of Sciences – Party Group Secretary Lu Jiaxi Presents Some Views on Work Arrangements for the Current Year', *Wenhui Bao* 21 May 1982, p 1.

42 This only appears in the Chinese version of the Constitution and not in its English translation. H. Kühner, 'Between Autonomy and Planning: the Chinese Academy of Sciences in Transition', p 23. The Chinese version of the 'Provincial Constitution' can be found in *KYGL*, no 3, 1981, pp 3-6 and the English version in *The Chinese Academy of Sciences: A Brief Introduction*, pp 219-226.

43 *CEN*, vol 12, no 4, 1984, p 30. By this time most CAS institutes had new directors and the average age was reduced from 60.7 years to 51.2. The Institute of Theoretical Physics is one of the key institutes in experimenting with organisational reform within the CAS structure.

44 Interview with Mr Luo Wei.

45 In 1977, as a result of the reorganisation of the Department of Philosophy and Social Sciences under the CAS, the Chinese Academy of Social Sciences was set up. At present, the Academy has 33 research institutes, three research centres, a postgraduate school and a publishing house under its jurisdiction. *The Chinese Academy of Social Sciences: An Introduction* (Beijing, 1984).

46 'Members of Division of Chemistry, Academy of Sciences Introduced' in *JPRS* 80189 - *S&T*-150, p 1.

47 'Zhonggong zhongyang guanyu kexue jishu tizhi gaige de jueding'. The ways in which this has affected financing within the CAS and personnel policy are dealt with in Chapters Four and Five respectively.

48 Interview with Mr Luo Wei.

49 *Xinhua* in English 16 March 1984.

50 'Making Science Serve Economy', *BR*, no 10, 5 March 1984, p 11.

51 Interview with Mr Luo Wei.

52 Thus, in 'Zhonggong zhongyang guanyu kexue jishu tizhi gaige de jueding' it is suggested that 'Party secretaries should themselves possess some scientific knowledge, be enthusiastic about S&T and implement Party policy towards intellectuals.'

53 Li Xing, 'Science Research Funding Overhauled', *CD*, 7 January 1985, p 1.

54 Interview with Mr Luo Wei.

55 Ibid.

56 Ma Longxiang, 'Ying shixing keyan he gaodeng jiaoyu tongyi de guanli tizhi' ('A Unified Management system Should be Adopted for Scientific Research and Higher Education'), *GMRB*, 21 June 1984, p 2.

57 The figure for 1985 is from the Interview with Liu Jidong, those for end 1982 and end 1983 are from *Zhongguo Tongji Nianjian 1983* (*Statistical Yearbook of China 1983*) (Beijing: Zhongguo tongji chubanshe, 1983), p 515 and *Zhongguo Tongji Nianjin 1984*, p 484.

58 The break-down of the 805 institutions at the end of 1983 into categories was as follows: 36 comprehensive universities, 215 colleges of science and engineering, 56 agricultural colleges, 11 forestry colleges, 111 medical colleges, 210 teacher training colleges, 10 linguistic and literary colleges, 44 colleges of finance and economics, 10 colleges of politics and law, 13 physical culture institutes for study of minorities and 52 short-term vocational universities. *Zhongguo Tongji Nianjian 1984*, p 489.

59 Zeng Decong, 'Gaodeng xuexiao keyan guanlizhong de jige lilun wenti' ('Some Theoretical Problems in the Management of Scientific Research in Institutions of Higher Education'), *KYGL*, no 1, 1984, pp 56-60.

60   Liu Dizhong, 'Minister's Pledge on Education Spending', *CD*, 16 January 1985, p 1.
61   This figure does underestimate total spending as there has also been local spending for '*min-ban*' ('people-run') schools.
62   Wang Yingluo, 'Woguo keji tizhi gaigezhong de jige zhanlüe wenti' ('Some Strategic Questions in China's S&T Reforms'), *KXX*, no 6, 1985, p 3.
63   'Zhonggong zhongyang guanyu jiaoyu tizhi gaige de jueding' ('Decision of the Central Committee of the Communist Party of China on the Reform of the Education System'), *RMRB*, 29 May 1985, p 3.
64   Wan Li, 'Zai quanguo jiaoyu gongzuo huiyishang de jianghuo' ('Speech to the National Education Work Conference'), *RMRB*, 31 May 1985, pp 1 and 3.
65   *Xinhua* in English, 13 June 1985 in *SWB:FE* 7978.
66   For example, the five Vice-Ministers are drawn from leading personnel of the State Planning Commission, the State Economic Commission, the SSTC, the Ministry of Finance and the Ministry of Labour and Personnel. *Xinhua* in Chinese, translated in *SWB:FE* 7990.
67   *Xinhua* in English, 18 June 1985 in *SWB:FE* 7982.
68   *Xinhua* in English, 13 June 1985 in *SWB:FE* 7978.
69   *Xinhua* in English, 18 June 1985 in *SWB:FE* 7982.
70   For example see, Commentary, 'Daxue gao keyan dayou kewei' ('There is Much to be Gained from Universities Engaging in Research'), *GMRB*, 23 March 1978, p 1 and Zeng Decong 'Gaodeng xuexiao keyan guanlizhong de jige lilun wenti'.
71   'Zhonggong zhongyang guanyu jiaoyu tizhi gaige de jueding'.
72   Interview at the Ministry of Education, 17 January 1985.
73   Wang Yihung, 'Tasks Set for Educational Reform', *BR*, no 51, 23 December 1985, p 22.
74   D F Simon, 'Rethinking R and D', *The China Business Review*, July–August 1984, p 27.
75   *CEN*, vol 13 no 2, 1985, p 37. These universities and laboratories are as follows:
       Nanjing University: a solid state micro-structure physics laboratory;
       Shandong University: a crystal material laboratory;
       Fudan University: a genetic engineering laboratory;
       Jilin University: an enzyme engineering laboratory;
       and
       Zhongshan University: an ultra-high speed laser laboratory.
       A total of 10 'key laboratories' have been designated for direct funding from the state and it is expected that a further 20 will be selected. Interview at the Ministry of Education.
76   'Zhonggong zhongyang guanyu jiaoyu tizhi gaige de jueding'.
77   'Universities Contribute to Economy', *CD*, 6 February 1984, p 1.
78   Interview at Fudan University, Shanghai, 23 January 1985.
79   Qinghua University, 'Guangfan kaizhan keji xiezuo, wei zhenxing jingji duo zuo gongxian' ('Extensively Develop Scientific and Technical Cooperation, Make a Greater Contribution to Upgrading of the Economy'), *KXX*, no 2, 1984, pp 5-6
80   Zhang Binglu and Zhang Yifu, 'Jiang xiaolu, qiu xiaoyi, yan zeren – shanghai jiaotong daxue keyan guanli gaige diaocha zhisan' ('Stress Efficiency, Seek Benefits, Pay Attention to Responsibilities – Part Three of a Survey of Reforms of Scientific Administration at Shanghai's Jiaotong University'), *GMRB*, 19 July 1984, p 2.
81   Qinghua University, 'Guangfan kaizhan keji xiezuo, wei zhenxing jingji duo zuo gongxian'.
82   Interview at Tongji University, Shanghai, 24 January 1985 and Interview at Qinghua University, Beijing, 18 January 1985 and Dongbei Technical College, 'Daxue keyan de fangxiang' ('The Direction for University Scientific Research'), *KXX*, no 2, 1984, pp 9-10.

83 Zeng Decong, 'Gaodeng xuexiao keyan guanlizhong de jige lilun wenti'.

84 Fang Yi, 'Zai quanguo kexue daihuishang de baogao' ('Report to the National Science Conference'), *RMRB*, 29 March 1978, pp 1 and 4.

85 Apart from these major academies there are other academies under ministerial control, namely, the Academies of Forestry Sciences, Geological Sciences, Railway Research, Petroleum Exploration and Development, and Space Technology, there are also Research Institutes of Coal Mining, Aeronautics and Petro-Chemical Engineering.

86 Interview with Mr Liu Jidong.

87 Ibid.

88 'Reforming Science Research System', *BR*, no 26, 25 June 1984, p 11. See also, Commentator's Article, 'Yao jiji tuiguang zhuzhoushi dianzisuo de gaige jingyan' ('It is Necessary to Actively Popularise the Experience of the Zhuzhou Electronics Research Institute in Carrying Out Reform'), *GMRB*, 24 May 1984, p 1.

89 Li Yongzeng, 'Research System Undergoing Reforms', *BR*, no 12, 25 March 1985, pp 18-20.

90 Zhao Ziyang, 'Report on the Work of the Government (Delivered at the Second Session of the Sixth National People's Congress on May 15, 1984)' *BR*, no 24, 11 June 1984, Documents p.x.

91 Zhou Peiyuan, 'Make Concerted All-Out Efforts, Strive to Modernise China's Science and Technology', 15 March 1980, in *SWB:FE* 6387.

92 The figure for 1984 is from 'Scientific Groups Urged to Promote Academic Exchanges', *CD*, 4 December 1984, p 3 and that for 1980 is from 'Chinese Scientific and Technical Association', *BR*, no 14, 7 April 1980, p 3. In addition to the societies, there are also research associations and centres, and organisations for the popularisation of science affiliated to the CAST.

93 R P Suttmeier, *Science, Technology and China's Drive for Modernisation*, p 28 and Zhou Peiyuan, 'Make Concerted All-Out Efforts, Strive to Modernise China's Science and Technology'.

94 Zhou Peiyuan, ibid.

95 For details of the Congress see *SWB:FE* 6387 and 'New Impetus', *BR*, no 14, 7 April 1980, p 3.

96 See R P Suttmeier, 'Chinese Scientific Societies and Chinese Scientific Development', *Developing Economies*, vol 11, no 2, 1973, pp 146-163.

97 Zhou Peiyuan, 'Make Concerted All-Out Efforts, Strive to Modernise China's Science and Technology'.

98 Hu Yaobang, 'Speech at the Second National Congress of the Chinese Scientific and Technical Association (Excerpts)', *BR*, no 15, 14 April 1980, p 15.

99 Zhou Peiyuan, 'Make Concerted All-Out Efforts, Strive to Modernise China's Science and Technology'.

100 Ibid. See also 'New Impetus'.

101 See, for example, 'Scientific Groups Urged to Promote Academic Exchanges'.

102 For details see Chapter Two.

103 'Scientific Groups Urge to Promote Academic Exchanges'.

CHAPTER FOUR

BETTER VALUE FOR MONEY: REFORM OF THE S&T FUNDING SYSTEM

While it is difficult to calculate precisely the level of spending on S&T in China, it is clear that it is far too low for the modernisation programme set out by the nation's leaders. To improve this situation reforms of S&T financing have centred around three basic problems. First, the low level of state expenditure on S&T means that the government is committed to expanding it as rapidly as possible. However, it is recognised that state expenditure cannot be increased as swiftly as is desirable. This means that, secondly, there is stress on making sure that money spent on S&T is put to more efficient use than in the past and, thirdly, that new channels for funding are to be exploited.

State Expenditure on Civilian Science and Technology

One clear indicator for assessing S&T and its development is that of the level of spending. However, even the relatively simple exercise of quoting a faintly accurate figure for state expenditure is fraught with difficulties. Although increasingly more statistics are being published by the Chinese authorities, often classifications are used so loosely that it can be difficult to find comparable data. Often no indication is given of how a composite figure is made up. Also, it is still very difficult to build up a series of data for S&T over time. The diversification of funding channels will make it even more difficult in the future to calculate a total figure for S&T funding. For example, it is estimated that while in 1982 99% of scientific research funds were allocated by the state, in 1985 state fund allocations had dropped to about 90% of the total amount.[1] An official of the Science Policy Department of the SSTC summed up the situation in the following manner:

> There is no reliable statistical data on funding. We can only say that it occupies roughly so much of the spending. Many speeches are contradictory, especially concerning funding from enterprises. In the past, very little funding came from enterprises and therefore figures were in terms of state allocations. Sometimes in the past when enterprises applied to the Ministry of Finance for money for research and development (R&D), one did not know whether it was all used for R&D or for other purposes. Definition was a matter of the technique of the accountant. Therefore, personally I am suspicious about the reliability of the figures.[2]

The lack of statistics (less than one per cent of statistical compilations are related to S&T) and also their reliability is thus clearly recognised by the SSTC. It was decided that during the current reform of the SSTC a statistical bureau would be set up and it was hoped that during 1985 a general survey of the S&T system would be carried out.[3] Despite such problems, some general observations on S&T financing can be made and the broad trends can be outlined.

Spending on S&T was yet another major casualty of the Cultural Revolution. Table 1 shows that between 1965, the eve of the Cultural Revolution, and 1978, two years after its officially designated end, spending on civilian scientific research had virtually halved when expressed as a percentage of the total industrial and agricultural gross output value. The abysmally low figure of

Table 1: State Expenditure on Civilian Science and Technology until 1979

Period	Amount spent unit: billion yuan	Amount as percentage of total industrial and agricultural output value
First 5 Year Plan (1953-1957)	0.764	0.13
Second 5 Year Plan (1958-1962)	3.94	0.46[a]
1965	1.50	0.8[a]
1966-1976	4.76	0.4[b]
1978	2.70	0.48[c]
1979	3.44	0.54[d]

Source: Based on figures given in Yu Hongjun, Wang Zonglin and Cheng Hengmo, 'Kexue jishu yu jingji jiegou' ('Science and Technology and Economic Structure'), in Ma Hong and Sun Shangqing (eds), *Zhongguo Jingji Jiegou Wenti Yanjiu (Research on the Problems of China's Economic Structure)* (Beijing: Renmin chubanshe, 1981), p 614.

(a): These figures should be taken as very rough estimates.

(b): Calculated from figures in *Zhongguo Tongji Nianjian 1983 (China Statistical Yearbook 1983)* (Beijing: Tongji chubanshe, 1983), p 16. This calculation gives a slightly higher figure since the figures in the yearbook are expressed in 1980 prices.

(c): Ibid. The figure of 5.3 billion *yuan* given by Yu Hongjun et al is clearly wrong. It is either a miscalculation or more probably represents total S&T spending including that for the military sector and covers the same areas as mentioned by Zhang Jingfu when talking about the 1979 Draft Budget (see below).

(d): Ibid. This figure is almost the same as that of 3.3 billion *yuan* given in Yu Hongjun et al: 'Science and Technology and Economic Structure', p 612. The figure of 3.3 million *yuan* is given also in Tong Dalin and Hu Ping, 'Science and Technology', in Yu Guangyuan (ed), *China's Socialist Modernisation* (Beijing: Foreign Languages Press, 1984), p 659.

0.48% for 1978 compares very badly with international standards. These figures for funds for scientific research on projects include operating expenses, capital construction investments and money for new product development, pilot plant production and subsidies for major research items.[4] This level of spending is very clearly insufficient for a country committed to the kind of modernisation programme which China has set for itself. That spending is too low has been recognised by China's leaders but it is pointed out that it can only be expanded gradually. Commenting on the plans for the 1980 budget, Wang Bingqian, the Minister of Finance, remarked that spending on education and science was the key to the modernisation programme. According to Wang, since these two fields had been starved of funds for a number of years, the outlay should be increased by as much as the country's finances would allow.[5] In December 1982, Wang reiterated the same sentiments but again pointed out the problem that the necessary funds could only be increased to a limited extent because 'present financial difficulties make it impossible for the state to allocate huge sums'.[6]

Despite these constraints, the financial allocations have been expanding. For example, since 1978 there have been consistently large increases in the total amount of funds allocated by the state for culture, education, science and public health. It is worth noting that not only did this budgetary allocation not suffer during the period of economic retrenchment from 1980 to 1982 but it experienced a sharp rise in the proportion of spending as a percentage of the total state expenditure from 10.4% in 1979 to 17.1% in 1982 (see Table 2). By contrast state allocations for certain sectors did decline during the same period. In fact, the 2.56 billion *yuan* by which the category of culture, education, science and public health increased during 1982 was equivalent to 36.9% of all additional state expenditure for 1982.[7]

However, within this compound figure, the direct budgetary allocation for science is very small. It accounts for only the operating expenses of the Chinese Academy of Sciences (CAS) and the SSTC and their affiliated organisations. In the draft budget for 1979, this amount came to only 619 million *yuan* out of a projected total spending of 12.08 billion *yuan*. Yet it seems that preferential treatment has been given for scientific work in terms of increased spending. For example, in 1981 operating expenses for education, public health and science increased by 8.1%, 7.2% and 21.3% respectively[8] while in the draft budget for 1983 it was estimated that they would go up by 7.3%, 7.0% and 9.3% respectively.[9] In fact, actual spending on science went up by 13.9% in the 1983 budget.[10] If we assume that since 1979 the science component in the budget has expanded at around 15% per annum – a reasonable and possibly conservative estimate – we would arrive at a figure for 1984 of 1.25 billion *yuan* for the science component out of a total allocation for culture, education, science and public health work of 26.34 billion *yuan*.

In his comments on the draft budget for 1979, the then Finance Minister, Zhang Jingfu, estimated that total state expenditure on scientific research would amount to 5.87 billion *yuan*, an increase of 10% on 1978. This figure includes

Table 2: State Expenditure on Civilian Science and Technology, 1977-1984

Year	State expenditure on culture, education, public health and science	Percentage increase over previous years' spending	Percentage of Total State Budget	Expenditure on civilian S&T work	Expenditure on civilian S&T if 0.7 per cent of total agricultural and industrial output value	Expenditure on civilian S&T if 1.0 per cent of total agricultural and industrial output value
	unit: billion yuan			unit: billion yuan	unit: billion yuan	unit: billion yuan
1977	9.02	5.4	10.7			
1978	11.2	24.2	10.1	2.7		
1979	13.2	17.9	10.4	3.4		
1980	15.6	18.3	12.9			
1981	17.1	9.6	15.4		4.9	7.1
1982	19.7	15.2	17.1		5.3	7.9
1983	22.35	13.5	17.3		5.8	8.3
1984	26.34	17.9	17.4		6.4	9.2
1985	29.3	11.2	18.7			

Source: Figures and calculations based on those in *Zhongguo Tongji Nianjian 1983*, pp. 16 and 448-449 and *Zhongguo Tongji Zhaiyao 1984 (China Statistical Abstracts 1984)* (Beijing: State Statistical Publishing House 1984), pp. 7 and 73. Figures for 1984-1985 are calculated on the basis of those given by Wang Bingqian 'Report on the Execution of the State Budget for 1984 and on the Draft State Budget for 1985', *BR*, no. 17 (29 April 1985), pp. i-iii.

investments in capital construction allocated to the CAS and the SSTC and the expenses and investments earmarked for scientific research by other departments, but it does not include expenditure on scientific research in the 'grass-root units'.[11] It should also be noted that this figure includes allocations for the defence sector. In 1979, funds for scientific projects for civilian purposes totalled approximately 3.3 billion *yuan*, about 0.54% of the gross output value of agriculture and industry.[12] According to Tong Dalin and Hu Ping, the state authorities in charge of S&T have called for an increase in spending on scientific research for civilian projects.[13] A preliminary plan suggested that funding be increased to between 0.7% and 1% of the gross output value of agriculture and industry in a period of five to ten years. Taking the lower percentage would give a spending on civilian scientific research of 6.4 billion *yuan* in 1983 while the higher percentage would indicate a spending level of around 9.2 billion *yuan* (see Table 2). It is not possible to verify whether these objectives have been fulfilled, although other evidence suggests that while spending as a whole has increased, as a percentage of the gross output value of agriculture and industry, significant progress has not been made. Figures have recently become available on China's R&D expenditure and while this category does not include all state spending it does include spending on the military sector and is thus considerably higher than spending on the civilian sector alone. In 1982, R&D expenditure accounted for 0.76% of the gross output value of agriculture and industry and was projected to reach 0.9% in 1983.[14] This would give a state expenditure of 6.3 billion and 8.2 billion *yuan* respectively, but, in fact, R&D expenditures in 1983 only totalled 7.4 billion *yuan*.[15]

The need to increase the science budget rapidly can be attributed initially to the strengthening of the S&T organisational structure and subsequently to the improvement of wages for personnel after a lengthy period of stagnation and to the arrangement of promotions. For example, the expansion of the CAS both in terms of the number of institutes and staff totals since the late seventies has eaten up much of its increased allocations in the state budget. Also the total wage bill for those classified under the category of science, culture, education and public health has virtually doubled from the end of 1978 to the end of 1983, from 5.28 billion to 10.28 billion *yuan*.[16]

At the end of 1983, 1,531 capital construction projects were under construction for the category of natural scientific research while 544 had been completed.[17] In 1983, the investment in fixed assets for scientific research was 1.21 billion *yuan*. Of this figure, 1.06 billion *yuan* was invested in capital construction, of which investment related to the natural sciences comprised 0.98 billion *yuan*, a slight fall from the total of 0.88 billion *yuan* in 1982 (see Table 3).[18] Investment in technical updating, transformation etc. in 1983 was 0.15 billion *yuan* and in 1983 there were four projects under construction absorbing over 10 million *yuan*.[19]

A provincial breakdown of the figures for investment in capital construction reflects, not surprisingly, the concentration of scientific research in a number of

Table 3: Selected Figures for Investment in Scientific Research Sector

unit: 100 million *yuan*

	Investment in Fixed Assets	Investment in Capital Construction	Investment in Technical Upgrading, Transformation etc.	Newly Increased Assets through Capital Construction
Total All Sectors	951.96	594.13	357.83	453.10
Scientific Research	12.08	10.59	1.49	8.19
of which:				
Natural Sciences		9.84		
Social Sciences		0.59		
Seismology		0.16		

Source: Compiled from statistics in Section Six 'Investment in Fixed Assets' in *Zhongguo Tongji Nianjian 1984*, pp. 299–344.

key provinces and the paucity of research institutions particularly in China's 'backward' Autonomous Regions. Of investment in 1983, around 20% was in the municipality of Beijing (20.49), reflecting the capital's clear predominance in the scientific research sector. Apart from Beijing, four other provinces and one municipality received over 5% of the investment: Sichuan (8.78%), Shanghai (7.08%), Liaoning (6.6%), Shaanxi (6.04%) and Jiangsu (5.19%). At the other end of the scale, seven provinces (or their equivalents) received under one per cent of the total investment: Inner Mongolia, Guangxi and Guizhou (all 0.94%), Jiangxi and Qinghai (0.84%) and Ningxia and Tibet (0.28%).[20]

The need to increase state spending on S&T is taken note of in the Party Decision on the Reform of the S&T Management System. In this document it is stated that for a given period, central and local finance allocations will be increased gradually at a higher rate than the growth in regular financial revenues. In fact, apart from increased central financing, evidence suggests that provincial government allocations for S&T are also being increased. Hebei province announced that in 1983 funds budgeted for S&T would increase by 45%, exceeding previous records. These funds were to be used primarily for 26 S&T projects and other key S&T projects organised during 1983.[21] Xinjiang Autonomous Region allocated an extra 30 million *yuan* in 1985 in its budget for education, science, culture, journalism and publishing, making a total invest-ment of 670 million *yuan*. Among other projects these new funds were for scientific research, construction of an electronic research laboratory, a new laboratory for studying crops and a science hall.[22]

A major problem at the provincial, and indeed at all levels, is that the inflexibility of the system means that even if money is available it takes a long time before it is actually allocated and it makes the issuance of extra funds a major problem. For example, in Gansu province it is said that it took the relevant provincial authorities almost one year to make arrangements for a one-year S&T plan and it took the planning commission and the financial office one to two months to examine the drafts. Now in Gansu they have started convening specialist meetings to discuss the problems and to speed up the process. It is stated that once the experts have made their suggestions decisions can be taken more swiftly concerning resource allocation. Thus, following one such meeting the one to two month period that was necessary for assessment of the S&T plan noted above was cut to only two days.[23] To help improve flexibility at the provincial level, special funds are being set up such as the Shanghai industrial technology development fund (17 December 1984). The objective of this fund is to help co-ordinate Shanghai's production, scientific research and education by providing funds and other forms of economic support. It is also expected that the funds will help spread research results to promote the upgrading of traditional industries, to spur the growth of new industries and service trades, and to offer consultancy services.[24]

Using State Allocations More Efficiently

Under the unreformed system of allocation the state did not distinguish between various levels or types of S&T activity but issued funds uniformly from the higher-level administrative departments according to the research unit and the number of people. Thus, research institutes would receive a lump sum from the state through the various departments to cover the operating expenses of the institute. However, very little control could be exerted by the state to ensure that the funds were used in the most constructive manner. This system was said to 'ensure stable yields despite drought or floods' but now it is dismissed as encouraging all to 'eat from the same big pot'.

In particular, the system is criticised for the fact that funds expended are not linked to results nor are wages nor promotion opportunities for researchers linked to their work performance. Instead of being dependent on their own efforts for expansion and research work, institutes are depicted as just having looked to the state for their investment funds. The lack of contact between research institutes and the self-sufficient mentality has meant that many have sought to acquire all the equipment and personnel they might conceivably require within their own unit. This has put an added, unnecessary burden on state funds in paying for boarding, overstocking and duplication of purchases. It also helps explain the very low utilisation rate of equipment and why a lot of fixed assets remain idle in many research institutes. One practical suggestion to resolve this problem is the sharing of equipment, but without an adequate system of compensation for use this is difficult to implement. The cost of import of large advanced equipment takes up two-thirds of total expenses of research units and thus duplication and under-use of the equipment are very costly. Not only is a more careful monitoring of purchases suggested but also the sharing of frequently used equipment. For precise, complicated, rare and expensive pieces of equipment, it is suggested that a public laboratory, or laboratory centre, be set up.[25]

In the future, most of the state allocations will go to finance major S&T projects, the construction of key laboratories and experimental bases included in the central or local plans. Given the situation outlined above, it is not surprising that the state wants to ensure that it gets better value for money when funding these projects. A consultation document prepared for the Science and Technology National Work Conference (March 1985) suggested a number of ways in which the situation might be improved.[26] First, the contract system is to be extended where possible to cover such projects. It is intended that, in the future, these contracts will use a compensatory rather than a non-compensatory form. Where possible the amounts stipulated in the contract should be repaid, but with approval, the consultation document stated, exemption could be made for those unable to repay. Secondly, a system of responsibility for tasks is to be implemented by industrial ministries. Industrial departments that originally received the three operating expenses for S&T and administered them by themselves will have as their basic allocation the amount received in the first year of implementing this reform. From then on, increases will be decided on the basis of the ministry's remaining profits. Thirdly, the system of opening up state key S&T projects to public bidding is to be gradually implemented. Fourthly, it suggests that a S&T contract law be formulated. This is to be drafted by the SSTC and the State Economic Commission with the relevant departments and to be implemented after being approved by the state.

Finally, the consultation document echoes the calls for a greater role for banks in ensuring not only sufficient financing levels but also that the money is put to good effect. While research funds for basic research, for example, will still be appropriated by the state, it is suggested that operating expenses can be entrusted to the supervision of the bank. The bank will be responsible for allocating the funds as they are needed and ensuring that they are used for the purpose intended. Funds temporarily not in use can be kept in the bank and used as revolving funds. The banks would retrieve the recovery capital which would not have to be turned over to the higher financial authorities but could be used to finance further S&T undertakings.[27] The part of operating expenses to be repaid is to be administered by the bank in accordance with the state's credit guidelines. A second consultation document from the National Work Conference dealt with this question. The bank, in accordance with an agreed contract, will assume responsibility for the supervision and investigation of the use of the credit. When the credit is due to be repaid the bank should recover it and return it to the ministry that allocated it. If it cannot be recovered on the date due then the relevant ministry and unit undertaking the project should conduct negotiations. The bank, for handling the credit, receives a low interest payment from the relevant unit or receives from the ministry concerned, in accordance with the annual payment, a 3% to 5% handling fee. This same document called for the establishment of S&T credit quotas in the state credit plan and that the quota be increased in line with the development of S&T work.[28]

Banks can also provide a further source of S&T financing through loans. In particular, this method is being encouraged to launch a project that could not be sufficiently financed through other means. For example, the Hunan People's Bank allocated 2.5 million *yuan* for S&T between January and September 1984.[29] It has even been suggested that specialised S&T banks be set up, similar in function to the agricultural banks, to meet the needs of reform. An article in mid-1984 outlined the advantages of creating such banks. In addition to applying economic levers as noted above by checking up on loan projects the banks would be able to control the unnecessary repetition of research topics. Also, the banks would play the role of mediator between scientific research institutes and production units to ensure that any contract implemented was fair to both parties. The fact that these banks could do the professional economic and legal work concerning the contracts means that the S&T research institutes would not have to establish their own departments to carry out such work.[30] One Chinese writer has stated that the fact that China did not have a S&T bank system testified to China's past failure to regard S&T as a productive force.[31]

Scientific Funds

Despite the increase in state allocations for investment in S&T and attempts to ensure that these funds are used more efficiently, it is clear that they remain insufficient to meet China's need. To rectify this situation it has been decided that other channels must be tapped to finance the modernisation of the S&T research sector. To ensure that institutes can take advantage of the new opportunities they are being allowed much greater financial autonomy as a part of the decentralisation of the decision-making process.

The Decision on the Reform of the S&T Management System foresees a threefold system for funding scientific research institutes.[32] As has been discussed in Chapter Two, in future developmental research will be financed through the contract system with the intention that developmental research institutes become financially independent within a five-year period. It is hoped that with these institutes providing their own revenues for operating expenses, more of the state allocations can be redirected towards support of basic research. The policy emphasis on the need to link research work more directly to production has clearly led to problems for basic research work. Emphasising the commercialisation of technology creates a tendency for researchers to focus on short-term projects that yield quick results. This problem is recognised and reassuring noises are made in the Chinese press about the need to protect long term basic research work.[33] According to one writer, how basic, and applied research work is reformed and how stability of the basic and applied S&T ranks is maintained have become very prominent problems.[34]

Clearly research institutes primarily engaged in basic and applied research do not have the opportunity to make a contract to derive their own revenue. Neither is there always a clear end in sight to their work. To deal with this problem a system of science foundations is to be gradually introduced on a trial basis to support basic and applied research projects. One of the first funds to be set up is the seismology science fund. This was founded by four organisations pooling their funds, along with the wages of the concerned personnel, for basic and applied research in the field. In addition to these funds, the 'higher authorities' allocated 500,000 *yuan* in support, bringing the total fund to 3.08 million *yuan*.[35]

In particular, a national natural science foundation is to be established. The relevant institutes would compete to draw their research expenses primarily from this, and other, foundations with the state only providing directly limited funds to support their necessary operating expenses and public facilities expenditures.

Initially, the bulk of the funding for the national natural science foundation will come from government allocations. Its funds will be derived primarily from the following sources: state allocations to the CAS administered science fund (in 1985 this was 50 million *yuan*); the expenses devoted to basic research within the funds for three operating expenses managed by the SSTC (in 1985 this was 10 million *yuan*); S&T funds annually transferred by the CAS and other relevant units for basic and applied research; and special state subsidies and increases for

S&T expenses and any relevant increases in basic and applied research funds.[36] However, it is expected that other units and individuals will also contribute to the funds so that, over time, the percentage of funds from government appropriations will decrease. While the foundation will rely heavily on government funding, it is stated that it will be autonomous in deciding which projects to support. These kinds of decisions will be made by a specially convened committee.[37]

The foundation will draw on the experiences derived from the administration of the Science Fund by the CAS. This fund, set up in 1982, was the first of its kind to be established in China. According to the CAS, it has three advantages over the old method of allocating lump sums to various units. It is open to all scientific workers in China to apply directly for the funds they need for their research programmes. The scope of support is clearly defined; it is mainly intended to support basic research in the natural and applied sciences. Finally, the projects to be supported are themselves by necessity concretely defined.[38]

Primarily, the CAS funds were intended to go to those projects that broke new ground and that could produce their results within a specified period of two or three, or at most five years. The funds were also to be used for advancing important branches of science that were not sufficiently developed within China. While the fund was drawn mainly from national revenues, donations by individuals or units within China or from abroad were also accepted.[39]

From its foundation in March 1982 until the end of 1984, the CAS Science Fund Committee gave out grants totalling 120.33 million *yuan* to subsidise 2,696 research projects. This was roughly 30% of the total funds applied for and about 51% of the total number of research projects sent in.[40] This means that either the less costly projects were accepted or, more probably, those applying did not receive the full amount asked for. Of the projects approved, 87% involved applied research on technical problems in the national economy while approximately 11% were involved with basic research.[41] The percentage of projects being funded that deal with applied research is rising. In 1982 such projects accounted for 72% of the total and 89% in 1983.[42] In keeping with the original intentions, the overwhelming majority of the funds have been allocated to organisations outside the CAS structure; in fact, only 10.26% of the total funds have gone to projects from affiliated institutes. The main beneficiaries of the fund were institutions of higher education. Institutions of higher education directly under the Ministry of Education[43] received 46.36% of the funds while research units belonging to industrial, communications, agricultural, medical and national defence departments and institutions of higher education under local control accounted for 42.16%. Only 1.75% of the funds was allocated to national large-scale projects.[44] In fact, the percentage of funds that went to institutions of higher education, including those institutions not directly under the jurisdiction of the Ministry of Education, came to 79.4% of the total funding granted.[45]

If all other factors were equal, it is intended that preference be given to middle aged and younger applicants and those from 'remote areas'. This policy has shown some results, but the latter aspect has not been entirely successful. Over 80% of the projects that have received funds were presided over by people under 55 years of age. While units that have won awards, 406 in all, are from various corners of China, it is worth noting that no unit in either Tibet or Qinghai province has won an award.[46]

The extension of the method of financing research through the foundation system signals a further major break away from the old system of research financing. Individuals, or groups of scientists, will apply to the foundation for the funding of a particular project and, perhaps most importantly, applications will be assessed through a system of peer group review. The process appears to be consciously modelled on that used in the USA. Such a system would run sharply against China's hierarchical structures where age and political factors have usually played a key role in dictating who has the power of decision making. It will presumably take some time for people to adjust to a different kind of system and opposition may be expected. However, the apparent success of the CAS Science Fund would suggest cautious optimism.

Whether this system works to its full effect will also depend on the success of reforms of the personnel system which are developing in tandem with the financial reforms. Once a grant has been won, unless the scientist or institute is able to recruit the best people available for the project it will undermine the project's viability. Despite discussion of this point, it remains unclear whether new personnel can be recruited for the project from outside the original institute or whether one must make do with those people already working inside it. There appear to be too many bureaucratic barriers to allow a sufficiently free flow of skilled personnel. At the moment this may not be important as within the institutes, especially within the CAS, there is said to be an abundance of skilled personnel that can be redeployed. However, this will not always be the case and things could become very difficult as more new fields of research open up that require scientists from different disciplines to co-operate.[47]

There will remain, though, some institutes which supply vital services but are unable to take advantage of either the contract or science foundation system. These institutes, such as those engaged in medicine, family planning and meteorology, will continue to receive state appropriations. They will, however, be expected to show greater accountability for the way in which they use these appropriations.[48]

Financial Reforms Within Scientific Research Institutes

To make sure that research institutes and institutions of higher education can get the most out of the reform programme, it is important that they are given greater control over their own financial affairs. This will help institutes to be able to conclude the kinds of agreements most suited to their particular field of work. Also, it is hoped that better use of funds will be made within institutes in the future. The contract system is intended not only to regulate relations between the individual research institute and other organisations but also, as far as is possible, to regulate relations within the institute.

The new possibilities for research institutes will mean that in the future many of them will receive their funds from a variety of different sources ranging from state allocations to the incomes derived from the contract, consultancy and training work they undertake. The CAS has been busy diversifying its sources for funding. While the overwhelming amount of the Academy's funding, some 95%, still comes from the national budget, the remainder is derived from contracts signed with enterprises, ministries and local authorities.[49] Clearly some institutes within the CAS structure have far more to gain from this diversification of funds than others, as have the polytechnical institutions of higher education. For example, Tongji University, in Shanghai, has developed strong links with local industry and in 1984 derived almost one-third of its income from projects signed with outside units. The 1984 annual research budget was approximately 3.5 million *yuan*. This was comprised of three broadly equal parts with money from the Ministry of Education; money from other industrial ministries, the SSTC and the Shanghai Municipality; and revenue from contracts with outside enterprises.[50]

Money derived by institutes from the outside contracts does not have to be handed over to higher authorities but is used to set up a variety of funds. According to the temporary regulations on technology transfer, incomes that scientific research institutes and institutions of higher education derive from such endeavours will be exempt from taxes for three years.[51] Institutes that derive money from contracts with outside units use it to establish three funds: a S&T development fund, a welfare fund and a reward fund. The institute itself has the power to decide how the money received will be distributed between the three funds.[52]

To ensure that funds are used more effectively within research institutes the contract system is also being promoted, as are other financial reforms including decentralisation of decision-making powers. It is expected that the use of the contract system will improve efficiency and lead to a more prudent use of funds with less money being used to conduct more projects. Within the institutes, research project contracts and other job economic responsibility systems are to be used in dealing with their laboratories, shops and individuals. It is hoped that this will provide a framework for rewarding people in terms of wages and bonuses according to the quantity and quality of work done. This would bring research workers into line with the reward system already operating in the countryside and now being extended throughout the industrial sector.[53] However, there have been warnings that the responsibility system adopted should not simply ape that used in other sectors but should be adapted to suit scientific research. In particular, it has been stressed that factors other than economic revenue should be taken into account when devising a scientific research responsibility system. Academic, practical and sociological values are also to be taken into account. Similarly, with respect to the training of personnel it is urged that the judgment of success should not be solely limited to the total number trained but should also include the quality of the training provided and the levels of skills taught.[54]

The CAS has undertaken a number of reforms geared to improving the use of research funds by those institutes under its jurisdiction. In a major effort to break away from the old system of allocation of funds, the CAS has introduced a reform for the funding of theoretical research. The state funds received by the CAS are distributed in two ways: 20% is allocated directly by the Academy for key or important projects; 80% is distributed among the different institutes.[55] In theory, the different qualities and contributions of the institutes are taken into account when the funds are distributed, but in practice it is said that such factors have made very little difference to the allocation of funds. In practice, the size of an institute's funding has depended mainly on the total of its S&T staff. This has led, not surprisingly, to frustrations on behalf of those institutes that were producing better quality work more efficiently. To overcome this problem, in 1985 the CAS began to experiment with a research fund for institutes engaged in theoretical studies in both pure and applied sciences that prove to be the most successful or advanced. To finance this fund, the amount of money distributed direct to the institutes has been cut by 17%. This 17% is being held back to finance the new fund.[56] This is intended to be an initial experiment and the intention is that the size of this fund will be increased over time. Indeed, it seems that the CAS leadership would have liked to introduce the experiment on a larger scale but that two main considerations appear to have held them back. First, opposition to the reform exists from institutes that are either naturally cautious or that feel they may lose out under the new system. Secondly, a limited reform provides a period of experimentation to give people time to get used to it and to iron out faults before it is implemented on a larger scale.

Also, in 1985 the CAS decided to introduce a contract system to fund non-theoretical and development projects in applied science studies. These projects are intended to be ones that are most likely to help solve key problems: the country's construction and technical renovation, the absorption of imported expertise and the gaining of social and economic benefits. Some of these projects will be put in the state plans and institutes will be able to apply for funding for others. The institutes that are assigned the projects will sign a contract and receive their funds from the Academy.[57]

The CAS leadership has also decided to set up a President's fund and a Director's fund. To finance these funds, a further 3% of the total research fund is being withheld. These funds will be used for bonuses for researchers and scientists engaged in key research programmes, awards for those who make great contributions and for financing those scientists who have difficulty in raising money from other sources. The funds will also be used to support talented young researchers with their projects.[58] In fact the CAS had already been experimenting for a couple of years with setting aside funds for targeting on specifically designated areas for support. In August 1983 it was announced that the CAS had decided to allocate 5% of its scientific research funds to supporting a number of key young and middle-aged S&T personnel. The biology division of the CAS took a leading role in this experiment. It appropriated some 1.73 million *yuan* to be used mainly by 40 such scientists and technicians.[59] The biology division has also experimented with the giving of small grants of less than 5,000 *yuan* in order to assist important exploratory research by staff under 45 years of age.[60]

Financing within institutions of higher education is also experiencing a major shake-up. In the future, universities are going to be free to shape their own budgets. Previously funds received from the Ministry of Education came in three major parts, for personnel, research and operating costs. Now the institutions will receive their funds from the new Commission, for Education in a lump sum and the universities themselves will be responsible, within broad guidelines, for deciding how this money will be allocated within the institution. The budget will still have to be approved by the Commission but the institution will be allowed to retain any surplus funds and will be held accountable for any overspending of the budget.[61] It is unclear how rigorously this accountability will be enforced, but it is within the power of the Commission to make the institution devote a portion of the subsequent financing to clear the deficit.[62]

At the forefront of the reform programme for higher education and the subject of numerous articles in the Chinese press is Shanghai Jiaotong University.[63] Before the introduction of financial reforms in 1981, funds for scientific research were concentrated within the central university administration and the various departments and research institutes would simply draw on these funds for their needs without being held properly accountable for their use. In fact, it seems that departments would apply for far more than their needs. At the end of the year, the phenomenon common to all organisations working on an annual budget occurred – the rush to spend remaining funds before they are reclaimed by higher authorities. In Jiaotong, the lack of control and co-ordination meant that not only did this annual spree result in the usual waste but also in year-end financial deficit. The 1979 outlay of funds for scientific research, for example, was 150% of the total funds made available for that year. Who footed the bill is unclear. Also, according to statistics for the first half of 1980, of the 315 pieces of equipment costing over 10,000 *yuan*, one-quarter were not used during the period.[64]

To resolve this problem, in 1981 the university introduced regulations to devolve administration of certain aspects of research funds to the departments and research units. With these units responsible for their own research budgets, they were able to retain any surpluses but any overspending was deducted from the following year's allocation.[65] This reform produced successes and provided the basis for further experimentation. Statistics for 1981, by comparison with those for 1980, show that while the total number of research topics went up by 49.1%, total spending went down by 23.6%. The savings were most probably made by reductions of circulating capital, depreciation of fixed assets and by cutting back on the overstocking of expensive equipment.[66] If this was the case, it would not necessarily mean that less money was available for actual research. This would explain why there was no resistance to the reduction in spending from the academic staff. The reform particularly enabled the departments within the university to attract more work from the Shanghai Municipality. Such research topics increased by 65.2% in comparison with a much smaller increase of 7.5% in topics undertaken for the various ministries etc.[67]

On the basis of these perceived successes, more powers have been devolved to departments and institutes to allow them greater ability to act on their own initiative. For example, the head of the department has the power now to examine, approve and purchase instruments and equipment that is of a value of less than 50,000 yuan per item and of educational equipment and materials below a value of 20,000 yuan. Also he or she can, within the state and university guidelines, authorise allowances for staff business trips, and can decide on the use of the department's development funds.[68]

The new reforms that are being introduced will clearly have a different impact on the various types of institutes. Within the CAS structure they will favour some institutes rather than others as they will favour some departments within an institution of higher education. As a consequence, it is recognised that some form of redistribution should take place to help finance departments or institutes that cannot easily take advantage of the new system. Redistribution of money will vary and clearly this will become a focus of bargaining between institutes and the Academy, and between departments and the university. For example, both Qinghua University and Fudan University operate a redistributive mechanism within the university.[69] One reason for the support of individual departments for the creation of a faculty system in the universities, apart from purely academic considerations, might be that it would strengthen their power against the central university authorities. This would improve the bargaining position of the individual departments over the redistribution of funds derived from external earnings. It is clear that a lively form of politics will emerge within institutions of higher education and the CAS as a result of these reforms. To facilitate this process it is necessary for them to develop a system that enables such discussions to be aired freely and for decisions to be made on a rational basis.

Notes

1   Ma Lili, 'The Concept of China's Scientific Research System Reform; A Visit to Wu Mingyu, vice-Minister of the State Science and Technology Commission', *Gaige Zhisheng (The Voice of Reform)*, no 4, 1985, p 31, translated in *JPRS - CST - 85 - 028*, p 2.

2   Interview with Mr Xu Zhaoxiang of the Science Policy Department of the State Science and Technology Commission, 15 January 1985.

3   Ibid.

4   Tong Dalin and Hu Ping, 'Science and Technology', in Yu Guangyuan (ed), *China's Socialist Modernisation* (Beijing: Foreign Languages Press, 1984), p 659.
5   Wang Bingqian, 'Report on Financial Work', *BR*, no 39, 29 September 1980, p 17.
6   Wang Bingqian, 'Report on the Implementation of the State Budget for 1982 and the Draft State Budget for 1983', in *Fifth Session of the Fifth National People's Congress* (Beijing: Foreign Languages Press, 1983), p 204.
7   Wang Bingqian, 'Report on the Final State Account of 1982', in *The First Session of the Sixth National People's Congress* (Beijing: Foreign Languages Press, 1983), p 99.
8   Wang Bingqian, 'Report on the Final State Accounts for 1980 and Implementation of the Financial Estimates for 1981', *BR*, no 2, 11 January 1982, p 18.
9   Wang Bingqian, 'Report on the Implementation of the State Budget for 1982 and the Draft State Budget for 1983', p 204.
10   Wang Bingqian, 'Report on the Final State Accounts for 1983 and the Draft State Budget for 1984', in *The Second Session of the Sixth National People's Congress* (Beijing: Foreign Languages Press, 1984), p 88.
11   Zhang Jingfu, 'Report on the Final State Accounts for 1978 and the Draft State Budget for 1979', *BR*, no 29, 20 July 1979, p 22.
12   Tong Dalin and Hu Ping, 'Science and Technology', p 659. Yu Hongjun *et al.* use the same figure but do not make it clear that it is only for civilian projects. Yu Hongjun, Wang Zonglin and Cheng Hengmo, 'Kexue jishu yu jingji jiegou' ('Science and Technology and Economic Structure') in Ma Hong and Sun Shangqing (eds), *Zhongguo Jingji Jiegou Wenti Yanjiu* (*Research on the Problems of China's Economic Structure*) (Beijing: Renmin Chubanshe, 1981), p 612.
13   Tong Dalin and Hu Ping, 'Science and Technology', p 659.
14   Yang Weizhe, 'Improving Science and Technology Capability: Some Chinese Impressions', in R Lalkaka and Wu Mingyu (eds), *Managing Science Policy and Technology Acquisition: Strategies for China and a Changing World* (Dublin: Tycooly International Publishers Ltd, 1984), p 28.
15   Interview with Mr Xu Zhaoxiang.
16   *Zhongguo Tongji Nianjian 1984 (China Statistical Yearbook 1984)* (Beijing: Tongji Chubanshe, 1984), p 458.
17   Ibid, p 322.
18   Investment in fixed assets of state-owned units consists of two parts: investment in capital construction and in technical updating and transformation. Capital construction refers to construction, expansion, transformation and restoration projects of all sectors of the national economy, as well as purchases and installation of equipment. The investment in capital construction shows the amount of work done in capital construction in money terms, or the scale and progress of capital construction during a certain period of time. It is a comprehensive indicator, to be obtained by multiplying the actual progress of the project and the budget price (the price adopted during the preparation of the budget for a project's working drawing). Building materials that have not yet been used and equipment not yet installed are excluded. The accomplished investment in capital construction differs from financial appropriations for capital construction in that the former is the volume of work done, to be calculated at the budget price, while the latter is the actual amount of money allocated. Technical updating and transformation refer to projects or purchases by state-owned enterprises and institutions to renew or modernise their existing fixed assets (excluding major repairs or maintenance). Investment in technical upgrading and transformation shows, in value terms, the amount of work done in these aspects. *Zhongguo Tongji Nianjian 1984*, pp 565-567.
19   Ibid, p 340.
20   Ibid, p 317. The high percentage for Sichuan is probably a reflection of its large population.

21 Hebei Provincial Radio, 17 March 1985, in *JPRS* - 84524 - *S&T* - 210, p 191.

22 *Xinhua* in English 16 May 1985 in *JPRS* - *CST* - 85 - 019.

23 Ke Hua, 'Implement New Science and Technology Principles to Reduce Deficits and Increase Profits of Enterprises', *Lanzhou Keji Qingbao (Lanzhou Science and Technology Information)*, translated in *JPRS* - *CST* - 85 - 019, p 52.

24 *SWB:FE*, W 1319.

25 Du Shunxing, 'Kexue yanjiu danwei de jingji guanli' ('Economic Management of Scientific Research Institutes'), *KYGL*, no 4, 1984, pp 73-76.

26 'Guanyu gaige keji bokuan guanli banfa de zanxing guiding' ('Temporary Regulations Concerning the Reform of the Administrative Method for Science and Technology Allocations'), *National Science and Technology Work Conference Consultation Document No 1*, pp 2-3.

27 See also 'Excerpts of Governor Chen Lei's "Report: Reform the Science and Technology System and Make Science and Technology Serve the Economic Construction" ', *Heilongjiang Ribao*, 11 May 1985, translated in *JPRS* - *CST* - 85 - 023, p5.

28 'Guanyu jiji kaizhan yinhang keji xindai de jueding' ('Decision Concerning Enthusiastically Developing Bank Science and Technology Credit'), *National Science and Technology Work Conference Consultation Document No 2*, pp 1-2.

29 Wu Xinghua, 'Hunan geji renmin yinhang jiji fafang keji daikuan' ('Hunan's People's Banks at Various Levels Positive About Granting Science and Technology Credits'), *RMRB*, 19 October 1984, p 3.

30 Wang Sanhou, 'Xiwang jianli keji kaifa yinhang' ('In Hope of the Establishment of Science and Technology Development Banks'), *GMRB*, 7 May 1984, p 1.

31 The author notes favourably that certain East European countries (the German Democratic Republic, Bulgaria and Hungary) have basically adopted the system of borrowing from banks. Yang Peiqing, 'Jingji tizhi he keji jinbu' ('Economic Reform and Scientific and Technological Progress'), *KXX*, no 1, 1985, p 13.

32 'Zhonggong zhongyang guanyu kexue jishu tizhi gaige de jueding' ('Decision of the Central Committee of the Chinese Communist Party on Reform of the Science and Technology Management System'), *Renmin Ribao*, 20 March 1985, pp 1 and 3.

33 See, for example, 'Technical Markets are the Key to Reform of the Science and Technology System', *Jingji Ribao*, 27 December 1984, pp 1-2, translated in *JPRS* - *CST* - 85 - 009, p 4.

34 Chen Yong, 'Fund System will Promote China's Basic Science Development', *KXX*, no 3, 1985, translated in *JPRS* - *CST* - 85 - 020, p 49.

35 Ibid.

36 'Guanyu gaige keji bokuan guanli banfa de zanxing guiding', p 5.

37 'Zhonggong zhongyang guanyu kexue jishu tizhi gaige de jueding' and interview with Mr Xu Zhaoxiang.

38 'Science Fund Established', *BR*, no 1, 6 January 1982, p 9.

39 Ibid.

40 The total amount of money applied for was 416.11 million *yuan* and the number of projects was 4,770. 'Jichuxing yanjiu shixing jijinzhi de qingkuang huibao' ('Report on the Conditions of Implementing a Fund System for Basic Research'), *National Science and Technology Work Conference Exchange Materials No 6*, p 4. See also Hu Xian, 'Jijinzhi de shixing shi dui keji tizhi de yixiang zhongyao gaige' ('Trial Implementation of Fund Systems is an Important Reform of the S&T System'), *KXX*, no 5, 1985, p 43. The fund is administered by a committee of 23 people drawn from within and outside the CAS.

41 Ibid. The applied research projects are said to comprise mainly basic research work in the applied research.

42   Chen Zujia and Chen Dong, 'Kexueyuan kexue jijin kashi fahui zuoyong' ('The Science Fund of the Chinese Academy of Sciences has Begun to Play a Role'), *RMRB*, 12 January 1984, p 3.

43   The figures refer to the period before the State Education Commission was established.

44   'Jichuxing yanjiu shixing jijinzhi de qingkuang huibao', p 5.

45   Hu Xian, 'Jijinzhi de shixing shi dui keji tizhi de yixiang zhongyao gaige', p 43.

46   'Jichuxing yanjiu shixing jijinzhi de qingkuang huibao', p 5.

47   Reforms of the personnel system are discussed in detail in Chapter Five.

48   The Decision on the Reform of the S&T Management System also mentions research institutes involved in labour protection, disaster prevention and control, environmental science and other public welfare undertakings and institutes engaged in basic technical services and research, such as information gathering and supply, standardisation and surveying 'Zhonggong zhongyang guanyu kexue jishu tizhi gaige de jueding'.

49   Interview with Mr Luo Wei, Deputy Director of the Science Policy Study Office of the Chinese Academy of Sciences, 16 January 1985.

50   Interview at Tongji University, Shanghai, 24 January 1985.

51   'Temporary Regulations on Technology Transfers Issued by the State Council (10 January 1985)', *Anhui Ribao (Anhui Daily)*, 16 January 1985, p 2, translated in *JPRS - CST - 85 - 012*, p 13.

52   Interview with Mr Liu Jidong of the Scientific Management Department of the SSTC, 14 January 1985.

53   Wu Lantian and Zhang Guangren, 'A Model for Reforming the Economic Management of Scientific Research Units', *KXX*, no 4, 1983, pp 19-23.

54   See, for example, Na Baokai, 'Keyan danwei de zerenzhi wenti' ('The Question of a Responsibility System in Scientific Research Units'), *KYGL*, no 1, 1984, p 71.

55   Interview with Mr Luo Wei.

56   Ibid and Li Xing, 'Science Research Funding Overhauled', *CD*, 7 January 1985, p 1.

57   Ibid.

58   Li Xing, 'Tie Science to Nation's Needs, Says Hu Yaobang', *CD*, 14 January 1985, p 1.

59   Of these 40, 27 had studied abroad and the grants awarded ranged from 10,000 to 100,000 *yuan*. The highest award of 100,000 *yuan* was awarded to Hong Guofan who returned from Great Britain in 1983 to the Shanghai biochemistry institute. The award enabled Hong to continue his work on nucleic acid research. See 'Zhongguo kexueyuan bochu jingfei ze you fuchi zhongqingnian keji gugan' ('The Chinese Academy of Sciences Allocates Funds for Supporting Young and Middle-Aged Scientific and Technical Personnel'), *RMRB*, 25 August 1983, p 3.

60   Chen Zujia and Chen Dong, 'Kexueyuan kexue jijin kashi fahui zuoyong'.

61   Interview at the Ministry of Education, 17 January 1985.

62   Ibid and interview at Fudan University.

63   A book on the reform experience at Jiaotong has been published providing a rich source of materials. Party Committee Office (Compilers), *Shanghai Jiaotong Daxue Guanli Gaige Chutan (First Explorations of Reform of Management at Shanghai's Jiaotong University)* (Shanghai: Jiaotong daxue chubanshe, 1984), pp 1-633.

64   Zhang Binglu and Zhang Yifu, 'Jiang xiaolü, qiu xiaoyi, yan zeren - shanghai jiaotong daxue keyan guanli gaige diaocha zhisan' ('Stress Efficiency, Seek Benefits, Pay Attention to Responsibilities - Part Three of a Survey of Reforms of Scientific Administration at Shanghai's Jiaotong University'), *GMRB*, 19 July 1984, p 2.

65   Ibid.

66   See the suggestions made in Zhu Chuanbo, 'Zenyang ba yanjiusuo gao' ('How to Make Research Institutes Lively'), *KXX*, no 6, p 18.

67 While the total of topics undertaken for ministries increased by 7.5% costs went down by 20%, costs for projects for the Shanghai Municipality went down by 50.3% and while other co-operative projects went up by 62.3% costs went down by 10.7%. 'Guanyu woxiao 1981 nian shixing keyan jingfei yusuan baogan qingkuang de baogao' ('Report Concerning the Circumstances of Our University Implementing in 1981 a Budget for Scientific Expenses'), 3 April 1982, in *Shanghai Jiaotong Daxue Guanli Chutan*, p 534.

68 'Shanghai jiaotong daxue guanyu shixing zerenzhi, kuangda xi(suo) zizhuquan de zanxing guiding' ('Concerning Implementing the Responsibility System at Shanghai's Jiaotong University, Temporary Regulations for Expanding the Autonomous Powers of Departments (Institutes)'), June 1983, in *Shanghai Jiaotong Daxue Guanli Chutan*, pp 39-40.

69 Interview at Fudan University and interview at Qinghua University, Beijing, 18 January 1985.

CHAPTER FIVE

REFORMS OF THE PERSONNEL SYSTEM

Problems relating to S&T personnel have received considerable attention in the Chinese media. In fact, Deng Xiaoping, in his speech to the 1985 National S&T Work Conference, highlighted this when he stated that 'the most important problem in the reforms of either the research management system or the economic system is that of talented people'.[1]

It is a common theme of Deng's that China can make enormous progress towards its goal of economic modernisation by solving problems concerning the nation's limited qualified personnel. For the S&T sector, the problems boil down to improving both the quantity and the quality of the labour force and making sure that the best use is made of personnel already trained.

China's leadership have decided that it is this latter aspect that is the most pressing problem. Over time both the size of the S&T workforce and its quality can be increased. However, such improvements will not be fully felt unless a more flexible system for allocating the labour force can be developed to ensure that the right people finish up doing jobs for which they are properly trained. To quote Deng again: 'it is not that we do not have talented people, the problem is whether we can better organise them and tap their initiative and use their talents to the full extent'.[2]

Premier Zhao Ziyang has signalled his agreement with this assessment. In March 1985, noting that the 'biggest obstacle' for the reform programme was the lack of talented people, he continued by saying that the most pressing problem was to make better use of the existing personnel.[3]

The Size and Structure of the S&T Labour Force

As with other topics, statistics concerning the total size and composition of the S&T labour force are incomplete, contradictory and confusing. It is best to start with those figures that seem the most complete and reliable - fortunately they happen to be those most relevant to this study - figures for natural scientific and technical personnel in state-owned units. This category relates to two sets of people. The first are those who have graduated from departments of science, engineering, agriculture and medicine in colleges and secondary technical schools and acquired titles of technical and scientific posts or those who have been promoted from among workers and peasants and are doing research or are engaged in education of production techniques in the fields of science, engineering, agriculture and medical work. Secondly, there are those with the same qualifications who are engaged in administrative work that is related to S&T in the government organisations, enterprises and institutions.[4]

At the end of 1984, there were 7.35 million people[5] in these categories, an increase of 59.1% over the total number in June 1978. Thus the policy to increase the total number of the workforce has met with a degree of success. More importantly, the increase means that the number of technical personnel as a proportion of the total staff and workers has risen from 59 per 1,000 in June 1978 to 86 at the end of 1984 (see Table 1).

The 7.35 million total clearly does not represent the total natural science labour force but it is difficult to get a clear picture of those working outside the state sector. In 1979, according to Hu Ping, 84.7% of the total natural science S&T labour force were working in the state sector.[6] If this percentage has remained roughly the same, although with the emphasis on the development of the collective and individual sectors it may have declined a little, we would have a total natural science labour force of around 7.9 million in 1983 rising to 8.5 million at the end of 1984. These seem reasonable figures. We know that at the end of 1983, 392,430 technical personnel in the fields of engineering, agriculture and public health were working in collectively owned units belonging to the various departments at county (city) level and above[7] and 6.85 million in state-owned units. The remaining 0.65 million could well be accounted for by those engaged in such work at levels below that of the county.

The projection for the natural science S&T labour force in state-owned units is that it will grow to 9.3 million by the year 2000.[8] This is a relatively modest increase and represents a slowdown in the expansion during the late seventies and early eighties. The projected increase would mean a 26.5% rise in the total at the end of 1984, an average annual rise of between 1.5% and 1.75%. This should easily be attainable given current expansion of training and would mark a considerable slowdown in the average annual increase of around 11% between 1979 and 1984.

The natural science S&T labour force in state owned units accounts for around 70% of what China describes as its total technical contingent.[9] This technical contingent is essentially a combination of those working in the natural and the social sciences. If the percentages have remained the same since 1982, this would mean that China had a total technical contingent in state-owned units of around 9.5 million at the end of 1984.

In the eighties, the Chinese authorities began to release more figures concerning the social composition of the natural science S&T personnel, the sectors in which they worked and their provincial distribution (see Tables 2 and 3). As Orleans has pointed out, these statistics tend to throw up new questions rather than to answer old ones.[10] Following Orleans, the vertical column in Table 2 is taken to refer to the economic and government sectors in which the personnel are employed while the horizontal columns refer to the activity and academic field.

Table 1: Natural Scientific and Technical Personnel in State-Owned Units: 1978-1984

unit: 1,000 persons

	June 1978 Total Personnel 4,345			1979 Total Personnel 4,705			1980 Total Personnel 5,276			1981 Total Personnel 5,714			1982 Total Personnel 6,264			1983 Total Personnel 6,852			1984 Total Personnel 7,466		
	A	B	C	A	B	C	A	B	C	A	B	C	A	B	C	A	B	C	A	B	C
Engineering	1,571	36.1	21.5	1,667	35.4	21.7	1,862	35.3	23.2	2,077	36.4	24.8	2,354	37.6	27.3	2,802	40.9	32.0	3,163	42.4	
Agriculture	294	6.8	4.0	324	6.9	4.2	311	5.9	3.9	328	5.7	3.9	362	5.8	4.2	405	5.9	44.6	435	5.8	
Public Health	1,276	29.4	17.4	1,396	29.7	18.2	1,530	29.0	19.1	1,680	29.4	20.1	1,807	28.8	20.9	1,934	28.2	20.1	2,079	27.8	
Scientific Research	310	7.1	4.2	317	6.7	4.1	323	6.1	4.0	338	5.9	4.0	372	5.9	4.3	328	4.8	3.7	335	4.5	
Teaching	894	20.6	12.2	1,001	21.3	13.0	1,250	23.7	15.6	1,291	22.6	15.4	1,369	21.9	15.9	1,383	20.2	15.8	1,456	19.5	

Source:　Based on figures in Zhongguo Tongji Nianjian 1984 (China Statistical Yearbook 1984) (Beijing: Tongji Chubanshe, 1984), p.497.

Figures for 1984 are derived from China: A Statistics Survey in 1985 (Beijing: New World Press, 1985), p.109.

Key:　A - Total in the various state-owned units.

B - Percentage of total S&T personnel in state-owned units.

C - Technical personnel per 1,000 of staff and workers.

Table 2: Composition of the Natural Scientific and Technical Personnel in State-Owned Units by Sector of National Economy – 1983

unit: 1,000 persons

Sector	Total	Engineering	Agriculture	Public Health	Scientific Research	Teaching
National Total	6851.9	2802.3	404.7	1934.1	328.1	1382.7
1. Industry	1754.9	1486.5	06.2	221.3	14.2	26.7
2. Construction and resources prospecting	448.8	403.5	00.6	39.1	02.7	02.9
3. Agriculture, forestry, water conservancy and meteorology	509.0	207.4	263.5	31.1	03.5	03.5
4. Transport, posts and telecommunications	224.2	202.8	00.3	18.9	00.2	02.0
5. Commerce, catering and service trades, materials supply and marketing	82.8	53.8	13.2	14.9	00.2	00.7
6. Civil public utilities	40.2	33.4	00.7	05.7	00.1	00.3
7. Scientific research	410.1	101.5	05.2	14.5	288.1	00.8
8. Culture, education, public health and social welfare	2969.0	74.4	02.9	1534.0	16.9	1340.8
9. Banking and insurance	04.3	03.0	00.1	01.0	00.1	00.1
10. Government agencies and people's organizations	384.1	225.8	110.0	43.0	02.0	03.3
Female	2165.0	492.3	58.5	1139.1	92.2	386.4
Percentage	31.6	17.6	14.5	58.9	28.1	27.9
With Higher Education	3111.3	1425.2	145.5	506.0	251.9	792.7
Percentage	45.4	50.5	36.0	26.2	76.8	57.3
With Secondary Education	2759.5	1041.6	215.5	1017.7	57.9	426.8
Percentage	40.3	37.2	53.2	52.6	17.6	30.9
Senior Technical Personnel	81.	22.6	00.9	16.4	14.3	26.8
Percentage	1.2	0.8	0.2	0.8	4.4	1.9
Secondary Technical Personnel	1350.4	834.0	61.7	150.6	163.4	140.7
Percentage	19.7	29.8	15.2	7.8	49.8	10.2
Under 45 years	5128.	1998.1	305.3	1496.6	226.5	1101.5
46-60 years	1662.1	780.2	96.7	420.0	96.9	268.3

Source: *Zhongguo Tongji Nianjian 1984*, p.498.

As of the end of 1983, 31.6% of the personnel was female with, as one would expect, a higher percentage engaged in public health work (58.9% of the total labour force) and a relatively low percentage in the fields of engineering (17.6%) and agriculture (14.5%). Only 45.4% of the labour force had received higher education while 40.3% had received secondary education. Presumably this means that some 14% (959,000) did not receive or finish their secondary level schooling. Also as one would expect, the highest percentage of those with higher education are working in the field of scientific research (76.8% of the total), although even here 5.6% (180,000) would appear not to have finished their secondary education. The field with the lowest number of people with higher education is public health - 26.2%. This reflects the higher percentage of females working in the field and, as Orleans notes, the previous emphasis on the use of paramedics.[11] However, the recent stress on upgrading the professional level of public health personnel and decreasing the use of paramedics is not reflected in the statistics. Of those working in public health the percentage with higher education was 25.7% and 26.2% in both 1982 and 1983. This may not so much reflect the inability to recruit better qualified personnel as the fact that the upgrading of existing personnel is not taken into account in these compilations. Finally, it is interesting to note that during 1983, the number of people listed as doing scientific research fell from 371,000 to 328,000. This probably reflects the attempts to redistribute personnel to work in the more applied sectors of S&T work.

There are severe problems with respect to the internal structure of this S&T labour force and much criticism in the press has focused on the irrational structure of the existing pool. First, there are not enough senior people within the system, a problem deriving partly from the reduction in training during the Cultural Revolution and partly from the age structure of the S&T labour force. In 1983, people who were described as senior scientists and technicians totalled only 81,000, while those at the intermediate level (secondary technical personnel) were 1.35 million, with the bulk, 4.69 million, at the basic level. Clearly, the number of senior personnel is too small for current needs although there has been a small rise in their proportion in the total natural science S&T labour force in state owned units from 0.81% in 1979 to 1.03% in 1981, 0.96% in 1982 and 1.2% in 1983.[12] Given that most of those in the senior category are old, if not very old, it will be difficult to expand this percentage very rapidly.

A more serious problem is that there are too many people working in the wrong fields and in the wrong locations for the current policy priorities to be promoted effectively. The lopsided structure of the labour force is now attributed to the pursuit of mistaken economic policies in the past. To give this view credibility, Chinese writers have argued that in most societies change in S&T and change in the S&T structure bring about changes in the economic structure whereas in China since the late fifties the reverse has been the case.[13] One can argue about the verity of such a proposition but it is true that China's past priorities have left it with a personnel structure that is not conducive to promoting its new economic priorities.

In line with former economic priorities, preferential assignment of personnel was given to the military industry followed by heavy industry, with light industry and agriculture trailing well behind. A report in mid-1982 noted that only 1.9% of higher education graduates and 4.4% of technical secondary school graduates had been assigned to the light industry sector. In the relatively weak coal industry, engineering and technical personnel comprised only 1.9% of the total number of staff and workers.[14] Of the 851,000 engineering and technical personnel working in industrial departments in 1978, 14.5% worked in light industry and 85.6% in heavy industry. Moreover, 64.4% of the personnel were concentrated in the two fields of machine building and metallurgy.[15]

This bias in the structure of qualified personnel has hampered the development of light industry at a time when policy preferences were beginning to emphasise its importance. One picturesque example illustrating this problem was given in late 1981. At the time, Beijing was producing around two million dozen bottles of soft drinks but supply was still lagging behind demand. In part, this was blamed on the fact that the only efficient (sic) bottling machine was imported from Shanghai and was of 1930s vintage. Apparently the machine frequently broke down and had never been properly fixed.[16]

In agriculture the shortage of suitably qualified people is even more acute. The low wages and benefits and the poor work conditions, away from the bright city lights, for rural S&T personnel over the years have meant that many preferred not to work in the agricultural sector at all. Thus, since 1949, of the 800,000 agricultural scientists who had been trained, only 360,000 remained working in agriculture by the end of 1983, and only 50,000 were said to be 'serving in the frontline of promoting technical progress'. This means that there was, on average, less than one trained agricultural scientist per commune.[17] The author who cites these figures does not make it clear in the article that they refer only to state-owned units and, as a result, the picture might not be quite so bleak if those working in collective organisations in the countryside were taken into account. Most of these people, however, would have practical knowledge rather than paper qualifications. The tendency of specialists not to want to get their hands dirty is also noticed in the Municipality of Shanghai. According to one report, most of the specialists of the agricultural department are working in city or county level units, meaning that 'almost no one works for units in townships or lower units'.[18]

The level of the agricultural specialists is not very high. At the end of 1983, only 900 of the 404,700 natural science and technical personnel in state-owned units were described as senior technical personnel - just 0.2%. Those described as secondary technical personnel accounted for 61,700 (15.2%) of the total. This does mark an advance over 1982 when there were only 441 senior agricultural specialists (0.12% of the total). Conversely, while the number of those with higher education rose numerically from 133,500 to 145,500 between 1982 and 1983, as a percentage of the total it declined slightly from 36.9% to 36.0%.

The geographical distribution of S&T personnel is, as one would expect, very uneven with high concentrations in the three municipalities of Beijing, Shanghai and Tianjin and the more industrial north-east (the provinces of Liaoning, Jilin and Heilongjiang). This is particularly evident with respect to engineering personnel and, for Beijing and Shanghai, for scientific research personnel. By contrast, the poorer provinces such as Anhui and the more remote and border provinces such as Tibet and Yunnan have relatively few S&T personnel (see Table 3).

In Beijing and Shanghai the ratio of engineers in state-owned units to the total municipal population was 1:55 and 1:71 respectively, in Anhui it was 1:649 and in Tibet 1:1037. Given the differing levels of industrialisation this is not surprising but even in a field such as public health the urban and industrial areas fare considerably better. Here the ratios for Beijing and Shanghai were 1:137 and 1:169 while those for Anhui and Tibet were 1:869 and 1:335. 'Urban' Beijing even had a better ratio for S&T personnel in agriculture (1:1803) than 'rural' Anhui (1:3810). The shortage of senior personnel is acute in the backward regions. In the six remote border provinces of Tibet, Xinjiang, Qinghai, Gansu, Ningxia and Inner Mongolia there were said to be only 2,583 people with advanced professional titles in 1983, and of these only 60 were in Tibet.[20] What is even more of a problem is that these provinces find it difficult to keep the trained personnel under their jurisdiction. In 1978, in Qinghai province, the outflow-inflow ratio for S&T personnel was 20:1 while Guangxi province in 1980 lost 2,530 qualified people and the city of Huhehot in Inner Mongolia lost over 200 during 1981 and 1982.[21] These figures are probably deceptive as they may well include the large numbers of 'educated youth' sent down to the countryside and the remote regions during the Cultural Revolution who were subsequently allowed to return to the cities.

Within particular sectors of the S&T system the distribution of personnel is also said to be wrong, especially with respect to the ratios of skilled and unskilled staff and to age groups. In agriculture, the balance between administrative cadres, technical cadres and workers is said to be incorrect. In Anhui province, for example, the ratio is said to be 1:2:4 meaning that there are too many workers and not enough technicians.[22] In industrial departments and research institutes there is an imbalance between high, medium and low ranking personnel, with too many medium ranking personnel and too few of the other two categories. This problem is compounded by the age structure of the S&T workforce. For example, in the Seventh Ministry of Machine Building, those between 40 and 45 years of age are 60% of the workforce. In some research institutes the percentage is as high as 70%.[23] The effect of this is that promotion prospects are often limited and many people finish up doing work that should be done by those with lesser qualifications. Thus, at 'a certain institute' with 3,000 S&T personnel,

Table 3: Natural Scientific and Technical Personnel in State-Owned Units by Province 1983

Province	Total Population unit : 1,000	Total	Index^A	Engineering	Agriculture	Public Health	Scientific Research	Teaching
National total	1,024,950	6,851,877	100	2,802,255	404,736	1,934,904	328,074	1,382,718
Beijing	9,340	361,599	579	167,642	5,178	68,090	73,018	47,671
Tianjin	7,890	164,984	313	80,418	2,306	42,767	10,079	29,414
Hebei	54,020	316,802	87	123,082	21,753	89,424	9,315	73,228
Shanxi	25,720	193,804	113	83,172	12,678	50,967	4,835	42,152
Inner Mongolia	19,550	159,413	122	62,142	14,737	45,748	3,987	32,799
Liaoning	36,290	429,034	177	214,064	15,053	107,725	19,091	73,101
Jilin	22,700	221,588	146	91,031	12,063	62,638	7,996	47,860
Heilongjiang	33,060	335,590	152	135,538	24,721	94,521	10,383	70,427
Shanghai	11,940	317,639	398	166,701	2,499	70,266	30,140	48,123
Jiangsu	61,350	339,929	83	149,134	14,432	89,390	14,310	72,693
Zhejiang	39,630	173,599	66	64,200	10,491	59,158	5,785	42,965
Anhui	50,560	202,450	60	77,840	13,267	58,126	4,674	48,543
Fujian	26,400	145,986	83	62,976	13,223	33,453	3,124	33,210
Jiangxi	33,840	186,954	83	70,084	10,878	60,090	3,729	42,173
Shandong	75,640	339,210	67	119,241	24,697	102,358	9,105	83,809
Henan	75,910	320,777	63	105,384	20,420	107,862	9,046	78,065
Hubei	48,350	367,566	114	133,064	17,165	112,873	16,979	87,485
Hunan	55,090	283,398	77	106,711	21,200	78,530	9,700	67,248
Guangdong	60,750	289,047	71	114,584	22,046	83,017	11,694	57,706
Guangxi	37,330	190,429	76	68,157	17,189	63,546	5,706	35,831
Sichuan	100,760	542,871	81	221,727	28,495	166,792	25,258	100,689
Guizhou	29,010	151,345	78	63,374	14,176	47,053	3,157	23,585
Yunnan	33,190	168,988	76	61,241	15,426	62,199	6,646	23,476
Tibet	1,930	10,328	80	1,861	1,880	5,757	229	601
Shaanxi	29,310	270,629	138	123,186	13,291	64,086	18,216	51,850
Gansu	19,880	135,230	102	58,549	9,418	38,208	6,292	22,763
Qinghai	3,930	43,634	166	18,911	3,670	12,770	1,427	6,856
Ningxia	3,980	35,176	132	13,726	3,038	10,551	836	7,025
Xinjiang	13,180	153,887	175	44,515	19,526	55,159	3,317	31,370

Source: Zhongguo Tongji Nianjian, 1984, pp.84 and 499.

A – Index figures of S&T personnel to provincial populations taking the national level as 100.

over 2,000 were engineers, many of whom were doing work that should have been done by technicians and laboratory assistants.[24]

Because of these problems, reforms have been introduced to increase the numbers of the S&T workforce, to raise its general educational level and to deal with the irrational structure.

Relevant Reforms of the Education Sector

a) Higher Education

Attempts to improve both the quantity and quality of the personnel depend primarily on the capacity of the education system to deliver people with the requisite skills in the necessary numbers. Constraints on the amount of money that can be spent on education have brought into sharp relief the question of how that money can be best spent. As Orleans has remarked, China is faced with the classic dilemma of improving the quality of higher education without dis-regarding the quantity of those trained; and increasing the number of students without lowering educational standards.[25] At the present time a new institution of higher education opens in China every three days. Although spending is increasing for education, financing such an expansion is a daunting task. According to a recent account, even this rapid expansion will fall short of the target of quadrupling the number of graduates in China.[26]

Higher education suffered badly during the Cultural Revolution years. For four years (1966-1969 inclusive) no students were admitted, with the result that enrolment fell from 674,436 in 1965 to 47,815 in 1970, including the 41,870 new students admitted that year.[27] Since the universities were closed during those four years one can only guess what kind of qualifications the several hundred thousand students had who 'graduated'. Presumably they were considered graduates merely because they had been on the institutes' books for a sufficient period of time. Although admissions picked up during the early seventies to 217,048 in 1976 with a total student body of 564,715, the quality of the students and the education provided was dubious. Admissions policy stressed being 'red' over 'expert' and favour was given to those from 'worker, peasant, soldier' backgrounds. While many of those entering university had dubious claims to being from such backgrounds, they were not sufficiently prepared for higher education. Standards in secondary schools had fallen badly and much of what was learned was forgotten during the 'compulsory' two- or three-year work periods before entering university.[28] Once in the university, standards were low and a large amount of time was spent on political study or working in the fields or the factories.

In an attempt to assess standards and to give force to the arguments of those who wished to overhaul the education system, a test was given to 1977 graduates who were working in the Shanghai area. The questions covered the basic secondary school syllabus and those tested were informed of the questions beforehand. The results shocked even those who had administered the test: 68%

failed mathematics, 70% failed physics and 76% chemistry.[29] To improve the educational system, initial policies set about restoring the pre-Cultural Revolution structure. Subsequently, as in other spheres, the limitations of such structures were recognised and a further phase of more wide-ranging reforms was introduced.

Higher education is now based on an extremely competitive system to gain scarce places in the various institutes.[30] With the rapid expansion of the education system, measures were introduced to ensure a degree of uniformity across the system. In October 1977, success in unified national examinations was restored as the key criterion for gaining a college place rather than the Cultural Revolution emphasis on workplace recommendation and having the correct political attitude. Within the institutes, postgraduate education and research training have been revived and in May 1980 the first exams were held for those wishing to enrol for postgraduate work. To ensure uniformity of the system within China and to facilitate comparison with foreign systems for placing those students going to study abroad, a system for regulating academic degrees was introduced. As of January 1981, new regulations for awarding the degrees of bachelor, master and doctor came into force.[31] According to the then Minister of Education, Jiang Nanxiang, these measures would 'help raise academic and education levels, stimulate national interest in scientific research, promote the training of specialists and expand international academic exchange'.[32]

From the introduction of these titles until the end of 1983, 29 people had been awarded doctorates, 18,143 master's degrees[33] and over 300,000 had received their bachelor's degrees. In 1984, a total of 57,000 postgraduates were taking advanced courses for master's degrees and doctorates in institutions of higher education[34] – a marked increase over the 1983 total of 37,166. In 1983, the overwhelming majority of postgraduates (82%) were studying in institutions of higher education that fell under the then Ministry of Education (see Table 4). For those taking higher degrees, there is a marked preference for the scientific and engineering fields rather than for the social sciences and the humanities (see Table 5). Thus, for example, of the first batch of 420 students who enrolled for doctoral degrees, 191 were majoring in science, 237 in engineering, 60 in medicine, 16 in literature, 11 in history, two in philosophy, two in pedagogy and one in agronomy.[36]

A similar structure for admissions and enrolments is found at the under-graduate level (see Table 6). By far the most popular courses remain those in engineering which accounted for 34.7% of the student enrolment in 1983. The natural sciences, agriculture, and medicine and pharmacy accounted for 6.6%, 6.7% and 11.6% of enrolments. Table 7 gives a more detailed breakdown of the sub-fields of study for those majoring in the broad category of engineering. Given China's former priorities in its development strategy, it is not surprising to find that almost 30% specialise in mechanical engineering. The two other major sub-fields are radio and electronics, and civil engineering and architecture with around 15% each. In terms of China's current priorities, it is worth noting

Table 4: **Number of Institutions Training Postgraduates and Number of Postgraduates**

Year	Total	Inst. of Higher Education	Chinese Academy of Sciences	Chinese Academy of Social Sciences	Ministries & Commissions under the State Council	Research Organisations under Provinces & Municipalities
Number of Inst. Training Postgraduates						
1962	173	114	49	10	—	—
1963	190	121	60	—	9	—
1964	219	129	76	—	11	—
1965	234	134	81	—	19	—
1978	370	208	73	18	71	—
1979	508	300	84	20	79	25
1980	586	316	89	21	102	58
1981	593	338	98	1	101	55
1982	633	330	111	1	134	57
1983	680	345	115	1	162	57
Number of Postgraduates						
1962	6,130	5,711	382	37	—	—
1963	4,938	4,399	583	—	46	—
1964	4,881	3,973	819	—	89	—
1965	4,546	3,528	943	—	75	—
1978	10,934	8,396	1,381	405	752	—
1979	18,830	15,539	1,307	557	1,253	174
1980	21,604	17,728	1,393	594	1,577	312
1981	18,848	15,575	1,158	321	1,467	327
1982	25,847	21,284	2,089	259	1,924	291
1983	37,166	30,571	3,025	425	2,788	357

Source: *Zhongguo Jiaoyu Chengjiu – Tongji Ziliao 1949–1983*
(*Achievement of Education in China – Statistical Documentation 1949–1983*)
(Beijing: Renmin Jiaoyu Chubanshe, 1985), p.112.

Table 5: Number of Postgraduates by Field of Study

Field	Year					
	1978	1979	1980	1981	1982	1983
Engineering	4,011	6,102	7,206	6,889	10,414	14,932
Agriculture	276	510	618	947	1,375	1,964
Forestry	55	88	106	74	167	197
Medicine & Pharmacy	1,474	3,651	3,651	2,442	2,558	3,781
Teacher Training	693	1,138	1,704	1,347	1,732	2,204
Humanities	1,358	2,495	2,628	1,825	1,822	2,253
Natural Sciences	2,774	4,507	4,705	3,979	6,088	8,930
Finance & Economics	49	339	451	738	917	1,500
Pol. Science & Law	—	122	171	358	582	1,137
Physical Culture	62	169	200	168	92	123
Art	182	247	164	81	100	145
Total	10,934	18,830	21,604	18,848	25,847	37,166

Source: *Zhongguo Jiaoyu Chengjiu – Tongji Ziliao 1949–1963*, pp.114–115

Table 6: Enrolment, Admissions and Graduates in 1983 – Institutions of Higher Education

unit: 1,000 persons

	Enrolment	Percent of Enrolment	Admissions	Percent of Admissions	Graduates	Percent of Graduates
Engineering	418.5	34.7	131.3	33.6	111.4	33.2
Agriculture	67.9	5.7	21.3	5.5	16.7	5.0
Forestry	13.5	1.1	04.5	1.2	2.7	0.8
Medicine and Pharmacy	140.1	11.6	31.8	8.1	55.5	16.5
Teacher Training	313.3	26.0	114.	29.1	90.1	26.09
Humanities	67.9	5.6	24.5	6.3	17.8	5.3
Natural Sciences	79.8	6.6	21.9	5.6	21.0	6.3
Finance & Economics	71.1	5.9	29.4	7.5	13.0	3.9
Pol. Science & Law	18.3	1.5	6.9	1.8	3.1	0.9
Physical Culture	10.0	0.8	3.2	0.8	2.7	0.8
Art	6.3	0.5	1.9	0.5	1.3	0.4
Total	1206.7	100	390.7	100	335.3	100

Source: Compiled from statistics in *Zhongguo Jiaoyu Chengjiu – Tongji Ziliao 1949-1983*, pp.54-55, 62, 68-69, 76, 80-81 and 88.

Table 7: Percentage Distribution of Engineering Students by Sub-field of Study

Field	Year							
	1976	1977	1978	1979	1980	1981	1982	1983
Applied Geology	5.36	4.48	3.34	4.53	4.61	4.38	4.63	4.29
Mining	4.97	5.14	2.96	3.63	3.46	3.79	3.76	3.89
Power Engineering	4.42	3.08	3.13	3.66	3.91	4.31	4.44	3.82
Metallurgy	4.92	4.19	3.19	3.68	3.05	4.28	3.55	4.13
Mech. Engineering	26.61	30.96	29.47	27.68	28.27	25.88	27.75	28.68
Electrical Engineering & Instruments	2.73	3.13	2.07	1.94	1.63	1.30	1.46	1.79
Radio & Electronics	12.39	11.52	18.74	14.99	16.10	16.58	18.38	16.64
Chem. Engineering	8.16	8.56	6.71	7.30	7.07	6.71	7.67	7.5
Grain Processing & Food Industry	0.99	0.95	1.00	0.86	1.23	1.28	1.46	1.76
Light Industry	2.18	1.87	2.41	2.52	3.01	3.59	3.65	4.1
Mapping, Surveying & Hydrology	0.91	1.05	0.82	0.76	0.80	0.75	0.81	0.73
Civil Engineering & Architecture	9.65	8.58	10.26	10.99	12.06	12.58	13.09	15.18
Transport	2.12	1.88	1.88	2.79	2.58	2.45	2.75	2.99
Telecommunications	1.17	1.51	1.37	1.31	1.17	1.02	1.15	1.06
Others	13.42	12.65	12.18	11.34	10.69	10.79	3.78	2.83
Unclassified	—	—	0.47	2.02	0.36	0.31	1.67	0.61
Total	100	100	100	100	100	100	100	100

Source: *Zhongguo Jiaoyu Chengjiu – Tongji Ziliao 1949-1983*, pp. 78-79.

the low percentages of those specialising in the engineering sub-fields of light industry (although this has grown from 1.87% in 1977 to 4.1% in 1983), transportation (22.99) and telecommunications (1.06%).

In quantitative terms, China seems well capable of meeting the targets that it has set for the higher education sector. Most of the targets of the Sixth Five Year Plan (1981-1985) for training in higher education had been met in 1984. The plan called for an admission of 400,000 new students by 1985 with a total student body of 1.3 million. It was expected that 1.5 million students would graduate during the period.[37] In 1984, China admitted 475,000, making a total of 1,396,000,[38] while the total number of graduates until the end of 1984 was only just short of the target figure - 1,218,884. With respect to graduate students it was expected that in 1985 admissions would total 20,000 with a student body of 50,000 and with 45,000 finishing their studies during the period.[39] By the end of 1984, the first two of these targets had been achieved with some 23,000 new postgraduates entering to make a total of 57,000.[40] In the three years 1981 to 1983 just over 20,000 finished their studies.[41] This would mean that some 44% of those enrolled in 1984 would have to finish their studies by the end of 1985. This seems to be a difficult target to meet.

The Seventh Five Year Plan (1986-1990) projects a continued rapid growth in the number of graduates turned out, with 2.6 million expected to graduate from regular or special college courses and 200,000 from postgraduate courses.[42] This would mean an average graduation total of 500,000 for the former and 40,000 for the latter. To meet these targets, a continued steady expansion of the higher education sector will be necessary. The 500,000 figure may be more easily met by the expansion of short-cycle, special courses. In 1983, 23% of the student body and 34.4% of newly admitted students were on such special courses (*zhuanke*). In fact, the projections should just about be feasible. If one assumes that all students admitted to the regular programme graduate four years later, this would give a combined graduation total of 798,000 for the years 1986 to 1988.[43] If we assume an annual graduation of 175,000 over the same period for those on short-term courses[44], the graduation total for the years 1986-1988 would be 1.3 million. This would mean that around 650,000 students would have to graduate in each of the two remaining years. If a reasonable rate of expansion can be maintained this should be possible. Similar expansion would have to be maintained to reach the figure for postgraduates, but this too appears to represent a realistic assessment.

b) Quality Problems in Higher Education

Having looked at the quantitative aspects of higher education it is necessary to make some sort of assessment of what kind of graduates are being turned out. Before looking at this, however, two weaknesses should be highlighted concerning current training programmes within higher education, First, apart from strengthening traditional courses, it is necessary for China to open up a number of new fields of study that will become vital for its S&T development in the future. Thus, more attention must be paid to subjects such as electronics, computer science, biotechnology, materials science and information technology. An article from mid-1985 pointed out that China had 'accorded too much importance to the training of traditional scientists, technicians and engineers'. This, the article continued, was 'not suited to the requirements for the development of modernised industry and agriculture in the new era'. The article also suggested that even 'traditional S&T courses' should attempt to integrate a greater use of computing.[45] This prior concentration makes the problem all the more difficult to resolve as there are too few people in China capable of teaching these 'new subjects'. Also, those with the requisite skills are in heavy demand from other sectors of the economy.

The second weakness is the lack of specialists in fields such as law, economics and business management. If the reforms are to work, China's administrative system will have to be staffed by a new kind of person rather than one who is schooled in the old administrative planning system. If the market system is to be expanded, administrators and planners must be trained who can act in accordance with, and respond to, market demands. Also, for those institutions and industrial enterprises wishing to co-operate with foreign partners, a sound knowledge of foreign business practices and international law is necessary. Sufficient numbers of qualified people simply do not exist at present in China. During a visit in early 1985, one of the most commonly heard problems when visiting technology development corporations in Beijing and Shanghai was the shortage of trained legal and economic personnel. This problem was noted relatively early in the reform programme. In 1980, Fang Yi commented that 'for many years there has been a lopsided development of science and engineering departments in the institutions of higher learning, with the result that the training of professionals in liberal arts, law and business departments has been seriously neglected'.[46]

Slow progress has been made, however, in redressing the balance. Since 1976 the number of students reading finance and economics has risen form 1.2% of the total student body to 5.9% in 1983 and that for political science and law from 0.1% to 1.5%. More encouraging is the fact that in 1983 the percentages of total admissions for these two categories were 7.5% and 1.8% respectively.

A few preliminary observations can be made concerning the quality of the graduates. Clearly, the quality is improving, especially when compared with those who were recruited when the institutions first re-opened in the early seventies. However, a number of problems exist. For those studying in the sciences, particularly those sciences requiring expensive new equipment, there can be practical obstacles in the way of their ability to learn. Despite increased spending, it is clear to anybody who goes to a Chinese university that sufficient high quality equipment is sadly lacking. In some instances students may be reduced simply to watching teaching staff conduct experiments while they learn in theory what is to be done but get little opportunity for practice. This problem is compounded by the present lack of suitably qualified teachers.

As Orleans has pointed out, a number of problems exist with respect to the curriculum,[47] particularly the narrowness of the courses of study and the reliance on rote learning systems. With respect to the first of these problems Orleans quotes a discussion from a National People's Congress panel meeting on education where it was noted that 'often a student majoring in physics does not understand chemistry'.[48] Other reflections of this problem are that science and engineering students receive no liberal arts training and that very little theory is taught in the science and engineering courses. The traditional Chinese emphasis on learning by heart and being able to recite from memory is now recognised as a defect in educational terms. To an Englishman, Chinese classrooms smack terribly of the proverbial second-form Latin classes with the assembled throngs reciting 'amo, amas, amat'. While useful for language drills, such repetition does not stimulate the kind of independent, inquisitive scientist that China now says that it wants to produce.

It seems that the competition to get into university has produced a mentality among the successful students that they have arrived and need no longer make any real hard effort while at college. Recently enrolled students have been compared unfavourably with those enrolled immediately after the Cultural Revolution in 1977 and 1978. The latter students are said to have had a much better motivation, presumably as they may have been adversely affected by the events of the years 1966-1976. To many it may have been an unexpected, last chance to become upwardly mobile.[49] Enthusiasm may have been rekindled by knowledge that on graduation they would receive a well-paid job and have a choice about the kind of work they could do. But with the imperfections in the job allocation system, it is possible that a graduate will have difficulty in getting a job in which he or she will be able to use his or her special skills.

c) The use of foreign training

In an attempt to raise educational and research standards, the sending of students abroad for periods of study has been playing an increasingly important role. The numbers involved have been rising rapidly and have already surpassed those for the fifties, the major difference being that the United States is the number one choice rather than the Soviet Union.

From the beginning of 1978 until the end of 1983, the government has sponsored some 18,500 students to go abroad for training. Of this total, 12,642 were sponsored by the Ministry of Education.[50] The total of government-sponsored students had risen to 29,000 by mid-1985. By comparison, from 1972, when Chinese students began to go abroad again after the impact of the Cultural Revolution, until the end of 1977, the Ministry of Education sponsored only 1,217 students for foreign training.[51] However, the totals noted above do not represent all those who have gone abroad for study in recent years. China's thirst for knowledge from abroad has led to the authorities allowing Chinese nationals to study abroad at their own expense. In 1985, 7,800 students had taken advantage of this possibility.[52] The vast majority of these are in the USA and are mostly supported by relatives living outside China.

To make it easier for self-supporting students to study abroad, the relevant regulations have been gradually relaxed. Initially such prospective students had to work for two years in the job assigned to them by the state before they could apply to study abroad.[53] However, in January 1985 the State Council adopted new regulations modifying these conditions. Following these regulations, it is possible to apply to go abroad for study regardless of one's school record, age or length of employment, so long as the applicant can show evidence of financial support and a letter of acceptance from a foreign institution. Approval will still have to be given by the individual's unit and students graduating whose jobs are assigned by the state should go first to their new workplace before applying. The problem for the authorities is that many of these 'self-financing' students may not come back to China. To try to deal with this eventuality, as long as students return within five years their study period will be included in their employment record. Also, once back in China, they are to be given jobs in their specialities and they are to receive the same wages and treatment as government-supported students.[54]

Of the students who have gone abroad to study most are trained in S&T fields. For example, of the 6,709 students sent abroad by the Ministry of Education from the end of 1976 until 1981 about 80% were studying science and engineering.[55] Towards the end of 1984, a more detailed breakdown was given concerning those studying abroad. This was based on a total of 26,000 government-sponsored students. Of these, 78% were engaged in advanced studies with 18% enrolled as graduate students and 4% undergraduates. In terms of subjects, the spread was 39.6% in engineering, 28.5% in natural sciences, 11.1% in medicine and pharmaceutics, 7.7% in forestry and agricultural sciences, 6.6% in social sciences and 6.5% in linguistics.[56]

Although the total numbers are relatively small, the impact of this training programme should not be underestimated as most of those trained abroad will eventually find their way into leadership positions. A considerable number of these students have returned to China and it is clear that they are already beginning to make their presence felt. By the end of 1984, 14,000 of those students sent since 1978 had returned to China.[57] The majority are said to be 'playing leading roles in teaching, scientific research and production'. For example, at Jiaotong University, Shanghai, among the 63 returned students, one had been selected as vice-president of the graduate school, another 25 were heads or deputy heads of departments etc., and 22 more were postgraduate tutors.[58] Of the 82 task groups within the Shanghai branch of the CAS, in early 1985 72 were headed by people who had been abroad and 90% of such people were said to have taken 'positions of responsibility' either as task group or office heads.[59]

While on the whole the sending of students abroad has been beneficial, there are some drawbacks. Full use is clearly not being made of these students when they return to China. The most common problem is that often on returning to

China, advanced equipment is simply not available. Having worked with advanced technology abroad, sometimes on return, the people find themselves working with substandard equipment. Lu Jiaxi noted that for some, because no relevant equipment existed in China, they found themselves going back to the work which they had done before they left.[60] It may even be that the returned personnel are assigned to a completely different research project on their return. This is clearly wasteful of scarce resources and extremely demoralising for the individual or individuals concerned.

More broadly, the problems arise because, as one writer notes, the 'special fields they study abroad are not what China needs for S&T development'. The same writer complains that of the S&T personnel who have gone abroad to study, 70% to 80% have chosen basic or applied subjects to major in. This, it is said, has made it 'difficult to raise the professional level of S&T personnel engaged in production technology and developmental research'.[61] In major part, these problems stem from the lack of planning with respect to the foreign study programme. Thus, calls have been made to improve this situation to ensure that people undertake relevant work abroad and, in particular, work that they can continue with on their return to China.[62] Apparently no complete, long range study has been made of the programme for foreign training.[63] Also, on occasion, there appears to have been resentment from colleagues who have not had the opportunity to study abroad and this has hampered the development of some collective projects.

d) Vocational and Technical Secondary Education

While China stands every chance of being successful in meeting the targets for its higher education sector, the number of graduates will still fall short of providing the required numbers of skilled personnel for the S&T sector. As China modernises there will be a growing demand for the workforce as a whole to have a much higher technical knowledge. The burden of meeting this objective will fall on the secondary level of education which will have to provide the training for the vast bulk of those filling technical jobs. The Decision on the Reform of the Education System states that 'the socialist modernisation drive needs not only senior experts in science and technology but also urgently needs tens of millions of intermediate and primary technicians, managerial personnel and skilled workers, who have completed sound vocational and technical education'.

The decision recognises that without this trained workforce 'advanced science and technology, and equipment cannot be turned into practical productive forces'.[64] This has led to moves to diversify secondary education in China by decreasing the number of students who attend regular schools and increasing those who attend specialised secondary schools (*zhuanye xuexiao*) and, in particular, those who go to vocational secondary schools (*zhiye zhongxue*), including agricultural schools (*nongye zhongxue*). The serious imbalance in China's secondary education has also been highlighted by the World

Bank as a serious constraint on the country's ability to achieve the 'Four Modernisations'.[65]

The specialised schools train middle-level technicians for various professions through a mixture of two- to five-year courses at the upper secondary and post-secondary levels. Training is very specialised. Despite the name, the vocational secondary schools tend to be less specialised and have a common core of general subjects in all programmes. This sector of education was devastated during the Cultural Revolution. Enrolment in the specialised schools fell from 547,447 in 1965 to 63,976 in 1970 before the student numbers began to pick up again.[66] Vocational and agricultural schools suffered an even worse fate. In 1965 there were 54,332 agricultural schools and 7,294 vocational schools and all were closed down with the onset of the Cultural Revolution.[67] It was not until 1976 that these types of schools were revived and then only very slowly at first.

The dismantling of the schools had a devastating effect on training requirements for S&T personnel. One source calculates that between 15 and 20 million people missed out on this kind of education as a result of the Cultural Revolution.[68] It also meant that those entering the workforce did not have any relevant pre-employment training, thus intensifying the need for more apprentice training at the workplace. Obviously the Cultural Revolution policies created a major imbalance in the structure of secondary education. By the end of the seventies, China still compared unfavourably with other developing countries in this respect. In 1979 only 2.4% of China's secondary school students were enrolled in technical or vocational education as compared with an average for 1975 of 10.9% in other developing countries. This compares even more unfavourably with percentages of 27.1% for Europe and 42.1% for the USSR.[69]

Starting in the late seventies, China made concerted efforts to re-expand this sector of education. The number of specialised secondary schools has increased steadily, although not spectacularly, from 2,443 in 1976 to 3,090 in 1983 (see Table 8). At the end of 1984, the number of students was 1.32 million, roughly double the 1976 total of 0.69 million. Within this category of schools, the majority are technical secondary schools (jishu xuexiao), 2,229 (72%) out of the 1983 total, with the remainder being teacher training schools. Enrolment at these technical secondary schools has fluctuated since the mid-seventies. From a low of 385,521 in 1976 it reached a high of 761,280 in 1980 before declining again to 628,063 in 1982. However, recruitment has been stepped up again so that by the end of 1983 the student body was 688,438 (see Table 9). In line with current needs, admissions to schools of finance and economics have risen from 23,884 in 1976 to 76,559 in 1983 and in 1981 schools were opened for politics and law with an initial intake of 9,897 students, rising to 15,095 in 1983.

Growth in the number of vocational and agricultural schools has been fast, to say the least. From 1980 to the end of 1983, the total increased from 3,314 to

Table 8: Specialised Secondary Schools in 1976 – 1983
Secondary Technical Schools by Field of Study

Year	Total	Teacher Technical Schools	Secondary Technical Schools	Industry	Agriculture	Forestry	Health	Finance and Economics	Politics and Law	Physical Culture	Art	Others
1976	2443	982	1461	103	260		548	164	—	19	32	35
1977	2485	1028	1457	414	273		512	181	—	15	39	23
1978	2760	1046	1714	532	302		520	231	—	16	65	48
1979	3033	1053	1980	627	337	35	543	297	—	23	70	48
1980	3069	1017	2052	643	337	36	555	319	—	26	83	53
1981	3132	962	2170	658	352	38	556	360	44	30	95	37
1982	3076	908	2168	672	349	38	526	363	64	29	93	34
1983	3090	861	2229	670	365	39	520	375	82	31	97	50

Source: *Zhongguo Jiaoyu Chengjiu – Tongji Ziliao 1949–1983*, pp. 147–148.

Table 9: Enrolments in Secondary Technical Schools: 1976–1983

unit: 1,000 persons

Field	1976	1977	1978	1979	1980	1981	1982	1983
Industry	117.3	120.6	181.5	242.9	263.0	203.4	215.7	233.9
Agriculture	69.0	71.8	86.5	110.4	113.8	82.8	77.1	78.2
Forestry	—	—	—	11.3	12.2	11.1	13.2	13.7
Health	137.6	133.1	158.7	210.2	244.7	183.2	163.2	163.3
Finance & Economics	45.9	50.3	75.4	105.5	107.5	106.8	109.7	145.6
Politics & Law	—	—	—	—	—	17.5	22.1	27.4
Physical Culture	2.5	2.4	3.6	5.1	6.2	6.6	6.9	6.8
Art	8.4	9.3	12.2	12.9	15.6	15.5	15.2	16.8
Others	4.7	3.9	11.4	15.7	18.2	5.1	4.8	2.7
Total	385.5	391.3	529.3	714.2	761.3	630.5	628.1	688.4

Source: *Zhongguo Jiaoyu Chengjiu – Tongji Ziliao 1949–1983*, pp. 150–151.

5,481. Of the total, agricultural schools increased from 2,094 to 4,073 and vocational schools from 390 to 1,408 (see Table 10). Total enrolments have increased from 453,700 (320,024 for agricultural schools and 133,649 for vocational schools) to 1,220,100 (681,447 and 538,647). In 1984 the total enrolment stood at 1,745,000. Dramatic though these increases are, they will not succeed in meeting the targets of the Sixth Five Year Plan. This envisaged 1.4 million new students enrolling in 1985 with a total student body of 2.28 million for agricultural and 0.87 million for vocational schools.[70] In 1983, the number of admissions was 756,800 and it was unlikely that this figure could have been doubled by 1985. The total student body was still some 1.4 million short of the target figure.

For vocational training, workers' training schools are also important. These schools provide mainly three-year technical-vocational courses at the upper secondary level or, if the schools do not take in enough such students, they are expected to train in-service workers or possibly even 'job-awaiting youth', i.e., the unemployed. In 1984, there were 639,000 training at these schools and this total was said to be an increase of 114,000 over that in 1983.[71]

If one combines these three elements, the technical secondary schools, the vocational and agricultural schools, and the workers' training schools, an idea of the technical force being trained at the secondary level can be built up. The total enrolment for 1983 was approximately 2.5 million. However, one source suggests that only 0.14 million of those in the technical secondary schools were studying at the secondary level.[72] If this is correct, the total enrolment would amount to 1.9 million. Using the total of 2.5 million this would account for 28.5% of those enrolled in upper secondary education and 5.4% of all secondary level students; the lower total would give percentages of 23.5% and 4.2% respectively.

This is a creditable achievement in redressing the balance within secondary education but it is necessary to push ahead still further with the programme of expanding vocational and technical education. In fact, it is hoped that by 1990 around 50% of students at the upper secondary level will be in some form of technical-vocational programme,[73] a figure that would be about right for China's developmental stage. This will require a further major effort in terms of planning and administration on the part of the education authorities. The major constraints on such development are precisely those that apply to other sectors of the education system: shortages of funds, staff and equipment. The Decision on the Reform of the Education System especially pointed out that 'the current lack of teachers is an outstanding problem in the development of secondary vocational and technical education'.[74]

Stirring up the Stagnant Pool: Measures to Improve Labour Mobility

Crucial to the reform of personnel are the moves being introduced to ensure that scientists are allocated to jobs more rationally and to help graduates find jobs in which they can use their training to the best advantage for all concerned. What lies at the core of these problems is that there is no job mobility and that the

Table 10: Agricultural and Vocational Schools

unit: 1,000 persons

	Agricultural Schools				Vocational Schools			
	No. of Schools	No. of Graduates	No. of Admissions	Enrolments	No. of Schools	No. of Graduates	No. of Admissions	Enrolments
1980	2924	78.3	185.4	320.0	390	01.1	121.7	133.6
1981	2094	77.5	149.6	267.8	561	16.7	117.0	213.1
1982	2253	75.2	215.3	346.7	851	55.3	210.7	356.9
1983	4073	101.4	436.5	681.4	1408	114.3	320.3	538.6

Source: *Zhongguo Jiaoyu Chengjiu – Tongji Ziliao 1949–1983*, pp. 208–209.

method of job allocation has been dominant. Once a scientist or technician has been assigned to a job it is, to all intents and purposes, theirs for life. It provides them with an 'iron rice bowl' that cannot be broken. The situation has prompted S&T leaders such as Lu Jiaxi and Fang Yi to liken the labour force to a 'pool of stagnant water'.

Calls are now being made and policies devised to stir up the water and get the water flowing. Fang Yi, speaking to the Scientific Council of the CAS in January 1984, stated that:

> Only with the mobility of research personnel is it possible to speed up the dissemination of knowledge and transfer of technologies. The Chinese Academy of Sciences should make positive efforts to recommend some outstanding personnel and backbone workers to work in other departments and localities where their service is needed. At the same time, it should call on and encourage scientific and technical personnel to take up concurrent jobs of technical guidance and teaching in other units.[75]

The question of how scientists and technicians could be encouraged to work in more remote areas was dealt with in January 1983 at a National Conference on Rural Scientific Research and Application. With the termination of the programme of sending 'educated youth' to the countryside, it is clear that shortages of qualified personnel have been exacerbated. Shen Qifu, the Secretary of the Chinese Association of Science and Technology, noted that:

> Under the present situation in which university students cannot be sent to rural areas, measures should be adopted to get scientists and technicians to the rural areas. We should do a good job of training rural youth so that they master science and technology and assume the task of transforming the objective world.[76]

The January conference proposed that those who did accept posts in remote areas would receive special benefits in the way of higher wages, more annual holidays, better living conditions and better placement for their children in schools and jobs. Importantly, these people would retain their urban registration and residence cards and they would be permitted to return to their original place of residence after a fixed period of time.[77]

It will be interesting to see if such incentives will work. It is clear that salary incentives introduced over the past few years have been insufficient to persuade enough scientists and technicians to move to less developed regions of the country to work on key construction projects. In late March 1984, the Science and Technology Leading Group took actions to redistribute personnel away from the more developed areas to work on major construction sites in interior, rural and border regions. It is not clear how the people were chosen for the projects but they may not have gone voluntarily. The first group of transfers involved 363 individuals going to 13 'major construction projects' for energy, communications and the raw materials industry. The process was to have been completed by August 1984. In mid-1984, Shenyang, Liaoning province, 'assigned' 500 outstanding young cadres to leading technical and managerial posts in county and township enterprises. The period of work was provisionally set at two years. To sweeten the taste of the pill, those who had been transferred to work in villages and towns on the outskirts of the city had their salaries raised by two grades and were to enjoy the same labour protection and welfare as other workers and staff.[78]

Tibet has been benefiting from an influx of engineers and technicians from the contracts it has signed with nine provinces and municipalities. During February and March 1985, some 12,000 such people arrived in Tibet from Chengdu and Shanghai to carry out work for the various contract projects.[79] These people will not, of course, settle in Tibet but will return to their original units on completion of the contract.

Certainly if the price is right, scientific and technical personnel can be persuaded to move. In the eighties, the Ministry of Labour and Personnel and the State Science and Technology Commission (SSTC) began promoting the use of a contract system between peasants and scientists. Through the contract, scientists are paid directly by the peasant for technical expertise and services rendered over a particular period of time. Those rural areas that are well situated, such as those on the outskirts of a major city, and which show sufficient initiative have been able to take advantage of the new opportunities. Changping County on the outskirts of Beijing has been able to recruit 1,358 technical personnel to help improve commodity production. Among this number were 130 professors, research fellows, senior engineers and agronomists.[80] Such examples are no doubt what led Tao Kai and Ceng Qing to state that 'it is incorrect to draw a sweeping conclusion that all intellectuals in China are hankering after big city life'.[81] Their assessment might well be true, but examples of scientists voluntarily uprooting and heading off to the poorer regions do not abound in the Chinese press. Most of those who do move are going to the suburban counties and communes and flourishing small and medium-sized towns. For example, in Zhejiang province, there have been some successful attempts to persuade technicians to go and work in rural factories. Also, technicians in colleges and research institutes are allowed to work in these factories in their spare time and, 'in the main', are allowed to keep the remuneration.[82]

Small and medium-sized towns that have been successful in introducing reforms have been given wide coverage - for example, Changzhou in Jiangsu, Xiangfan and Shashi in Hubei, and Siping in Jilin. These cities have managed to import significant numbers of urgently needed scientific and technical personnel from outside large cities and units. Around 1,500 people have been transferred to Changzhou and more than 600 each to Xiangfan and Shashi.[83] The towns have also recruited retired engineers and technicians along with working technicians to teach specialised courses on a contract basis.[84] Within the towns, the old allocation system has also been reformed by breaking down the departmental and industrial boundaries. This has enabled existing personnel and newly recruited personnel to be employed in accordance with their special skills and the needs of the particular city. Changzhou and Wuxi have reassigned over 1,500 of their scientific and technical personnel, transferring the greater part of them to light and textile industry and 'quite a few' to collective enterprises. Siping has transferred personnel from the metallurgical and machine industries to the light, textile and electronics industries.[85]

It is important to note that, as a part of the reforms to ensure a better distribution of personnel, in February 1984 the Bureau of Scientific and Technical Cadres was transferred from the Ministry of Labour and Personnel to the SSTC. To ease the problem of labour flow, the system of job allocation is being chipped away at and experiments are being carried out to expand the job invitation system. The Party Decision on the Reform of the S&T Management system allowed research and planning institutes and institutions to adopt such a system on an experimental basis.[86] This built on the experience of trial reforms introduced in the previous year.

In July 1984, the SSTC made a series of decisions to help improve labour mobility. The most important was the introduction of the trial use of a job invitation system. Under this system organisations offering jobs have the right to invite personnel and to sack them, as well as the right to refuse personnel, while the employees have the freedom to accept a job or to resign from it.[87] This decision was implemented initially on a trial basis in Shanghai, Chongqing, Xiangfan, Xian and the CAS and the Chinese Academy of Social Sciences. Relations between the various parties are regulated by the ubiquitous contract. In Shanghai, the length of the appointments for S&T personnel is generally two or three years. Neither of the parties can break the contract without due reason but the state can make direct re-allocations by breaking the hiring contracts if the personnel is urgently needed in key construction projects for the state or in the Shanghai Municipality.[88] As long as contractual obligations are fulfilled, the scientists and technicians are encouraged to take on outside consultancy work. Should both parties agree, the contract can be renewed.[89] This system is said to combine 'state plan requirements, the voluntarism of units and certain rights of individuals to select a work unit and it rationally adjusts the three-sided relationships among the state, units and individuals in the question of personnel allocation'.[90]

A second related set of reforms was designed to loosen the job assignment system. In particular, this affected those who had studied abroad. Such people, as long as the state plan is guaranteed, will have the freedom to choose jobs. This, it is hoped, will ensure that best use is made of this personnel and that there will be more circulation of personnel. In fact, lack of job mobility has been identified as a major problem in research institutes. A vice-Chairman of the CAS, Zhou Guangzhao, has attacked 'inbreeding' as being a major reason why China's young research personnel 'do not easily stand out'. Bright students are generally recruited as teachers' assistants and, on becoming teachers, they begin the process again.[91] Clearly such a system is not conducive to the spread of academic ideas as within academic units viewpoints tend to become the same and reproduce themselves. This is reinforced by the traditional Chinese system of the pupil learning from his master and is not favourable for students developing their own ideas. Even when they do develop separate ideas, the patron–client relationship makes it unlikely that the client would express ideas that differed radically from those of the patron.

This leads Zhou to suggest that:

> Universities and research organisations should in general cease the practice of employing students whom they have themselves trained but should instead release them so that they may go to other units. This way, they will understand dissimilar viewpoints, co–operate with people who received their training elsewhere, compete academically and mature professionally, try out new ideas and develop them.[92]

Reforms in this direction have, in fact, been introduced. Regulations drafted by the Science and Technology Leading Group and discussed at the Science and Technology Work Conference in March 1985 suggested that the number of graduates retained by institutions of higher education and research institutes should be restricted and, where high, reduced. It also suggested that, except under special circumstances, those students retained should work for a fixed period of time in another unit.[93] One institute already operating this system is the Institute of Theoretical Physics under the CAS. PhD graduates from the institute are no longer automatically assigned work there but are now expected to work outside it. Indeed, it is expected that they will have worked in one or two other places before they can receive a permanent work assignment in the institute itself.[94] This notion is also being extended to post–doctoral fellowships. The SSTC announced that, during 1985-1986, 250 post–doctoral places would be created. These places would not be counted as permanent staff of the centre concerned and the researchers would not be permitted to stay for more than four years – the usual time being two years. They will be expected to move on completion of their fellowship. To make the moving more palatable, their husbands or wives and children will be able to move with them. It is expected that after completing the 'mobile period', they will find a regular post.[95]

A third area of policy reform is seeking to make sure that scientists and technicians who are working in the wrong fields for their qualifications can be reassigned to more fruitful work. Research institutes have not only in the past hoarded equipment that they seldom, if ever, used but have also stored up personnel. This tendency was reinforced by financing being closely related to the size of staff of a particular unit – thus the maxim 'the more the merrier' seems to have applied. This, of course, leads not only to exaggerating the over-concentration of skilled personnel in a limited number of key centres, but is extremely wasteful in that it means that many either do work unrelated to their qualifications, or spend a lot of time simply sitting around doing nothing. Now personnel departments at the various levels have been instructed to investigate and intervene in those organisations that have a surplus of qualified staff or that use them inappropriately. It is hoped, however, that research institutes themselves will take the initiative by sending their excess personnel to other units and that they will inform the relevant administrative departments.[96]

To maximise the use of the limited pool of skilled labour, a number of other initiatives have been taken. As long as their official work requirements are fulfilled, scientists and technicians are being encouraged to take up work assignments outside their own units.[97] This also helps improve the remuneration of S&T personnel who are, on the whole, still not particularly well paid given their importance within the new development strategy. Support is also given to ensuring that those who are retired and still capable of making a positive contribution can do so. A discussion document at the National S&T Work Conference entitled 'Regulations Concerning Continuing to Give Play to the Role of Retired Intellectuals' addressed this question.[98] In particular this document calls for state organisations to give support to locally organised retired engineers' associations, retired S&T workers' associations, retired teachers' associations, etc. These associations are to be organised on the principle of 'run by the local people and subsidised by the state'. However, state help is to play a limited role. They are to be responsible for making their own plans and for their profits and losses. Only those that truly find themselves in difficulties will be able to seek the necessary help from the relevant government departments.[99] A number of these organisations have sprung up, one of the first being the Chongqing City Association of Retired Engineers. In 1982, the Guangzhou City Association of Retired Engineers was established and by early 1984 it had a membership approaching 200 people. The association covers a wide range of engineering disciplines and 40 of its members are said to be senior level engineers.[100]

These recent reforms should begin to break through some of the problems of the current employment system. For example, previously an employee did not have the right to apply for another job without the permission of the unit. However, problems with implementation will remain. For example, it is still difficult to resign from a job as many formalities have to be completed first. This may in itself deter some from making the effort. Also, it is unclear what the reaction of units would be to taking on people who have resigned from another position. For those with scarce, highly valued skills resignation might not make much difference but for others the prospective employers may see it as a sign of somebody who might not readily accept labour discipline.

Units can make it very difficult for individuals to move should the unit wish to retain their services. A *Xinhua* report outlined the three most common barriers put in the way of people wishing to move.[101] First, the workplace in China is also a social environment and, to date, a good unit provides housing, medical care and even schooling for children. Thus, some units who do not wish personnel to move demand that housing is returned. This can make particular problems for someone moving from the state sector, where security and welfare benefits are better, to the collective sector. It may also restrict the ability of new corporations to recruit better personnel. They may be in the position to offer better salaries and work conditions but may not be able to provide living space, indeed many have chosen deliberately not to do so.[102] A second barrier is that units will demand compensation for the loss of personnel to cover training costs. Finally, units may just hang on to their personnel for a rainy day stating 'we maintain an army for a thousand days to use it for an hour. We will use you some day.'

On the other hand, unscrupulous poaching of personnel has taken place. Apparently with respect to recruiting personnel:

> Some units have lacked the overall idea and have used the method of undermining other people to employ backbone technicians from some other places and units so that production, scientific research and educational work in the units of which qualified persons have flowed are affected.[103]

Cases have been reported in the press involving problems caused by inopportune resignations. The most widely covered was the case of the resignation of certain S&T personnel in Shanghai. It seems that four key technical members from a Shanghai plant left to work in a small factory. This withdrawal of expertise caused the key project on which they had been working to collapse. The case was even referred to by Premier Zhao Ziyang as a warning that the process of transfer of skilled personnel should be handled carefully.[104] It seems that the publicity given to this case gave those who were opposed to the reform a weapon with which to counter-attack. People complained of 'serious consequences' of resignations, some even referring to 'an unhealthy trend' and accusing the units employing those who resigned of 'undermining socialism'. The adverse reaction caused the *People's Daily* to run a story about how, on the whole, transfers had not caused problems in Shanghai and indeed how limited the work of transferring personnel had been.[105] This latter point testifies to just how difficult it is to reform the personnel allocation system despite conscious attempts.

To help with the problem of transferring personnel and, in particular, to circumvent the power of units to retain personnel, exchange centres for S&T personnel have been set up. They use a variety of names such as Qualified Personnel Service Company (*Rencai fuwu gongsi*), S&T Development and Exchange Centre (*Keji kaifa jiaoliu zhongxin*) and Qualified Personnel Bank (*Rencai yinhang*) but have the same objectives. In June 1984, the Ministry of Labour and Personnel established, in Beijing, the Talents Exchange and Consultation Centre.[106] The main function of the centre is to move people from jobs where their talents are not being fully utilised to places where they are needed. People who feel that they are not being used properly can register at the centre in the hope of finding more suitable employment. People can also, if they have the permission of their units, register for part-time work. In addition, the centre is intended to act as a go-between for units lacking skilled personnel to sign contracts with those units having a surplus.[107]

Much attention has been given to Shanghai's experience in this area. In March 1984, a municipal service department for talent exchange was set up[108] and in June preparations began for the establishment of the Shanghai Scientific and Technical Personnel Development Bank.[109] The bank was formally established on 31 August 1984,[110] although one account refers to it only having begun its work on a trial basis on 1 December.[111] The bank is for those who are not properly employed, those without permanent positions following reforms in the management system, those who were not recruited after the establishment of the recruitment system, those temporarily unemployed, those who have resigned for 'suitable reasons' and the exotic sounding category of those with 'unusual abilities'. To become a member of the bank it is necessary to pay a one-time fee of between 50 and 150 *yuan*. The bank comes under the authority of the Shanghai S&T Development Exchange Centre. Apart from trying to find the correct match, the bank can also provide opportunities for training, refresher courses and advanced studies.[112]

The experience of Shanghai shows just how limited, in practice, the increase in labour mobility has been. According to the *People's Daily*, the 20 talent-exchange organs in the Shanghai municipality had 'done a lot of work without, however, achieving much'. According to sample investigations, 20% of S&T personnel were not being employed in their speciality. The total flow of people in the municipality was said to have been 10,000 out of a total S&T workforce of 486,000, meaning that a major amount of the work remained to be done. By the end of 1984, 4,646 S&T personnel had formally applied for transfers but only 346 people were transferred out of their original work situation to a new one, a success rate of only 7.5%.[113] As of early 1985, the Shanghai S&T Personnel Development Bank had not contributed massively to the reforms. Between 1 December 1984 and mid-January 1985, 14 units had recommended S&T personnel for 'going into storage' and 64 individuals had applied themselves. The total number of job advertisements placed for all participating units was 1,084 and of the ten S&T personnel said to be formally 'in the pool' four had been placed in new work and four were taking part in S&T 'missions'.[114]

Even if mobility within cities can be improved, major problems will still exist when people try to move between cities. The new urban reform programme asserts that it is permissible to look for work in another city if this helps the person to reunite with his or her family. In general, there is not too much of a problem if somebody wishes to move from a major city such as Beijing to a smaller town. Moving in the opposite direction, however, is extremely difficult. The household registration system makes this particularly difficult. People can find themselves caught in a 'Catch-22' situation; to get an urban registration one would have to have a legally sanctioned job but one can only be given a job in a city if one already has a registration in that city. The growth of jobs in the collective and individual sector of the economy, where control is looser, will probably not hold out many possibilities for scientific and technical personnel, with the exception of consultancy work. Some institutions have the right to recruit from outside city boundaries but the numbers are restricted and often political influence is crucial in determining who gets the job. Such problems place restrictions on the new advertising system for jobs. The advertisers may well find themselves restricted to soliciting applications from people already resident in the city who do not have a job already or who have been allowed by their current employers to apply. In the latter case, if the person is any good it is unlikely that they would be released by their institution in the first place.

Improving the Situation of S&T Intellectuals

Intellectuals, and for our purposes this includes scientists and technicians, were one of the groups that suffered most as a result of the attacks on the status quo launched by the Cultural Revolution. During the height of the Cultural Revolution they were denounced as the 'stinking ninth category'. This does not mean that all intellectuals suffered, as the 'Gang of Four' tried to create their own intellectual force to support and explain their policies. It did mean, however, that most of those who had positions of authority in the pre-Cultural Revolution system based on their possession of specialised knowledge came under heavy attack. The current development strategy, by contrast, places a high premium on those people who possess precisely these skills, and indeed the contributions of such people are vital to the success of the strategy.

To ensure that intellectuals participate fully in support of the new policies, it has been necessary to give them certain freedoms to ply their trade more effectively. Thus, the current leadership have attempted to improve their political standing and to ameliorate their work and living conditions. The political implications of this policy will be dealt with in the concluding chapter and here remarks will be confined to moves introduced to improve the scientists' daily life. A survey conducted at a test reform institute, the Shanghai Laser Research Institute, found that to the question of what was considered the most urgent problem, 34.4% replied having a higher income, 34% improved housing and 27.4% improved research conditions.[115] Another survey, reported in early 1985, showed that 40.16% of the scientists and technicians asked highlighted wages as being too low, 44.95% mentioned title and rank problems and 39.15% had heavy family responsibilities.[116]

Those surveyed were not unduly impressed by reforms undertaken to improve the work environment. At the Shanghai Laser Research Institute, 44.6% of the respondents declared themselves to be indifferent to the trial reform programme, and only 13.4% felt that organisational reform would improve work efficiency. By contrast, 24.8% thought there would be no real change, although a further 31.2% thought that the reform would have a 'moderate promotional effect'.[117]

An important element in the reforms at the workplace has been the attempts to reduce administrative and political interference in the work of specialists. The attempt to reduce political interference was seen most clearly in the assurances given to scientists by Fang Yi during the Spiritual Pollution Campaign in late 1983.[118] The more reform-minded members of China's leadership would like the scientists' work to be judged, in future, on technical and professional grounds rather than in accordance with whether they had a good political standing or not. This is reflected in attempts to promote experts into leading positions and the increased use of peer group review to assess the value of particular research projects and by allowing scientists to devote most, if not all, of their time to their work. Scientists are now expected to be able to spend five-sixths of their time on research, thus reducing the time available for political activities.

This should mean that most scientists will be able to devote their time more fully to research, but not all. The policy of appointing experts to leading positions tends in the opposite direction, meaning that many senior staff members will get bogged down in administrative duties. As in many European research institutes, senior staff will become managers rather than researchers. Despite such reforms, many scientific and technical personnel would appear to remain dissatisfied with the way institutions are managed. In the survey reported in early 1985, 21.53% of the respondents complained that 'leaders interfered in everything' and 21.17% on the overuse of administrative orders.[119]

The living standard of most scientific and technical personnel means that much precious time is taken up on household chores such as shopping and cooking. It is no surprise that China's first supermarket opened in Beijing in the university and research institute area, Haidian. To give senior people more time for research, the CAS President, Lu Jiaxi, has called for the situation of the middle aged to be improved by relieving them of the 'four tasks' - professional, administrative, Party and household tasks.[120]

Housing is the most pressing problem in relation to living conditions, not just for the S&T community but for all urban dwellers. Housing provision has not received a high priority in China's development policies. In 1978, a survey of 192 big and medium-sized cities and towns showed that *per capita* living floor space totalled only 3.6 square metres, excluding kitchen, lavatory and corridor floor space, and it was suggested that one-third of the inhabitants were living in overcrowded conditions.[121] This will come as no surprise to anyone who has walked around Shanghai's back streets, but it may be more surprising to know that from 1949 to 1982 floor space actually decreased by 0.9 square metres per person.[122] In particular, the state seems to have tried to buy off their senior scientific personnel by improving their living space. Orleans states that 100 million *yuan* was provided for senior scientific, technical and education personnel working under the CAS and the Ministries of Education, Public Health, and Culture and the State Commission of Physical Culture.[123] This presumably accounts for the report toward the end of 1982 that during the previous two years over 5,000 professors, researchers and lecturers moved into new housing. Each had three or four rooms, a bath and a study covering a total of 70 to 100 square metres.[124]

The problem of wage levels has also been tackled and, as has been shown, other avenues for earning extra income have been opened up. Unfortunately, in a time series, figures are only available for the broad category of staff and workers in state-owned units working in the fields of science, culture, education and public health (see graph). It is noticeable that the average wage for those in this sector gradually declined from 1965 until 1971, as did the average wage for all those in the state-owned sector. Despite a brief rise in 1972, which brought wages for scientific personnel back to 1965 levels, wages steadily declined again until 1977, reaching a low of 559 *yuan*. Starting in 1978, however, this category's average wage began a steady climb surpassing the 1965, pre-Cultural Revolution, level in 1979 and surpassing the average annual wage for those in the state-owned sector in 1982 and 1983.[125] Figures for more recent years show that those engaged in scientific research have been faring even better than the composite figures suggest. Between 1980 and 1983, their average annual wage rose from 856 *yuan* to 986 *yuan*.[126]

In an attempt to stimulate high quality, relevant research, financial awards are given to scientists under schemes such as the Invention Awards or the Natural Science Awards. From 1979 until the end of 1984, over 900 items had won a national invention prize. Of the five first-class awards given in 1984, however, only one went to a civilian invention, the other four all going to items within the defence sector.[127]

The use of award systems has been expanding. In early 1985, the State Council announced that it would be offering cash awards for significant contributions to S&T advancement. These awards, made at the national and provincial levels, are in addition to the already existing awards given for scientific achievement. A first prize carries the value of 15,000 *yuan*, second prize 10,000 *yuan*, and third prize 5,000 *yuan*.[128] In January 1985, cash awards were given to 122 'outstanding geologists' at a ceremony in Beijing. The geologists were also awarded the title of 'model geologist of the PRC' and given medals, certificates and pay rises.[129]

However, egalitarian impulses exaggerated by the Cultural Revolution and feelings of envy and jealousy cannot be set aside with a simple flourish of the cheque book. Sufficient accounts have appeared in the Chinese press to indicate that what Orleans terms 'slicing' of awards takes place on a major scale.[130] Cases are reported of jealous cadres delaying the reward going to the individual and a case from Zhejiang province shows just how the value of an award can get whittled away.[131] By early 1983 scientists working for the Provincial Academy of Agricultural Sciences had received 91 awards but the actual 'winners' only received about 10% of the prize money. This was because first the political and administrative department took a 10% cut, then the service department took 12%, the information centre and library 3%, the research institute 15%, the farm 10% and the rest was divided among the team. Such practices are criticised

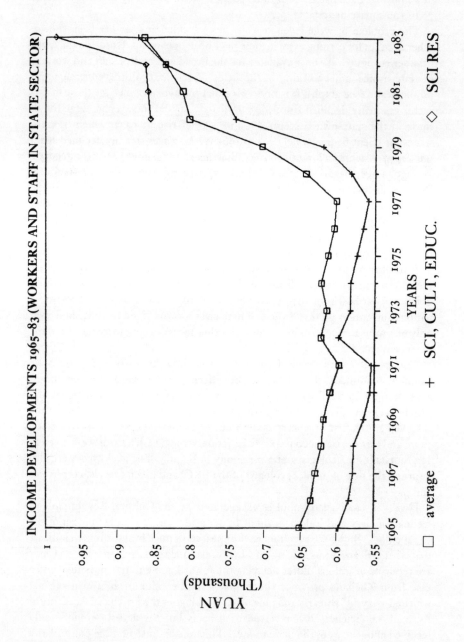

INCOME DEVELOPMENTS 1965–83 (WORKERS AND STAFF IN STATE SECTOR)

and in December 1984 new measures were introduced to deal with this problem. Wu Hong, the Director of the Records and Examining Committee for Inventions, announced that, in future, research chiefs were to receive at least 70% of the total sum awarded, with the rest going to partners who had helped with the project.[132]

Notes

1 Deng Xiaoping, quoted in 'Scientific System Due for Reforms', *BR*, no 11, 18 March 1985, p 6.
2 *Xinhua* in Chinese, 30 November 1982, translated in *FBIS*, 1 December 1982.
3 Zhao Ziyang, 'Gaige keji tizhi, tuidong keji he jingji, shehui xietao' ('Reform the Science and Technology System, Promote the Co-ordination of Science and Technology with the Economy and Society'), *RMRB*, 21 March 1985, pp 1 and 3.
4 *Zhongguo Tongji Nianjian, 1984 (China Statistical Yearbook, 1984)* (Beijing: Tongji chubanshe, 1984), p 570.
5 State Statistical Bureau, 'Communique on Fulfilment of China's 1984 Economic and Social Development Plan', *BR*, no 12, 25 March 1985, p vii.
6 Hu Ping, 'Education and Development of S&T Personnel' in Committee on Scholarly Communication with the People's Republic of China, *US-China Conference on Science Policy* (Washington DC: National Academy Press, 1985), p 285.
7 *Zhongguo Tongji Nianjian*, 1984 p 500.
8 Wang Haijiong, 'China's Prospects for the Year 2000', *BR*, no 44, 4 November 1985, p 18.
9 'Problems of the Present State and Existence of China's Scientific and Technical Contingent', *Jingji Ribao*, 9 January 1984, p 2, translated in *JPRS - CST - 84 - 003*, p 139.
10 L Orleans, *The Training and Utilisation of Scientific and Engineering Manpower in the People's Republic of China* (Washington DC: US Government Printing Office, 1983), pp 46-47.
11 Ibid, p 46.
12 The figures for 1979 and 1981 are calculated on the basis of information given in Hu Ping, 'Education and Development of S&T Personnel', p 285, and those for 1982 on the basis of information in 'Problems of the Present State and Existence of China's Scientific and Technical Contingent', p 139.
13 Yu Hongjun, Wang Zonglin and Cheng Hengmo, 'Kexue jishu yu jingji jiegou' ('Science and Technology and Economic Structure'), in Ma Hong and Sun Shangqing (eds), *Zhongguo Jingji Jiegou Wenti Yanjiu (Research on the Problems of China's Economic Structure)* (Beijing: Renmin chubanshe, 1981), pp 617-618.
14 Huang Wei and Zhang Jiexu, 'Woguo keji duiwu de jiegou ji dangqian de tiaozheng cuoshi', *KXX*, no 5, 1981, p 39.
15 Dai Guangqian, 'Lun keji duiwu de "bumen jiegou"' ('On the "Department Structure" of Scientific and Technical Ranks'), *KXX*, no 5, 1981, p 39.
16 Ibid.
17 'Problems of the Present State and Existence of China's Scientific and Technical Contingent', pp 139-140.
18 *SWB:FE* 8011.
19 Calculated on the basis of figures in Table 3. Even Shanghai has stated that its trained specialists are too few to meet the municipality's development needs up until 1990. The city had dropped to eighth place in its ratio of specialists in the total workforce. See 'Shanghai Faces Talent Shortage', *CD*, 24 November 1984, p 3.

20 'Problems of the Present State and Existence of China's Scientific and Technical Contingent', pp 139-140.

21 Gao Yulong, 'Guanyu heli rencai liudong de jige wenti' ('Concerning Several Problems with the Rational Movement of Talent'), *KXX*, no 7, 1983, p 36.

22 Zhu Ximin, 'Nongye keji renyuan guanli chutan' ('A Preliminary Study of the Management of Agricultural Scientific and Technical Personnel'), *KYGL*, no 1, 1982, pp 27-30.

23 Huang Wei and Zhang Jieyu, 'Woguo keji duiwu de jiegou ji dangqian de tiaozheng cuoshi', pp 4-5.

24 Ibid.

25 L Orleans, *The Training and Utilisation of Scientific and Engineering Manpower in the People's Republic of China*, p 15.

26 'The Challenge that Faces Higher Education in our Country', *Xinhua Wenzhai (Xinhua Digest)*, no 6, 1985, translated in *Inside China Mainland*, October 1985, p 18.

27 *Zhongguo Jiaoyu Chengjiu: Tongji Ziliao 1949-1983 (Achievement of Education in China - Statistical Documentation 1949-1983)* (Beijing: Renmin jiaoyu chubanshe, 1985), p 50.

28 For example, while studying at Nanjing University in 1977 the author found that although many students described themselves as 'workers, peasants or soldiers', their parents were government officials, lecturers or scientists. Their claim to be a 'peasant' or a 'worker' rested on the fact that they had been 'sent down' to a commune or a factory for a couple of years after graduating from high school. This unit then recommended them for college entry and they were classified as 'peasant' or 'worker' applications.

29 Bian Gu, 'Wenhua kaoshi henyou biyao' ('Educational Examinations are an Absolute Necessity'), *Renmin Ribao*, 23 October 1977, p 1.

30 For an analysis of the new educational policies in terms of their relationship to the needs of economic development see M Bastid, 'Chinese Educational Policies in the 1980s and Economic Development', *China Quarterly*, no 98, 1984, pp 189-219.

31 *SWB:FE* 6330 and 'Zhonghua renmin gongheguo xuewei tiaoli' ('Regulations of the People's Republic of China for Academic Degrees'), *RMRB*, 14 February 1985, p 2.

32 *BR*, no 8, 25 February 1980, p 5.

33 State Statistical Bureau, 'Communique on Fulfilment of China's 1983 Economic Plan', *BR*, no 20, 14 May 1984, p x.

34 State Statistical Bureau, 'Communique on Fulfilment of China's 1984 Economic and Social Development Plan', p vii.

35 *Zhongguo Jiaoyu Chengjiu: Tongji Ziliao 1949-1983*, p 112.

36 *SWB:FE* 7106.

37 *The Sixth Five Year Plan of the People's Republic of China for Social and Economic Development (1981-1985)* (Beijing: Foreign Languages Press, 1984), p 213.

38 State Statistical Bureau, 'Communique on Fulfilment of China's 1984 Economic and Social Development Plan', p vii.

39 *The Sixth Five Year Plan of the People's Republic of China for Social and Economic Development (1981-1985)*, p 216.

40 State Statistical Bureau, 'Communique on Fulfilment of China's 1984 Economic and Social Development Plan', p vii.

41 *Zhongguo Jiaoyu Chengjiu: Tongji Ziliao 1949-1983*, p 118.

42 'Proposal of the Central Committee of the Chinese Communist Party for the Seventh Five Year Plan for National Economic and Social Development September 23, 1985', *BR*, no 40, 7 October 1985, p xv.

43 This is based on admissions of 230,000 in 1982, 256,000 in 1983, and 312,000 in 1984.

44   In 1983, the total enrolment was 134,581 an increase over the figures of 84,405 in
     1982. See *Zhongguo Jiaoyu Chengjiu: Tongji Ziliao 1949-1983*, p 77.
45   'The Challenge that Faces Higher Education', p 18.
46   *Xinhua*, 6 June 1980 quoted in L Orleans, *The Training and Utilisation of Scientific
     and Engineering Manpower in the People's Republic of China*, p 21.
47   Ibid pp 27-28.
48   *Xinhua* 8 December 1981 quoted in Ibid p 27.
49   Yan Zheng, 'Daxue xinsheng wei shenmo bu shiying daxue jiaoyu' ('Why don't New
     University Students Adapt to University Education'), *GMRB*, 14 January 1983, p 2.
50   The figure of 18,500 is taken from 'Boom on Exchange Students', *CD*, 12 December
     1983, p 1 and the figure of 12,642 is taken from *Zhongguo Jiaoyu Chengjiu: Tongji
     Ziliao 1949-1983*, p 126.
51   *Zhongguo Jiaoyu Chengjiu: Tongji Ziliao 1949-1983*, p 126.
52   Li Xue, 'How Many PRC Students are Studying Abroad?', *Banyue tan*, 25 August
     1985, p 39, translated in *JPRS - CST - 85 - 037*, p 14.
53   On 16 July 1982, the State Council approved the Regulations Governing Studying
     Abroad at One's Own Expense. A translation can be found in *SWB:FE* 7094.
54   For a summary of these regulations see 'New Rules Help Students Go Abroad', *CD*,
     14 January 1985, p 3.
55   'Exchanges with Foreign Countries', *BR*, no 1, 4 January 1982, p 29. This article
     states that future priority should be given to sending abroad students in the fields of
     agronomy, animal husbandry, light industry, economic management and energy.
     Special consideration was to be given to those wishing to study law, other social
     sciences and humanities.
56   See Dai Beihua, 'China Will Send More Students Overseas', *CD*, 30 November
     1984, p 1, and K Rubin, 'Spotlight on Chinese Students Returned from Abroad',
     CEN, no 2, 1985, p 34 and Li Xue, 'How Many PRC Students Are Studying
     Abroad?', p 39.
57   'Returned Students Play Leading Role in Research', *Xinhua* in English, 2 December
     1984.
58   Ibid.
59   The Shanghai Branch of the CAS, 'Ruiyi gaige, wenbu qianjin' ('Keenly Desire
     Reform, Steadily Advance'), National Science and Technology Work Conference
     Exchange Materials No 2, p 9.
60   Lu Jiaxi, 'Guanyu dangqian keyan guanli de jige wenti' ('Concerning Several
     Problems of Current Scientific Research Management'), *KYGL*, no 3, 1982, p 6.
61   Shen Xiaodan, 'Cong fazhan jingjixue jiaodu yanjiu woguo zhili yinjin de fangzhen'
     ('A Study of Our Nation's Policy of Importing Brainpower Viewed from the Angle
     of Economic Development'), *KXX*, no 11, 1984, pp 24-25.
62   Lu Jiaxi, 'Guanyu dangqian keyan guanli de jige wenti', p 6.
63   Shen Xiaodan, 'Cong fazhan jingjixue jiaodu yanjiu woguo zhili yinjin de fangzhen',
     p 26.
64   'Zhonggong zhongyang guanyu jiaoyu tizhi gaige de jueding' ('Decision of the
     Central Committee of the Communist Party of China on the Reform of the
     Education System'), *RMRB*, 29 May 1985, p 3.
65   World Bank, *China's Socialist Economic Development vol 3. The Social Sectors
     Population, Health, Nutrition and Education* (Washington DC: The World Bank,
     1983), p 153. This emphasis of the World Bank is also clearly laid out in their 1985
     assessment of China.
66   *Zhongguo Jiaoyu Chengjiu: Tongji Ziliao 1949-1983*, p 146.
67   Ibid, p 208.
68   World Bank, China: *Long-Term Issues and Options, Annex A: Issues and Prospects in
     Education*, p 23.

69 World Bank, *China's Socialist Economic Development vol 3. The Social Sectors Population, Health, Nutrition and Education*, p 153.

70 *The Sixth Five Year Plan of the People's Republic of China for Social and Economic Development (1981-1985)*, pp 208-209.

71 State Statistical Bureau, 'Communique on Fulfilment of China's 1984 Economic and Social Development Plan', p vii.

72 World Bank, *China: Long-Term Issues and Options, Annex A: Issues and Prospects in Education*, p 25.

73 World Bank, China: *Long-Term Issues and Options, Annex A: Issues and Prospects in Education*, pp 21-22.

74 'Zhonggong zhongyang guanyu jiaoyu tizhi gaige de jueding', p 3.

75 For a report of the meeting see Jin Baohua, 'Scientific Research Given Tasks in Economy', *CD*, 6 January 1984, p 1.

76 'Wei quanmian kaichuang shehui zhuyi xiandaihua jianshe xin jumian gongxian liliang, zhongguo kexie bufen quanguo weiyuan xuexi dang de shier da wenjian faxin zhaideng' ('Devote Strength to Creating a New Situation in the Construction of Socialist Modernisation, Excerpts from Speeches Given by Members of the Chinese Association for Science and Technology on Studying the Documents of the Twelfth Party Congress'), *RMRB*, 5 October 1982, p 3.

77 See CEN, no 4, 1984. In Chongqing, Sichuan province, it was announced that those technical school graduates, engineers and technicians who worked in village and town enterprises below the county level would receive wages one grade higher as well as other fringe benefits granted by the state. Jin Qi, 'Technicians Go to Countryside', *BR*, no 29, 16 July 1984, p 4.

78 Jin Qi, 'Technicians Go to Countryside', p 4.

79 *JPRS - CST - 85 - 009*, p 17.

80 Jin Qi, 'Technicians Go to Countryside', p 4.

81 Tao Kai and Zeng Qing, 'Guanyu keji rencai de dingxiang liudong wenti' ('Concerning the Problem of the Directional Flow of Scientific and Technical Personnel'), *GMRB*, 12 July 1982, p 4.

82 *Xinhua* in English, in *JPRS - CST - 85 - 015*.

83 Huang Wei and Zhang Jieyu, 'Woguo keji duiwu de jiegou ji dangqian de tiaozheng cuoshi', pp 3-6.

84 Tao Kai and Zeng Qing, 'Guanyu keji rencai de dingxiang liudong wenti', p 4.

85 See Huang Wei and Zhang Jieyu, 'Woguo keji duiwu de jiegou ji dangqian de tiaozheng cuoshi' and Tao Kai and Zeng Qing, 'Guanyu keji rencai de dingxiang liudong wenti'.

86 'Zhonggong zhongyang guanyu kexue jishu tizhi gaige de jueding' ('Decision of the Central Committee of the Chinese Communist Party on Reform of the Science and Technology Management System'), *RMRB*, 20 March 1985, pp 1 and 3.

87 For further description of this system see 'Guanyu gaige keji renyuan guanli zhidu, cujin keji renyuan heli liudong de jixiang guiding' ('Several Regulations Concerning the Reform of the Scientific and Technical Personnel System and the Promotion of the Rational Flow of Scientific and Technical Personnel'), National Science and Technology Work Conference Consultation Document No 5, p 2.

88 'Shanghai bumen danwei shixing keji renyuan pinyongzhi. Zunao rencai jiaoliu jiang shou xingzheng ganyu' ('Some Units in Shanghai Departments Try Out the System for Hiring Scientific and Technical Personnel. Interference with the Flow of Personnel will be Dealt with through Administrative Intervention'), *RMRB*, 31 July 1984, p 3.

89 Lu Jianming, 'Shanghaishi jin yibu gaige keji tizhi' ('Shanghai Municipality Further Develops the Reform of the Science and Technology System'), *GMRB*, 4 September 1984, p 1.

90 Wang Kang, 'Shixing jihua zhidaoxia de keji rencai hetong pinrenzhi' ('Implementing the Contractual System for Hiring Scientific and Technical Personnel under Planned Guidance'), *RMRB*, 31 July 1984, p 3.

91 Zheng Haining, 'Xueshu yanjiu "jinqin fanzhi" nianqing housheng nan yu "bajian" ' (' "Inbreeding" in Scholarly Research Hinders Young People "Excelling" '), *GMRB*, 21 December 1984, p 1.

92 Ibid.

93 'Guanyu gaige keji renyuan guanli zhidu, cujin keji renyuan heli liudong de jixiang guiding', p 4.

94 Interview at the Institute of Theoretical Physics, 16 January 1985.

95 Zheng Haining, 'Woguo jiang shiban boshihou keyan liudongzhan' ('Our Nation Will Experiment with the Setting-up of Mobile Scientific Research Centres'), *GMRB*, 11 July 1985, p 1.

96 'Guanyu gaige keji renyuan guanli zhidu, cujin keji renyuan heli liudong de jixiang guiding', p 4.

97 Ibid, p 5.

98 This document was drafted by the powerful combination of the Organisation Department of the Central Committee, the United Front Department of the Central Committee, the Ministry of Labour and Personnel, the Propaganda Department of the Central Committee, the State Science and Technology Commission and the Chinese Association for Science and Technology. 'Guanyu jixu fahui tuilixiu zhishi fenzi zuoyong de guiding' ('Regulations Concerning Continuing to Give Play to the Role of Retired Intellectuals'), National Science and Technology Work Conference Discussion Document No 6.

99 Ibid, p 2.

100 Zhu Shu, 'Mobilise the "Remaining Enthusiasm" of Retired Scientific and Technical Personnel to Serve Construction of the Four Modernisations', *Yangcheng Wanbao*, 25 January 1984, p 2, translated in *JPRS - CST - 84 - 031*, p 43.

101 'Abolish all "Indigenous Policies" that Obstruct the Reasonable Flow of Talented People', *Xinhua* in Chinese, 4 December 1984, translated in *SWB:FE* 7820.

102 In a number of interviews conducted in Shanghai, in late January and early February 1985, with members of the Shanghai branch of the International Technology Development Corporation, the view was expressed that in the future new corporations etc should be just work units and should not be expected to provide the usual range of social amenities and living space.

103 Guangdong Provincial Service, 1 May 1985 in *SWB:FE*, 7 May 1985.

104 Zhao Ziyang, 'Gaige keji tizhi, tuidong keji he jingji, shehui xietao'.

105 Xiao Guangen, 'Dui keji renyuan cizhi yao zuo fenxi' ('We Should Analyse the Resignation of Scientific and Technical Personnel'), *RMRB*, 25 May 1985, p 1.

106 The Professional Service Corporation in Shenyang and the Talents Exchange Service Centre in Guangdong had already been established and were providing similar local services.

107 'Service Centre Created to Make Use of Talent', *CD*, 7 June 1984, p 1.

108 Xiao Guangen, 'Dui keji renyuan cizhi yao zuo fenxi', p 1.

109 Gu Wenxing, 'Shanghai keji tizhi gaige de wuxiang cuoshi' ('Five Measures for Reforming Shanghai's Science and Technology System'), *KXX*, no 4, 1985, p 17.

110 'Shanghai chengli keji rencai kaifa yinhang' ('Shanghai Establishes a Scientific and Technical Talents Development Bank'), *GMRB*, 31 August 1984, p 1.

111 Xiao Guangen, 'Shanghai chengli rencai yinhang dali cujin rencai liutong' ('Shanghai Establishes a Talent Bank to Vigorously Promote the Circulation of Personnel'), *RMRB*, 28 January 1985, p 1.

112 'Shanghai chengli keji rencai kaifa yinhang', p 1.

113 Xiao Guangen, 'Dui keji renyuan cizhi yao zuo fenxi', p 1. A more successful interpretation of these figures is given in Gu Wenxing, 'Shanghai keji tizhi gaige de wuxiang cuoshi', p 17.

114 Xiao Guangen, 'Shanghai chengli rencai yinhang dali cujin rencai liutong', p 1.

115 Article by Gu Jiugang in *KXX*, no 8, 1983, pp 10-12, translated in *JPRS - CST - 84 - 011*, pp 155-160, p 157.

116 Bian Diping, 'Making the Best Use of China's Limited Scientific Talent', *Jishu jingji yu guanli yanjiu (Research on the Economics and Management of Technology)* no 1, 1985, translated in *JPRS - CST - 84 - 022*, p 4.

117 In fact, according to the survey 7.6% thought that organisational reform would make things worse. Gu Jiugang, tranlsated in *JPRS - CST - 84 - 011*, p 157.

118 For details see Chapter One.

119 Bian Diping, 'Making the Best Use of China's Limited Scientific Talent', p 2.

120 Lu Jiaxi, 'Nuli kaichuang kexue gongzuo de xin jumian' ('Arduously Start the New Phase of Scientific Work'), *RMRB*, 23 September 1982, p 3.

121 Zhou Jin, 'Housing China's 900 Million People', *BR*, no 48, 30 November 1979, p 18.

122 Ibid.

123 L Orleans, *The Training and Utilisation of Scientific and Engineering Manpower in the People's Republic of China*, p 10. His source is an unpublished paper of the Policy Research Office of the CAS, 'Chinese Academy of Sciences in 1980'.

124 *SWB:FE* 7139.

125 *Zhongguo Tongji Nianjian*, 1984, p 459.

126 Ibid, p 456.

127 'Awards Go to Over 200 Top Scientists', *CD*, 4 December 1984, p 1. The award was for the propagation of woolly-headed crabs in salt water.

128 The first of these awards was given to Hu Daofan, a research fellow at the Beijing Academy of Agricultural and Forestry Sciences. She received 10,000 *yuan* for her success in breeding a new strain of winter wheat. *CEN*, no 1, 1985, p 32.

129 *SWB:FE* 7864. A further example is the President's Fund of the CAS which is outlined in Chapter Four.

130 L Orleans, *The Training and Utilisation of Scientific and Engineering Manpower in the People's Republic of China*, p 10.

131 'Science Award Cut to Ribbons', *CD*, 19 February 1983, p 3.

132 'Awards Go to over 200 Top Inventions', p 1.

CHAPTER SIX

SCIENCE, TECHNOLOGY AND THE REFORM PROGRAMME IN CHINA

The question of reform has dominated political and economic debates throughout the eighties in China. Differences about the scale, extent and nature of the reforms have been the major topics of discussion. This has not just remained at the level of theoretical discourse; indeed, so many new policies have been introduced covering all fields that it is difficult to keep track of them. No institution, organisation or sector of the economy has been left untouched by the reform drive. The reforms have moved beyond trying to deal with what are seen as the 'leftist' excesses derived from China's experimentation during the Great Leap Forward (1958-1960) and the Cultural Revolution decade to attempting to overcome the fundamental flaws in the overcentralised Soviet system which China chose to adopt in the fifties.

Not surprisingly, many of the specific measures introduced mirror those that have been tried in the Soviet Union and Eastern Europe with varying degrees of success. However, this is not true in all areas. While the reforms of the S&T sector and the urban industrial economy parallel those introduced first in the Soviet Union in 1962, the reforms of the agricultural sector reflect a radical new departure for a state-socialist society. Yet even in the case of S&T, the reforms have been introduced with a speed and a boldness that would be impossible in the Soviet Union and East European countries. Indeed China's independence from the Soviet Union since the late fifties, and its earlier independent revolutionary history, have meant that it has a greater degree of manoeuvre than other state-socialist societies that come directly within the Soviet sphere of influence.[1]

The reform programme is designed to turn China into a powerful, modernised, socialist state ready to move into the twenty-first century. Since the Third Plenum of the Eleventh Central Committee (December 1978), the key focus for Party work, and indeed all other work, has been defined as the promotion of economic development. However, it has become increasingly clear to many within China that its overcentralised, hierarchical state form and system of administrative planning are major stumbling blocks to further development. The need to develop a more flexible and democratic system and to rely on the market to fill in the large gaps left by the state plans is recognised by the whole leadership. Strong differences of opinion exist, however, about the extent of these necessary reforms.

A number of observers have attested to the inevitability of the process: that as the imperatives of economic modernisation come to the fore, the need for reform becomes irresistible. This process is often aided by the passing of the revolutionary generation and their replacement by a generation that has grown up under the new state and is more concerned for technocratic considerations - this is when, to use Kautsky's phrase, leadership passes from the 'revolutionary modernisers' to the 'managerial modernisers'.[2] In reality the process is rarely so clearly defined. One of the latest writers to outline the transitional phases of state-socialist societies is White. He sees China as having reached the phase where what he terms 'bureaucratic voluntarism' has become 'increasingly irrational economically and increasingly unacceptable politically'.[3] The need comes for the introduction of greater use of the market mechanisms and a larger role for democracy primarily for functional reasons. Once the decision is made to move in this direction of reform, it is necessary to give more autonomy, and possibly more power, to those with professional and technical skills and to try to restrict the power of the old administrative élite. This allows the possible emergence of a new élite that bases its power not on its position within the politico-administrative hierarchy but on its possession of scarce skills necessary for the modernisation programme. Conflict is inevitable and the most usual outcome is some sort of trade-off between the two. This sort of development can be seen most clearly with respect to scientists and technicians; a matter that will be returned to later.

Economic Reform and Science and Technology

Apart from the general trend noted above, the stress which the current leadership places on economic development has more specific causes deriving from China's immediate past. Three particular reasons are highlighted here. First, living standards in the late seventies had barely risen from those in the late fifties for much of the population. The government's overconcentration on accumulation at the expense of consumption meant that rationing, queuing and hours spent on laborious household chores were the daily fare for most. The lack of consumer goods was offset by the fact that few had sufficient disposable income to buy them. In fact, in 1977 the average wage of employees in the state sector was 5.5% lower than it had been in 1957; that for the category defined as industrial workers was 8.4% lower.[4] It seems no exaggeration to conclude that China's population had probably had enough of tightening their belts in return for the promise of a bright future.

Secondly, the failure of the initial post-Mao strategy to improve economic performance significantly caused the leadership to focus more sharply on the need for fundamental economic reform. The ascription of blame for economic failure to the policies of the 'Gang of Four' with the associated policy of returning to a 'golden age' before they existed was seen to lead to a dead end. It was increasingly recognised that the main problems were deep-seated structural ones. Also, the ambitious pursuit of 'maoism without Mao' had led to serious short-term problems such as a towering budget deficit, increasing inflation and inflationary pressures. The politically inspired measure of offering the urban labour force increased wages and bonuses to win their confidence and allegiance was exhausted. Future increases in earnings would only come after real increases in productivity. In January 1980, Deng Xiaoping complained of the indiscriminate handing out of bonuses that were not linked to productivity. He stated that some two million of the five million *yuan* paid out during 1979 was effectively wasted with the result that the 'lives of a few' were improved while 'very many more difficulties' were imposed on the 'people of the country as a whole'.[5]

Thirdly, the Party was faced with the problem of legitimacy. The continual twists and turns of policy since the mid-fifties left the Party's claim to be the sole body in society capable of mapping out the correct path to socialism looking a little thin, to say the least. The notion of the infallibility of the Party was strained to breaking point. This meant that the 'fine traditions' and the name of the Party could no longer be invoked to ensure allegiance to a particular set of policy preferences. This was compounded by the fact that people had the feeling that within a short space of time they might be expected to give total allegiance to a different set of policy preferences. The death of Mao Zedong and the dismantling of his personality cult meant that his name could not be effectively invoked to underpin legitimacy. As a result the Party chose the same option as most ruling groups when they have their backs against the wall; they began to promise a bright economic future for all within a relatively short period of time. By 1979, Deng Xiaoping and his supporters had tied their legitimacy to rule more closely to their ability to deliver the economic goods than had any other leadership group since 1949. This meant, in turn, that more freedom and power had to be given to those groups that could devise and implement the plans to bring this delivery about.

The failure of the Great Leap Forward, the Cultural Revolution and the initial post-Mao strategy to provide a viable alternative to the Soviet model of organisation that was capable of launching China on a path of self-sustaining economic growth led China's leaders to look for alternative sources of stimulating economic growth. This caused attention to be paid to the major role improvements in S&T could play in China's general economic progress. Technological change was identified as the main mechanism for improving economic performance and for maintaining economic growth. Increased productivity in the long term would, it was argued, depend on the capacity of China's research and development (R&D) establishment to provide the necessary innovation to make China's industrial and agricultural sectors realise more of their potential.[6] Indeed, at times China's thinking about the capacity of S&T to reach parts that other factors cannot reach has verged on the naive. As Simons has pointed out, at the end of the seventies S&T were regarded as a 'magic' ingredient that could 'automatically transform and modernise the Chinese economy and military'.[7]

The importance attached to S&T has brought China into line with the rest of the communist world where it is recognised that increased supplies of land, labour and capital are simply not enough to expand production. They must be accompanied by an increase in technical know-how. This has resulted in an increasing emphasis in policy making on the central role of technical advance in providing economic transformation.[8] Thus, for example, as long ago as 1975, the former Soviet leader Brezhnev, at the anniversary of the Soviet Academy of Sciences, stated that 'socialism and science are indivisible' and that 'only by relying on the latest developments of science and technology is it possible to build socialism and communism successfully'.[9] This has not just remained a verbal commitment as during the seventies the Soviet Union had a much higher investment rate for R&D than any 'Western' country.[10] While China has reached the same conclusion somewhat later, it now shares a similar enthusiasm, albeit one that cannot be matched by such high levels of spending. The importance attached to S&T in China is shown by the fact that they, as in the rest of the communist world, are now defined as productive forces.

The attention paid to S&T as the key promoters of economic growth is intensified by China's fast-growing awareness, and fear, of the 'new technological revolution'.[11] The fact that China feels that it has missed out on the industrial revolution makes it all the more eager to make sure that it is not left behind by the developments in new technology. In fact, China's list of key areas for research in new technologies is practically identical to those of the more developed countries. However, the flexibility within the S&T system necessary for response to new technology and the environment necessary for innovation have been seriously lacking in the PRC. This has forced China's leaders to take action to reform the system in certain ways, even if they may have wished to do otherwise or simply to do nothing at all.

These reforms are not taking place in isolation and their ultimate success will depend on how well reforms in related areas fare. As has been demonstrated, the major organisational problem is the lack of an effective link between R&D, on the one hand, and the production process on the other. Insufficient innovation has taken place to bring about the necessary technological change and where innovation has taken place in the research laboratories there have been great difficulties in transferring it to the productive sector. The relatively autonomous and isolated situation of the research sector is a problem in most countries but it is particularly acute in developing countries. The crude notion that more universities established and more money poured in will produce more research, leading to more technology to be absorbed in the production process, is now recognised as a fallacy.[12] It is clear that the research sector must be properly integrated with the broader socio-economic structure for optimal use to be made of scientific discovery and technical development.

The problem was magnified in China because of its adoption of a Soviet-type organisational model that erected administrative barriers between the various sectors. China's recent reforms in this respect are similar to the attempts introduced in the sixties in the Soviet Union and a little later in the East European countries. As early as 1962, the Soviets introduced a system to make independent research units support themselves from revenue earned from the sale of research.[13] Although this is now a well established practice, and it has removed the worst bureaucratic excesses, it is clear that it has still not fundamentally resolved the problem. Brezhnev, speaking to the Twenty-Fourth Party congress in 1971, commented that:

> We have to create conditions that would compel enterprises . . . literally to chase after S&T novelties, and not to shy away from them, figuratively speaking, as the devil shies away from incense.[14]

In the Soviet Union, the persistence of this problem can, in large part, be attributed to the failure of the industrial reform programme of the early sixties, the so-called Liberman reforms. However, even in Hungary, where the reform process has evolved further in terms of striking a better balance between plan and market, the problem persists. In June 1985, the Hungarian Prime Minister Lazar raised critical comments at a Comecon meeting during which he stated that it was vital to accelerate S&T progress and to get the results of new R&D into factory production lines.[15]

As we have seen, the problem has been recognised by China's leaders and reforms have been introduced with a speed that makes the Soviet Union look as if it has been moving at a snail's pace all these years. The contract system, joint research-production bodies, and consultancies are all designed to create horizontal links at lower levels of the hierarchical chain to break down the situation where such contacts only take place at the top levels of the various hierarchies. Yet it is not enough simply to reform the S&T sector in isolation. There must be sufficient demand, or pull, from the production sector to provide the stimulus and incentives for the S&T sector to undertake the kind of research that is necessary for the nation's economic needs. This means that success is ultimately dependent on effective reform of the economic sector as a whole.

Within the economic sector, the major problem is whether or not a successful reform of the urban industrial sector can be carried out. While rural reform has resulted in remarkable increases in both output and productivity, industrial reform has been a stop-go affair with consequently a far more limited impact. The success of the rural reforms has provided ammunition for those who wished to introduce much more wide-sweeping changes into the urban sector. In fact, as Bernstein has indicated, the centralised industrial system has not been able properly to meet the needs of the 'increasingly commercialised decentralised agriculture'.[16]

The need for reform was recognised by the October 1984 Central Committee 'Decision on Reform of the Economic Structure'.[17] This Decision chronicles the problems of the overcentralised industrial economy noting that 'defects in the urban economic sector . . . seriously hinder the development of the forces of production'. The measures proposed offered a more thoroughgoing reform than the piecemeal experimentation that had previously taken place. The Decision recognised that the 'new technological revolution had made vital the need for reform with its provision of new opportunities and challenges to economic growth. According to the Decision 'our economic structure must become better able to utilise the latest scientific and technological achievements, promoting scientific and technological advancement and generating new forces of production. Reform, therefore, is all the more imperative'.[18]

For the purposes of this study, two aspects of the urban reform programme are of particular significance. First, managers of factories and enterprises are to be given greater powers of decision making with respect to production plans and marketing, sources of supply, distribution of profits within the enterprise and hiring and firing of personnel. In part, the extension of this reform throughout the system is related to the replacement of the system of requisition of profits, or covering losses, by a taxation system. These managers will be expected to take advantage of the new opportunities provided by the extension of the market. The second reform is that of the pricing system to ensure that the market, as far as is possible, is a rational one.

While price reform is recognised in the Decision as the 'key to reform of the entire economic structure', an extremely cautious approach to the problem is suggested and progress to date has been slow. For the reform programme to work successfully, the price system must be overhauled, yet China's leaders fear the potential unrest caused by such an overhaul.

It is too early to state how successful the urban industrial reform programme will prove to be but the experience of other state-socialist societies is varied and not, on the whole, encouraging. Tremendous political will, coupled with good economic results, is necessary to sustain the reform momentum. While a reversal of the direction is highly improbable, a stop-go process is a more likely outcome, with spurts of activity being followed by temporary halts as results are assessed and ways are sought to try to deal with problems that arise.

In broad outlines, the measures are similar to the Liberman reforms introduced in the Soviet Union in the early sixties. The worst scenario would be that the reform programme gets bogged down, losing impetus through bureaucratic inertia. This could produce a system as in the Soviet Union, where administrative control and centralisation remain dominant. It will take a major change in thinking for state organs to adjust to their more withdrawn role and for enterprise managers to exert fully their new entrepreneurial functions. Cadres will not easily be persuaded to relinquish their power over economic affairs and, at present, China simply does not have enough people trained to exploit properly the market opportunities that do exist. According to the Decision, a new generation of cadres and competent managerial personnel is to be trained and, moreover, a reshuffling of leadership in enterprises, especially key enterprises, was to be completed before the end of 1985.[19] A more successful scenario would see China's industrial economy evolve in the direction of the more market-oriented economy of Hungary.

Full implementation of the reform programme will also depend on whether opponents can gather sufficient strength to halt them. While disgruntled bureaucrats may be able to frustrate the policies, there does not seem to be sufficient opposition at the centre, particularly since the removal of leaders of the People's Liberation Army at the special Party Congress in September 1985. This is not to suggest that there are no disagreements, indeed the present policies give cause for quite sharp disagreements over questions of speed and extent of reform. In fact the Decision on the reform of the urban economy can be read as a compromise document between those who seek gradual reform at the margins and those who seek more wide-ranging reforms.

Two main aspects of disagreement can be identified. First, there are those who are worried on economic grounds and these include veteran leader Chen Yun. Chen and others are worried about the destabilising effect of pushing the reforms too far too fast. They have criticised the over-reliance on the market and are worried about the 'over-heating' of the economy caused partly by the rapid growth of the rural industrial sector. They fear that current policies will deepen regional inequalities between China's poor hinterland and its more advanced coastal regions. Finally, they are concerned about the mushrooming of corruption that has sprung up as a result of the more liberalised policies and increased contacts with the West.[20] On this last concern, they are joined by a second group who are worried about the impact of the 'open door' policy on the socio-political fabric of China. The rise in corruption and the appearance of 'decadent bourgeois thinking' and 'practices' are attributed by these people to increased contacts with the West. As in the nineteenth century, China wants Western technology but wishes to divorce it from the social, economic and political matrix in which it is produced. To date, when forced to choose between closing the door to prevent such contamination or keeping it open to make sure that advanced technology comes in, Deng Xiaoping has been able to find a majority for the latter. The difference, thus, is more concentrated on the extent of the reforms and unwanted side effects than on the question of reform as a whole. Indeed, given the massive population that China will have to support by the year 2000, there seems to be very little alternative to continuing with the experimentation. Also, the popularity of the reforms with the majority of the Chinese makes it difficult for the process to be reversed.

The Party and the Scientists

As important as the success of the economic reforms is whether the Party can create an atmosphere that is conducive to scientific research. Party policy now gives the highest priority to the development of S&T and to facilitate this the Party has accepted the fact that it must withdraw from its overdominant position, allowing scientists and technicians greater freedom within their areas of professional competence. It has been stated that 'without democracy, there can be no science' and that 'science and culture cannot develop without free discussion'.[21] These sentiments reached their peak during the years 1979-1981, but in 1981 the Party clearly decided that some guidance was necessary, thus indicating that its commitment to science was conditional.

This raises, in this particular context, the classic dilemma of democratic centralism; how much freedom and autonomy should be given to the scientists and how much guidance and control should come from the Party. As in the Soviet Union, the heavy hand of Party control is an impediment to the development of an atmosphere conducive to scientific discovery and technical innovation. Kneen has remarked that in the Soviet Union, the Party's centralised structure and authoritarian style 'renders it incompatible with many aspects of the working situation it claims to supervise'.[22]

This situation is exacerbated by the fact that the Party professes to be the only organisation in society capable of defining the correct strategy for the attainment of communism. Yet the current leadership has chosen a strategy that relies heavily on the advice of those with scarce professional skills, skills that are conspicuously absent within the Party itself. With respect to the natural sciences, the Party accepts that questions of enquiry have a universal character, yet the scientists themselves are seen to belong to different social systems and thus subject to varying responsibilities. Further, while topics may be seen to have a universal character, the scientists' participation in the international scientific community is still seen as a reward for good work done and a reflection of their political reliability, rather than as a necessary part of their work.

The granting of greater freedom to scientists, the stress on the need for technical expertise and giving more autonomy to research institutes have called into question what overall Party control within the institute really means. In many instances, the members of the Party committee lack the detailed technical knowledge to be able to provide meaningful guidance to the institute's work. One Chinese writer poses the question of what Party control of cadres will actually mean in research institutes that have carried out reforms. He points out that, in the past, although the director assumed responsibility, the Party committee had the power to transfer cadres and assign them jobs. He then asks how the Party can control the cadres under the present circumstances where the director has the power to pick his or her own staff.[23]

If the Party wishes to continue with the current policy, it can employ one or more of three options. First, the Party can place more technically qualified people in leadership positions; secondly, it can attempt to upgrade the technical knowledge of existing Party members; and thirdly, the Party can recruit more scientists and technicians into the Party. At present, all three of the options are being promoted against considerable opposition from the existing Party cadres at the basic levels. Referring to the criticism of intellectuals during the Cultural Revolution, Orleans notes that 'ten years of propaganda had done its work'.[24] To this can be added the traditional resentment of intellectuals and, most importantly, the fear of Party cadres that an increase in the power of scientists and technicians in the institutes and enterprises will mean a corresponding decrease in their own power.

In China, the tendency in all organisations is to push decision making on even the most trivial of matters to the highest levels. The potentially adverse consequences of making an incorrect decision have far outweighed the potential gains of displaying initiative. In practice, this has meant referring all decisions to the Party committee. This not only means that Party committees become overloaded with matters that are not their proper concern but also that, with respect to technical matters, the quality of decision making is badly affected as committee members do not necessarily possess the requisite skills and information to handle them properly. To deal with this problem, calls have been made to appoint more experts to run research institutes and enterprises. For example, in November 1984 Premier Zhao, during an inspection tour, said that 'people with expertise' should run factories. He envisaged a situation where each factory would be led by a group of experts working under a 'good director' with full power to appoint suitably qualified personnel to posts under his or her leadership.[25] However, Zhao and other leaders are not seeing their wishes fulfilled. According to one report, 'in particular, the views of scientific and technical cadres on professional work, technology and employment issues often cannot gain respect and acceptance'.[26]

Within research institutions and other work units, there are clearly cases of conflicts emerging between cadres who owe their position to their political and administrative skills at working the old system and those who derive their power from their detailed technical knowledge. While those with technical skills push for greater autonomy, many administrative cadres have fought to exert greater control over the enterprise's work in order to maintain their own position. Even in situations where those with the necessary professional knowledge get into leadership positions, they will not necessarily have the power to implement their policies. As a last resort, a Party secretary can always invoke the ultimate authority of the Party to ensure getting his or her own way.

A case concerning a pharmaceuticals plant in Yangcheng City, Jiangsu province, gives a graphic example of this tendency. When an engineer was appointed manager he insisted that the plant must first test raw alcohol before using it in drugs. However, this was objected to by the Party Branch secretary who 'forcibly used' the alcohol without testing it. According to the report, he beat his breast saying 'I am responsible'. The result was that 80,000 bottles of cough mixture were ruined with a loss of 30,000 *yuan*.[27] Apparently, in Yangcheng City the phenomenon of intellectuals having leading posts but not being able to exercise proper authority was widespread. According to a survey conducted about intellectuals in leadership positions, 57.1 were said to be able to basically play their part, 28.2 could perform it only partially while 14.1 had had their 'enthusiasm stifled' and 'found it hard to work properly'. It is anyone's guess what these categories really mean but they do imply that a large percentage of skilled personnel is prevented from making a full contribution.

To tackle this problem, the Party is trying to upgrade the educational level of its existing members and is hoping to recruit more intellectuals. This enables it to exercise more realistic supervision over technical work and, in the eyes of others, makes it appear more capable of managing the modernisation programme. The ideal situation is that of the CAS, where the President, Lu Jiaxi, is both a highly respected professional *and* a Party member. This serves the dual function of subordinating the leading functionary of the CAS to the Party and of making sure that the Party receives better advice to aid its decision making.

The Party, however, does not possess a sufficient number of qualified members to make this the norm. Despite concentration since the end of 1978 on recruiting more intellectuals into the Party, the general education level remains low and obstacles persist with the implementation of this policy. According to statistics for the end of 1983, only 17.8% of the 40.95 million Party members had received education above senior-middle school level, while 52.2% of the membership was said to be still illiterate.[28] Only 4% of the membership had received a college education and Party members represented only 1% of all college students.[29] A November 1984 forum of the Organisation Department of the Central Committee called for this situation to be changed. It was remarked that:

> It is strategically important to recruit large numbers of outstanding intellectuals already qualified for membership into the Party so as to change its composition, to give it thousands of trained personnel who have mastered scientific subjects and to build the Party into a core of leadership for China's socialist modernisation.[30]

The Party's definition that intellectuals are an integral part of the working class and that many are thereby qualified for Party membership is clearly not accepted by all. Party cadres have moved to block applications for membership for precisely the same reasons that some have tried to keep intellectuals out of leadership positions - the fear that vested interests will be undermined. It is not simply due to the remnants of 'leftist thinking' as it is depicted in the Chinese press. Party cadres, jealous of intellectuals' possession of specialised knowledge, have tried to keep them out of the Party for fear that, should they join, the current policies will mean that their careers will advance more rapidly. By keeping them out of the Party, administrative cadres ensure that ultimate authority will rest in their own hands.

Thus there have been reports that some Party members have the attitude that 'if intellectuals are promoted to leading posts and then join the Party, they will have all the best jobs'. This results in the blocking of applications or putting qualified intellectuals on to unlimited probation periods while their 'complicated' family backgrounds are investigated.[31] Some Party cadres are said to think in the following terms, 'While you have an education, I have the Party membership in my hands. While you have knowledge, I have qualifications and record of service. No matter how capable you may be, as long as you are not admitted into the Party, you will remain under my leadership'.[32]

The number of press reports dealing with the fact that policies on intellectuals are not being properly implemented testifies to the scale of the problem. For example, in Henan province, between February 1984 and April 1985, the Party office for implementing the policies towards intellectuals received 5,000 letters reporting problems and interviewed some 1,800 people.[33] Consequently, the press has also paid attention to cases where Party cadres have been punished for their opposition to the policy. Thus, the Deputy Director of the Fengfeng Coal Mining Bureau in Hebei province, the Party Secretary of a Grassland Work Team in Gansu province and a Party Branch Secretary in a Jilin Chemical Fertiliser Plant have all been removed from their posts because of what is termed their deliberate obstruction of applications by intellectuals for Party membership.[34]

Despite these reported problems, more intellectuals are joining the Party and, while their total numbers remain small, intellectuals are over-represented in the Party if viewed in terms of their percentage of the population as a whole. Provincial and national figures indicate this trend and also show that the recruitment of intellectuals has been gathering pace since the Third Plenum of the Eleventh Central Committee (December 1978). In Beijing municipality in 1979, it was stated that 15% of new recruits that year were intellectuals[35] while in 1982 it was reported that from 1979 to 1982, 20% of new recruits were intellectuals. This trend gathered further momentum in 1984-1985. In 1984, in Guangdong province, 14,400 intellectuals with college or vocational secondary school education joined the Party, an increase of 130% over 1983.[36] In the Municipality of Shanghai, of those recruited between January and May 1985, 67% (13,624) had received education at or above technical secondary school level. Of the new members, 31.7% were described as having 'various professional skills'.[37]

Nationally compiled figures tell the same story. In the period between December 1978 and October 1984, the number of Party members recruited from among 'specialised personnel and skilled workers of various trades and professions' progressively increased to a total of 580,000. Not including recruits within the military, the proportion of the total recruited described as being 'specialised personnel and skilled workers of various trades and professions' has increased from 8.3% in 1978, to 23.6% in 1982 and 27% in 1983.[38] The co-option of intellectuals from central government departments and Party organs has also been taking place. A report in mid-1984 said that since the end of 1979, 6,887 'specialists and technicians' had been admitted to the Party, 53% of the total admitted.[39]

The Party now clearly recognises the importance of intellectuals, and scientists and technicians in particular, to the modernisation programme. This is reflected in their co-option in increasingly large numbers into the Party and in attempts to appoint more to leadership positions. The effect of this on the Party over the long term is unclear. With respect to the Soviet Union and Eastern Europe, it is often postulated that the Party is, or will turn into, little more than a pragmatic, technocratic machine managing the state. A similar scenario is now postulated for China. However, the recruitment of scientists and technicians into the Soviet Communist Party has still not fundamentally changed its nature and there is no reason to expect a different outcome in China. It will, of course, change the social composition of the Party with a smaller industrial worker membership but then the Chinese Party has never been a genuinely proletarian Party. However, the co-option of the scientific élite will give it more direct access to the decision making process, turning it into a powerful lobby group. It will also enable the Party to make better technically informed decisions. Yet, if the current policy line continues, more varied channels of career advancement will open up independent of Party membership. It may well be that many scientists and technicians will not be interested in taking on the extra burdens, and risks, of Party membership. If this proves to be the case, the Party might well find itself faced with a crucial group developing its work independent of direct Party control. It remains to be seen whether the Party will continue to grant this group such autonomy especially if it develops ideas hostile to the Party's monopoly of power and its theoretical monopoly of the truth.

Concluding Comments: China's Science and Technology Policy

Since 1949, the PRC has, despite political disruptions, built up a comprehensive S&T system that would be the envy of most developing countries. However, it is not without considerable problems and has proved inadequate to play the role which China's leaders expect from it. This has caused the need for reform and this study has focused on the key areas of organisation, finance and personnel, and has indicated that ultimate success depends on successful reform of the economy as a whole and on the Party creating and maintaining an attitude conducive to research.

The measures introduced have shifted the S&T system away from the Soviet model on which it was based in the fifties in the direction that evolved, not surprisingly, in the Soviet Union and Eastern Europe. Moreover, in broad outline, the policies and priorities now being pursued resemble those not only of other developing countries but also those of the more technologically advanced nations.[40]

First, there is a clear recognition of the important role that S&T plays in achieving economic and social objectives. This recognition is reinforced by China's awakening to the 'new technological revolution'. The realisation of the integral link between scientific discovery, technical innovation and economic growth has led to calls for a closer integration of plans for S&T development with those for economic and social development.

Secondly, it is clearly seen that S&T development cannot take place in isolation but needs to be properly linked with the broader society. Thus, reforms have been introduced in the organisational sphere to expand the horizontal links between the research, production, ministerial and military sectors. The creation of such links, it is hoped, will ensure that the technology being developed is actually needed and that the time it takes for research results to find their way into production can be cut drastically. By trying to break down the organisational barrier between the military and civilian research sectors, it is hoped that fuller use can be made of the more advanced military sector and the better qualified people who work in it to develop the civilian sector. To improve innovation, measures have been introduced to try to strengthen the industrial research and development sectors. The result of these policies has been to cause concentration on applied and developmental research sometimes at the expense of basic research.

Thirdly, it is recognised that China needs a much larger and better qualified S&T contingent as well as a higher general educational level among the population as a whole. Staffing the bureaucracy, research institutes and enterprises with sufficiently qualified personnel remains a major stumbling block to ensuring that correct policies are devised and properly implemented. The inadequacy of financing and the lack of sufficiently qualified personnel mean that China must pursue both a quantitative and a qualitative approach to developing the S&T sector.

Fourthly, China now recognises that a closer involvement with the international S&T community is necessary if its own capabilities are to be developed quickly enough. However, the failure of the large-scale technology import policy of the seventies to provide rapid technological development has caused China's leaders to have a more realistic perception of the role that technology transfer plays in advancing the indigenous S&T system. In fact, they have realised that a prior necessity is, in fact, a well developed indigenous system that can scan recent developments and select those most beneficial to China's current needs. China's continued dependence on technology import adds a further external constraint to its S&T development. Its success in attaining foreign technology will depend on export controls of Western countries and its continued good relations with these countries, especially the USA. This can make China a hostage to forces outside its control as exports to it may depend on the political climate and prevailing opinion within foreign countries. An example of this type of problem occurred in December 1985 when the US Senate voted to attach stricter conditions to the nuclear trade agreement with China than the Reagan administration, and the Chinese, had intended.[41]

Fifthly, the need to improve spending on S&T has been recognised. Fortunately, in this respect, China's leaders have appreciated that there is no high level of correlation between the amount of money thrown at the S&T sector and a markedly improved performance by that sector. Thus the attempts to increase the amount of money made available by the state and to open up more channels for S&T funding have been accompanied by reforms to try to make sure that the funds are used more effectively than in the past.

Sixthly, the PRC has realised that the S&T sector cannot be over-administered but that, at the same time, it cannot be left to its own devices. This has resulted in an attempt to find an appropriate balance between central control and delegation of powers. Thus, scientists and research institutes have been granted more autonomy over their work than at any other time since the founding of the PRC. However, in 1981 it was clearly recognised that this autonomy must take place within a general framework laid down by the central authorities. Coupled with the decentralising of powers there has been the creation of new central bodies such as the Science and Technology Leading Group and the Leading Group for Development of Computers and Large-Scale Integrated Circuits to devise and monitor policy implementation in crucial areas. While this is a rational development, elsewhere the continued reliance on the central bureaucracy will have, as Simon correctly points out,[42] its costs in terms of perpetuating inter-ministerial conflict and stifling initiative.

Finally, the process of reform has led to the realisation that much greater attention must be paid to the process of S&T development itself. Not only is it intended that more studies be carried out on the quality, effectiveness and relevance of S&T work in China and its organisation but also on the processes of scientific discovery and on the likely impact of new developments on China's economic and socio-political fabric.

Despite these recognitions and the introduction of measures based on them, the ultimate success of China's S&T reforms in providing what the leadership wants will depend on two external factors. First, the reform of the urban industrial economy must provide the necessary 'pull' to ensure that the appropriate research is undertaken and the necessary technologies developed. Secondly, the Party must ensure that an atmosphere that encourages the research environment is created. Progress has been made in this direction to date, but whether this progress can be maintained and built upon will, to a major degree, determine the ultimate success or failure of the reform of the S&T sector.

Notes

1   For a further discussion of this point see T Saich, *The Chinese Communist Party: The Search for a Suitable Form*. Working Paper no 31 (Amsterdam: University of Amsterdam, 1983), pp 1-3.

2   K Kautsky, *The Political Consequences of Modernisation* (New York: Wiley, 1971).

3   G White, 'Revolutionary Socialist Development in the Third World: An Overview', in G White, R Murray and C White (eds), *Revolutionary Socialist Development in the Third World* (Brighton: Wheatsheaf Books, 1983), p 32. According to White, the phase of 'bureaucratic voluntarism' occurs after the revolution has taken place and when it is becoming 'institutionalised'. An increasingly complex bureaucracy develops that attempts to stimulate and oversee rapid economic development.

4   M Korzec and T Saich, *The Chinese Economy: New Light on Old Questions*. Working Paper no 28 (Amsterdam: University of Amsterdam, 1983), p 16.

5   Deng Xiaoping, 'Sixteenth January Report on the Current Situation', *Cheng Ming*, no 29, 1980, translated in *SWB:FE* 6363.

6   Initially the tremendous surge in agricultural productivity derived from the realising of potential by relaxing constraints on the peasants and introducing organisational reforms such as the use of the production responsibility system. However, it is clear that any further major improvements will have to be brought about by reliance on better inputs and the adoption of more advanced techniques.

7   D F Simon, 'Science and Technology Reforms', *The China Business Review*, March–April 1985, p 31.
8   For a discussion of this point see R Volti, 'Science and Technology in Communist Systems: Introduction', *Studies in Comparative Communism*, vol xv, nos 1 and 2, pp 3–8.
9   Quoted in P M Cocks, *Science Policy in the Soviet Union* (Washington DC: Government Printing Office, 1980), p 2.
10 Ibid, p 3.
11 Yang Weizhe and Gan Shijun, 'Erlinglinglingnian zhongguo de kexue jishu' ('China's Science and Technology in the Year 2000'), *Jingji Ribao (Economic Daily)*, 11 November 1985, p 4.
12 See for example, A King and A Lemma, 'Science and Technology for Development', in M Goldsmith and A King (eds), *Issues of Development: Towards a New Role for Science and Technology* (Oxford: Pergamon Press, 1979), pp 20–22.
13 P N Cocks, *Science Policy in the Soviet Union*, p 136.
14 Quoted in P N Cocks, *Coupling Science with Production: The Architecture of Linkage*, Typed Manuscript, p 2-1.
15 'Hungarian Official Criticises Comecon', *International Herald Tribune*, 27 June 1985.
16 T P Bernstein, 'China in 1984: The Year of Hong Kong', *Asian Survey*, vol xxv, no 1, 1985, p 38.
17 See 'Decision of the Central Committee of the Communist Party of China on Reform of the Economic Structure', *BR*, no 44, 29 October 1984, pp i-xvi.
18 Ibid, p iv.
19 'Decision of the Central Committee of the Communist Party of China on Reform of the Economic Structure', p xiv.
20 See for example, Chen Yun, 'Zai zhongguo gongchangdang quanquo daibiao huiyishang de jianghua' ('Speech at the National Conference of the Chinese Communist Party'), *RMRB*, 24 September 1985, p 2; Chen Yun, 'Combating Corrosive Ideology', Speech at the Sixth Plenary Session of the Central Commission for Discipline Inspection, 24 September 1985, *BR*, no 41, 14 October 1985, pp 15-16; and *RMRB*, 4 October 1985.
21 Zhang Wen, 'Social Sciences: A Hundred Schools of Thought Contend', *BR*, no 14, 6 April 1979, p 10.
22 P Kneen, *Soviet Scientists and the State* (Basingstoke: Macmillan Press, 1984), pp 103-104.
23 Yang Peiqing, 'Jingji tizhi gaige he keji jinbu' ('Reform of the Economic System and Scientific and Technological Progress'), *KXX*, no 1, 1985, p 12.
24 L Orleans, *The Training and Utilisation of Scientific and Engineering Manpower in the People's Republic of China* (Washington DC: US Government Printing Office, 1983), p 6.
25 'Zhao Says Experts Should Run Factories', *CD*, 17 November 1984, p 3.
26 Sun Jian and Zhu Weiqun, 'Dangqian luoshi zhishi fenzi zhengce qingkuang jiujing ruhe? Jiangsu sheng de diaocha biaoming: "zuo" de yingxiang wangu, wenti yuanwei jiejue' ('What is the Current Situation in Implementing Policies on Intellectuals? An Investigation of Jiangsu Province Shows that "Leftist" Influences Stubbornly Persist and the Problem is Far from a Solution'), *RMRB*, 8 July 1984, p 3.
27 Ibid.
28 'More Intellectuals Should be Admitted as Party Members', *CD*, 16 January 1985, p 4.
29 'CPC to Recruit More Intellectuals', *BR*, no 49, 3 December 1984, p 10.
30 Ibid.

31 Sun Jian and Zhu Weiqun, 'Dangqian luoshi zhishi fenzi zhengce qingkuang jiujing
    ruhe? Jiangsu sheng de diaocha biaoming: "zuo" de yingxiang wangu, wenti
    yuanwei jiejue', p 3.
32 Cao Zhi, 'Cong zhanlüe gaodu kandai youxiu zhishi fenzi rudang wenti' ('Assess
    from the High Plain of Strategy the Question of Recruiting Party Members from
    Among Outstanding Intellectuals'), *Hongqi (Red Flag)*, no 23, 1984, p 18.
33 *SWB:FE* 7938.
34 'CPC to Recruit More Intellectuals', p 11.
35 'Why a Part of the Working Class?', *BR*, no 13, 31 March 1980, p 24.
36 *SWB:FE* 7933.
37 Ibid.
38 Cao Zhi, 'Cong zhanlüe gaodu kandai youxiu zhishi fenzi rudang wenti', p 16.
39 This report said that they were recruited from Party and state organs at the central
    level. This would mean that not all those working in such Party organs are Party
    members. 'Communist Party Increases Members', *BR*, no 29, 16 July 1984, p 7.
40 For an interesting comparison of S&T policy in the PRC and Taiwan see D F
    Simon, 'Chinese-style S&T Modernisation: A Comparison of PRC and Taiwan
    Approaches', *Studies in Comparative Communism*, vol xvii, no 2, 1984, pp 87-109. A
    study of five West European countries shows a remarkable similarity in their science
    and technology policies to those in China. See L Lederman, 'Science and
    Technology in Europe: A Survey', *Science and Public Policy*, vol 12, no 3, 1985,
    pp 131-143.
41 'Senate Restricts China Pact', *International Herald Tribune*, 11 December 1985, p 1.
42 D F Simon, 'Chinese-style Modernisation: A Comparison of PRC and Taiwan
    Approaches', p 109.

APPENDIX

Decision of the Central Committee of the Communist Party of China Concerning Reform of the Science and Technology Management System (Translated from 'Zhonggong zhongyang guanyu kexue jishu tizhi gaige de jueding', *RMRB*, 20 March 1985, pp 1, 3.)
(13 March 1985)

Following the gradual development of the reform of the urban and rural economic systems, it is necessary to reform correspondingly the S&T system. This is a major question having a vital bearing on our nation's modernisation programme as a whole. Thus, the Central Committee made the following decision.

One

The Chinese people are carrying out the great cause of socialist modernisation. By the end of this century, we must realise the task laid down by the Twelfth Party Congress of quadrupling the gross annual value of industrial and agricultural production and, moreover, make China's economy approach the level of the world's developed countries within a period of 30 to 50 years, and enable people's living standards to attain a relatively high level. The invigoration of the economy and the realisation of the Four Modernisations are the central task of the whole Party and the whole people. S&T work must closely focus on and serve this central task.

Modern S&T are the most dynamic and decisive factors of the new social productive forces. Following the vigorous development of the world's new technological revolution, S&T have daily permeated the various aspects of material and spiritual life of society. They have become an important source for raising the level of labour productivity and an important foundation stone in building a modern, spiritual civilisation. While building socialist modernisation, the whole Party must attach great importance to, and bring into full play, the tremendous role of S&T.

During the last 35 years, our nation's numerous S&T personnel have displayed the spirit of dedicating themselves to their cause and, through self-reliance and close co-ordination and by overcoming difficulties, have made an important contribution to socialist construction. Our nation's S&T undertakings have witnessed great developments and have accumulated a great deal of successful experience. However, we must realise that the S&T system that has gradually taken shape over a long period of time has serious defects mot only with respect to S&T work serving economic construction but also with respect to turning S&T achievements quickly into productive capacity. Making full use of the intelligence and creativity of S&T personnel has been hampered, thus making it difficult for S&T to meet objective needs.

In accordance with the strategic principle that economic construction must rely on S&T work and S&T work must serve economic construction, we must respect the laws of S&T development and, proceeding from our nation's actual situation, resolutely and gradually reform the S&T management system.

The most important contents of the current reform of the S&T management system are: in the field of operations, it is necessary to reform the funding system, open up the technology market, and overcome the bad practices of relying solely on administrative measures to manage S&T work and of the state exercising excessive and inflexible control. At the same time as implementing the planned management of the state's key projects, it is necessary to use economic levers and market regulation, to enable scientific institutions to develop their own capabilities and give the vitality to serve economic construction on their own initiative. With respect to organisational structure, it is necessary to change the situation where too many research institutions are separated from enterprises; where research, design and education are separated from production; where the military and civilian sectors are separated; and where departments and districts are separated from one another. Efforts must be made to strengthen greatly the enterprises' capability to absorb and develop technology and strengthen intermediate links in the transformation of technological achievements into productive capacity, promote co-ordination and integration among research and design institutions, institutions of higher education and enterprises, and, moreover, bring into being a rational S&T force in all fields. With respect to the personnel system, it is necessary to overcome the influence of 'Leftist' thinking, eliminate the situaion in which S&T personnel are subjected to too many restrictions, talented personnel cannot move rationally, and intellectual work is not given its due recognition. This will create conditions favourable to the training of a large number of talented people and using them in the best fashion.

Two

Reform the system of allocating funds to research institutes and, in accordance with the characteristics of different S&T activities, implement varying methods for managing funds.

For a given period of time, central and local S&T allocations should increase gradually at a rate higher than the growth of regular financial revenues. At the same time, other financial sources should be explored and departments, enterprises and mass organisations should be encouraged to invest in S&T.

With respect to major S&T research and development projects and the construction of key laboratories and experimental bases included in the central or local plans, funding will come from central or local allocations.

Planning and management must also make use of economic levers and respect the law of value, and introduce gradually, management methodssuch as public bidding and the contract system.

With respect to technology development work, and applied research work promising immediate practical benefits, a technological contract system should be introduced gradually. Independent research institutes primarily engaged in this sort of work should, in the process of providing economic benefits for society, earn income and accumulate funds through such methods as contracting for state planned projects, accepting research entrusted by other units, transferring technological achievements, running joint ventures in development, forming joint operations for exporting, and providing consultancy services. Operating expenses allocated by the state must gradually be reduced so that within three to five years' time the vast majority of this kind of research institute will be basically self-reliant for operating funds. Money saved from the reduction in operating expenses will be used by the state for the development of S&T.

For basic research, and some applied research, a science foundation system will gradually be introduced on a trial basis. This will rely primarily on state budgetary allocations. A national natural science foundation and other science and technology foundations will be established and, in accordance with the state S&T development plan, be geared to the needs of society. It will receive applications from all sectors, to be assessed by peer group review, selecting those most suitable for support. Institutions primarily engaged in this sort of research work should strive to ensure that after a few years they primarily rely on applications to such foundations for their scientific expenses, with the state providing only a fixed amount for operating expenses to guarantee necessary day-to-day expenses and public facilities expenditures.

With respect to research institutes engaged in medicine and public health, labour protection, family planning, disaster prevention and control, environmental science and other public welfare undertakings, and institutes engaged in information services, standardisation, meteorology, monitoring and surveying and other S&T services and technological basic work, they will still receive state allocations and implement a system of responsibility for their expenditures.

For high level technological development that involves rapid change and relatively high risks, new enterprise investment funds may be established for support.

Funding sources for institutions engaged in many different kinds of research work can, according to their specific conditions, be resolved by channels provided for in the regulations of the state capital construction management system.

Banks should actively launch S&T credit work and carry out supervision and management of the use of S&T operating funds.

Three

Promote the commercialisation of technical achievements, and expand the technology market, in order to suit the development of the socialist commodity economy.

S&T are primarily the product of human intellectual labour and the value thus created must be fully recognised and evaluated. Following the development of S&T, technology is playing a greater and greater role in creating society's commodity values. More and more technologies have already become independent commodities in the form of knowledge and a new knowledge industry has already appeared. The technology market is an important component part of our nation's socialist commodity market.

Through the expansion of the technology market and the unblocking of the channels for the flow of technological achievements to production, we must change the practice of uncompensated transfer for technological achievements by purely administrative means. Changing the flow mechanism of the S&T system will help link up the economically beneficial relations of research institutes and production units, promote competition, quickly transform S&T needs of production into research projects, and ensure the speedy application of research achievements to production.

Attention should be paid to resolving questions concerning technological achievements, commodity production and economically beneficial results, and other aspects, in order to provide technological commodities to meet the needs of the technology market. It is necessary to develop actively the transfer of technology, job-contracting for technological work, technology consultancy, technology services and many other forms of technological trade activities. It is necessary to change the mistaken concept that holds management work in contempt. It is necessary to train talented people who know how to develop industry through the use of technological achievements, how to administer technological commodities and, moreover, suitably develop agencies to administer technological commodities. Essentially, the development of the technology market depends on the demands of the buyers, and thus we should adopt various measures to fire the enthusiasm of the enterprises for making use of new technology and increase the enterprises' economic ability to buy technological achievements.

It is necessary to formulate relevant laws, regulations and a system to protect the legal rights of buyers, sellers and go-betweens. With the promulgation by the state of the patent law and other relevant laws and regulations, intellectual property rights are protected. The utilisation of taxes and administrative methods provides a limited protection for the domestic technology market. The market price for technological achievements will be fixed through negotiations between both parties to the transaction and the state will not impose restrictions. For the time being, income for the transfer of technological achievements will be exempt from taxation. New products may enjoy preferential treatment, such as tax reduction or exemption for a given period of time. Units with particular technological achievements may adopt the method of entering into partnerships with enterprises by contributing the technology. Technology development institutes and enterprises can reward personnel directly engaged in development work with a part of the income from the transfer of technological achievements.

S&T personnel, on the condition that they fulfil their primary work tasks and that there is no encroachment on the technolgical and economic rights and interests of their unit, may engage in spare time technological work and consultancy services. For such work they are entitled to payment. If they make use of the technological achievements, data and equipment, they must have their unit's approval and hand over part of the income derived to the unit.

If the achievement is worth popularisation, but not suitable for commercialisation or compensated transfer, the state and the departments concerned in the society will organise the popularisation of a useful technological achievement and reward appropriately the producer of the achievement.

Four

It is necessary to readjust the S&T system, encourage co-operation between research, education and design institutes with production units and enhance capability of enterprises for technological application and development.

Technology development institutes under the Chinese Academy of Sciences, institutions of higher education, the central ministries and commissions and the local authorities should be encouraged to set up various forms of partnership with enterprises and design institutes on a voluntary, and mutually beneficial basis. Some of these partnerships may gradually become economic entities. Some, on the basis of the co-operation, may become enterprises merged with research institutes or vice versa. Some research institutes may, voluntarily, develop themselves into research and production type enterprises, or associated technology development organs of medium and small sized enterprises. This kind of unit is permitted to set aside a certain percentage of the newly increased portion of profits as technology development funds.

While emphasising the partnership between research institutes and enterprises, attention should be paid to important intermediate and long term research and development for production. The departments and units concerned should adopt some necessary economic readjustment measures to support the institutes and personnel engaged in such research work.

While fully relying on S&T forces in society, enterprises should actively improve and strengthen their own technology development capability. They should bring effectively into play the backbone role of skilled technical workers and carry out mass technical innovation. Large key enterprises should gradually improve their own technology development departments, or research institutes. Suitable medium and small sized enterprises may also have their own necessary technology development forces. In particular, enterprises' technology development work should attach importance to the development of new products, intermediate tests, productive tests and to the solution of technological and equipment problems concerning quality, reliability, economy and the ratio of up-to-standard products in industrial production.

Enterprises may, in accordance with the relevant regulations, apportion, by stages, technology development funds into production costs. They may also apply to banks for credit loans for technology development. For special needs, they may, in accordance with state regulations, retain a part of the pre-tax profits for technology development funds. Efforts made to rely on technological progress to improve economic efficiency must be seen as an important criterion for evaluating enterprises.

Defence scientific research institutes must establish a new system of army-people co-operation. While guaranteeing the fulfilment of national defence tasks, they should serve economic construction, accelerate the transfer of military technological achievements to civilian use, and energetically engage in the development of products for civilian use.

In order to speed up the development of new industries, it is necessary to select some regions in China where there is a concentration of intellectual resources, adopt special policies for them and gradually turn them into new industrial development zones with different characteristics.

Five

It is necessary to reform the agricultural S&T system to make it help with re-adjustment of the rural economic structure and promote rural economic change in the direction of specialisation, commercialisation and modernisation.

In order to conduct large scale agricultural development projects or regional development projects, governments, at all levels, should break down the barriers between departments and regions, implement a public bidding system and entrust the project to those with the best bids. All localities should develop various forms of co-operation with all aspects of S&T forces, centred on establishing commodity production bases for agriculture, forestry, animal husbandry, sideline occupations and fishery. Agricultural scientific research institutes and agricultural colleges of higher education, at and above the provincial level, should strengthen their co-operation, devote a relatively large force to engage in more advanced research and development work, and, moreover, establish demonstration bases for the comprehensive use of S&T achievements. It is necessary to encourage, and promote, S&T personnel and organisations of various occupations and trades in urban areas to supply all kinds of technological achievements, information and technological services to the rural areas.

Agricultural technology popularisation organisations must work closely with research institutes and institutions of higher education and strengthen their ties with village and township enterprises, all kinds of co-operation organisations, specialised households, model technological households and skilled craftspeople. They should also make use of the experience of selected units to enthusiastically provide good technological services for supply, production, storage, transport and processing and in the popularisation of new technology. A system of technological responsibilities with remuneration linked to economic efficiency should be implemented, or the method of collecting fees for technical services. This will mean that the income of technology popularisation organisations and

S&T personnel will follow peasants' incomes and gradually increase. Technology popularisation organisations and research institutes may set up enterprise-type economic entities. Operating funds for agricultural popularisation organisations and research institutes may still be received from the state and they should practise the contract responsibility system. Units with the necessary conditions must be encouraged and supported to become self-sufficient for their operating expenses.

Six

Scientific research must be completely and thoroughly and rationally arranged to ensure long term economic and S&T development.

While vigorously promoting technology development work, it is necessary to strengthen applied research and ensure the steady and continuous development of basic research work. With respect to the different kinds of research work, it is necessary to adopt different policies and criteria for appraisal.

Applied research is a necessary link in the process of transforming basic research achievements into practical technologies. It is of major significance for developing new technology and new industries, and transforming old production technologies. As our focus, projects should be selected that promise major benefits and we should pool labour power and material resources to achieve breakthroughs as quickly as possible.

Contemporary scientific development shows that major breakthroughs in basic research often open up new channels for technological development and that the timescale for basic research achievements becoming technologies is shortening day by day. Attention must be paid to basic research with good prospects for application, especially research related to the special characteristics of our nation's natural conditions and resources. With respect to research with no immediate possible applications, but that is valuable to the understanding of natural phenomena and the law of nature, it should also be supported in accordance with the financial situation. With respect to basic research achievements, they should be appraised primarily in terms of their academic significance and scientific standard.

Institutions of higher education, and the Chinese Academy of Sciences, shoulder a heavy responsibility with respect to basic and applied research. In accordance with their needs, research institutes of industrial departments must strengthen applied research. All groups must work closely together so that personnel can concurrently hold different posts, develop co-operative research, and set up joint laboratories and research institutes. Basic and applied research must be closely linked to personnel training. Institutions of higher education with the necessary conditions may also set up a few highly qualified research institutes with their own special characteristics.

Seven

The autonomy of research institutes should be enlarged and the macro-level management of S&T work by government organs should be improved.

Independent research institutes should serve society and operate as research and development entities with the initiative in their own hands. With the exception of research topics entrusted by the state and the appointment or hiring of the president or director by higher levels, research institutes, within the limits laid down by the state laws and regulations, will have autonomy of decision making on such matters as planning, expenses, personnel management and internal organisation. With the exception of operating funds allocated by higher levels, research institutes should use most of their net income for the development of their undertaking, with the remainder being allocated to collective welfare and rewards. This latter amount is to be determined by the extent to which the institutes have achieved self-reliance with respect to operating funds. Institutes that are already completely self-reliant with respect to operating funds may distribute bonuses and reform wage scales as prescribed by the State Council regulations for enterprises.

Research institutes will implement the system of the director taking full responsibility. Within each research institute, the role of S&T personnel must be fully respected and brought into play, various kinds of responsibility system established, and democratic management strengthened. In particular, it is necessary to increase the powers of project team leaders. Project teams may be composed of people hired by the team leader or through free association.

Party organisations of research institutes must, through ideological and political work, guarantee and supervise the implementation of various principles and policies, support the effective implementation of the system of the director taking full responsibility, and promote the development of S&T work. Party committee secretaries must have a certain level of scientific knowledge and education, be enthusiastic about S&T undertakings, and conscientiously implement the Party's policy on intellectuals.

Relevant ministries and commissions under the State Council should simplify their administration and delegate authority to lower levels, improve the process of decision making for S&T work and use system engineering and other modern administrative methods to improve macro-level management. S&T development plans and national economic plans must be properly co-ordinated and closely integrated. It is necessary to study and analyse the trend of S&T development and social demands and formulate development strategy and other relevant policies accordingly. It is necessary to organise and co-ordinate properly major S&T projects. It is necessary to strengthen supervision over statistics and set up an information network to promote the exchange of information.

Collectives and individuals should be permitted to set up scientific research or technological service organisations. Local governments should exercise control over them and give them guidance and assistance. If profit-making is the goal of such organisations, they should be registered with industrial and commercial departments.

Eight

Opening up to the outside world and establishing contacts with other countries is the basic, and long term, policy for developing S&T for our nation.

Our technological development work must change. The important role of technology import should be recognised for the development of production and the upgrading of existing enterprises. The special economic zones and coastal cities should take advantage of their favourable situation and take the lead in importing technology. When importing technology, great efforts must be made to integrate foreign trade with technology and industrial production. Importance should be attached to importing patents, technical knowledge, and software, and to expanding the various forms of international co-operation in development, design and manufacturing. Relevant research and development projects in China should be integrated closely with the import of technology. Imported advanced technology should be digested and absorbed in order to raise the level of development of production technology, to develop innovations and expand the capability of independent development. Technological development projects that have the potential to compete on the international market must be supported by policies so that they can be completed at the earliest date and be put on the international market.

It is necessary to make active efforts to expand international academic exchanges, help outstanding scientists and engineers participate in co-operative international research, increase the number of people studying, receiving advanced training, practice sessions abroad or participating in study tours, and invite foreign specialists and other scholars to work in our country. Conditions should be created so that those relatively advanced research institutes be opened to the outside world and visiting scholars from abroad should be invited to join co-operative research projects. It is necessary to develop an on-line computer information retrieval system tied into international systems, import more books on S&T, and speed up international exchanges of S&T information so that the nation can be quickly informed about trends in world S&T development.

Nine

It is necessary to reform the system of management for S&T personnel and create an excellent environment within which large numbers of qualified personnel can be trained and people given full scope to exploit their potential.

S&T personnel are the developers of new productive forces. It is necessary to train thousands and thousands of scientists and technicians who have socialist consciousness and who have a firm grasp of modern science, technology and technical knowledge. Full scope must be given to the role which they can play.

S&T experts of the older generation have made indelible contributions to China's S&T development. It is necessary to create energetically conditions for them so that they can continue to play a role in training personnel, guiding research, writing books, providing information and participating in various social activities.

It is necessary to go all out to reinforce academic and technical work by placing a large number of professionally trained and energetic middle-aged and young people in important positions. Full play should be given to the role of middle aged scientists and technicians in their forties and fifties, who are the backbone linking the past to the future. It is necessary to dare to support the most promising young people to show their talents.

It is necessary to appoint to leading positions, S&T personnel who have organisational and managerial ability in addition to inquisitive minds. The purpose of this is to change, as soon as possible, the serious situation of the aging of leading bodies of research institutes. It is also necessary to adopt measures to train a large number of administrators, of all types, who are knowledgeable about modern S&T, and management.

We must change the situation of holding back and wasting talented personnel and promote a rational flow of S&T personnel. At present, many medium sized and small cities are becoming increasingly prosperous, commodity production is developing vigorously in the vast countryside and many border areas, and areas where national minorities live in tight-knit communities are being developed. It is necessary to adopt all kinds of policies and preferential treatment, to encourage S&T personnel to work in those areas. Research and design institutes, and institutions of higher education, may gradually adopt a hiring system on an experimental basis. S&T personnel may take up appropriate second jobs, with the proviso that they have accomplished their own work. This will promote the exchange of knowledge and full play will be given to their potential.

We must make positive efforts to improve the work and living conditions of S&T personnel. The principle of 'from each according to his ability, to each according to his work' should be conscientiously implemented, egalitarianism should be fought, and problems of paying S&T personnel rationally should be resolved, gradually and effectively. It is necessary to set up a proper system governing spiritual and material rewards. Pay, awards and honours should be closely linked to individual contributions. Those who make major contributions should be generously rewarded.

Free exploration and discussion in academic disciplines must be guaranteed in order to attain the objective that scientists and technicians are really respected, thus enabling them to pursue the truth without fear. It is necessary to encourage specialists from all different schools of thought to make contributions while opposing the use of administrative means to obstruct academic freedom. Academic verity or fallacy can only be determined correctly by way of free discussion and practical examination. The so-called academic criticism of the past that used one point of view to suppress free discussion of differing viewpoints should not be allowed to occur again. Only if we do this, can we successfully integrate the S&T workers' sense of social responsibilities and ambitions with the requirements of the state, or give full play to the S&T workers' wisdom and creative spirit.

The reforms of the S&T system, and of the economic system, are intimately linked, yet they both have their own characteristics. Leading Party and government organs at all levels must give meticulous guidance to these reforms. The basic goals of the reform of the S&T system are to apply S&T achievements to production quickly and on a large scale, to bring the role of S&T workers into full play, to liberate greatly the productive forces of S&T, and to promote economic and social development. All reforms must aim at achieving these objectives and should not be diverted from these goals. During the reforms, it is necessary to rely fully on the conscious actions of S&T personnel, respect the innovations of basic-level units, earnestly sum up experiences, and promptly study ways in which to settle the new problems that appear during the process of reform. After a period of experimentation, all kinds of reform must be gradually popularised in accordance with different situations. It should not be expected that we can achieve quick results nor should the reforms be carried out by force. Major reforms affecting the whole situation will be planned by the State Council. Reform of the S&T system in the national autonomous regions and for the military should be organised and carried out in accordance with their situation. The Central Committee is deeply convinced that after having gone through several years of unceasing efforts, our nation can establish a new S&T system that will, moreover, be perfected in the course of implementataion and that the large numbers of S&T personnel will make, in the future, a glorious contribution to achieving the great cause of developing S&T, invigorating the economy and building a prosperous and affluent socialist society.

SOURCES

i) Journals

The following journals were used regularly for the research project:

> *Beijing Review* (formerly *Peking Review*)
> *China Daily*
> *China Exchange News*
> *Foreign Broadcast Information Service*
> *Guangming Ribao (Guangming Daily)*
> *Jingji Ribao (Economic Daily)*
> *Joint Publication Research Services*
> *Kexuexue yu Kexue Jishu Guanli (The Science of Science and S&T Management)*
> *Keyan Guanli (Scientific Research Management)*
> *Renmin Ribao (People's Daily)*
> *Summary of World Broadcasts: the Far East*

ii) Interviews

During a research visit to the PRC in January–February 1985, the following interviews were conducted:

A. *Visits to foreign embassies in Beijing.* All people interviewed were responsible for S&T relations.

Date	Country	Function of Interviewee
7 January	Denmark	Counsellor
	Sweden	Counsellor
8 January	Australia	First Secretary
	USA	S&T Officers
9 January	Hungary	First Secretary
	Belgium	First Secretary and Consul, Attaché for Development and Culture
10 January	Great Britain	Science Officer
	Canada	First Secretary
11 January	West Germany	Second Secretary

B. *Visits to Chinese institutions in Beijing*

Date	Institution	Name	Function
12 January	Chinese Academy of Social Sciences	Mr Ru Xin	Dep Director
		Mr Su Shaozhi	Prof of Grad School, Director of Inst of Marxism-Leninism-Mao Zedong Thought
		Ms Wu Lingmei	Head of European Division, Foreign Affairs Bureau
14 January	1) SSTC	Mr Mei Jinfang	Head of the West Europe Dept
	2) SSTC Scientific Management Dept	Mr Liu Jidong	Head of Scientific Management Dept
15 January	1) SSTC Policy Dept	Mr Xu Zhaoxiang	Head of Science Policy Dept
	2) China International Technology Development Corporation	Mr Zeng Ping	President
		Mr Ding Renjun	Vice-President
16 January	1) CAS	Mr Luo Wei	Dep Director of the Science Policy Study Office
	2) Chinese University of Science and Technology (Grad School)	Mr J F Tang	Vice-President of the Grad School, Prof of Particle Physics
17 January	1) Min of Educn, Science and Technology Office		
	2) Beijing University		Head of Foreign Affairs Bureau
18 January	1) Qinghua University	Mr Liu Caiquan	Head of Scientific Management Office, Prof of Inst of Thermal Energy, Dep Secretary-General of Engineering Thermophysics Soc of China
	2) Chinese Academy of Agricultural Sciences		
19 January	Chinese Academy of Medical Sciences	Mr Gu Fangzhou	Pres, Prof of Virology
		Mr Liu Shilian	Dean of Capital Medical College, Dir of Inst of Basic Medical Sciences of CAMS
		Mr Chen Miaolan	Dir of Dept of Scientific Research
		Mr Shen Ning	Dep Dir of the Dept of Foreign Affairs

C. Visits to Chinese institutions in Shanghai

21 January	Shanghai Science and Technology Commission	Mr Yan Chengzun	Dep Sec General
		Mr Zhang Qibiao	Dep Dir of the Comprehensive Planning Dept
		Mr Zhou Luping	Official of the Dept of International Co-operation
22 January	Shanghai Branch of CAS	Mr Huang Weiyuan	Pres
23 January	Fudan University		Foreign Affairs Dept Scientific Management Dept
24 January	Tongji University	Mr Zhu Zhaohong	Head of Science Policy & Management Office
25 January	Shanghai Branch of the China International Technology Dev Corp	Mr Fang Ruyu	Dir, Chairman of Board of Directors, Dir-Gen of the Shanghai Steel Technology Structures Corp
26 January	Shanghai Science	Mr Zhou Luping	Official of the Dept
27 January	& Technology Commission		of International Co-operation
28 January	Shanghai Science & Technology Commission	Mr Yan Chengzhun	Dep Sec Gen
		Mr Zhang Qibiao	Dep of the Comprehensive Planning Dept
		Mr Zhou Luping	Official of the Dept of International Co-operation

iii) Selected Bibliography

Anon 'Guanyu jiakuai gongye fazhan de ruogan wenti' xuanpi' ('Selected Criticisms of "Some Problems in Accelerating Industrial Development" '), *Xuexi yu Pipan*, no 4, 1976, pp 28-35.

Anon 'On the General Programme of Work for the Whole Party and the Whole Nation', in Chi Hsin, *The Case of the Gang of Four* (Hong Kong: Cosmos Books, 1977) pp 203-238.

Anon 'Some Problems in Accelerating Industrial Development', in Chi Hsin, Ibid, pp 239-272.

Anon 'On Some Problems in the Fields of Science and Technology, Selections from an Outline Report', in Chi Hsin, Ibid, pp 277-286.

Anon 'Peking University Professor Exposes Crimes of "Gang of Four" in Obstructing Research on Basic Theories of Natural Sciences', *Xinhua*, 15 January 1977.

Anon 'China's New Priorities for Technology Development', *The China Business Review*, May-June 1978, pp 3-8.

Anon 'Guofang kegongwei tizhi gaige bangongshi Bai junde, Zhu minjin tongzhi shuo: "Junshi jishu de keyan ye yao jinxing tizhi gaige" ' ('Comrades Bai Junde and Zhu Minjin of the National Defence Science and Industry Commission System Reform Office Say: "Scientific Research on Military Technology Also Should Undergo System Reform" '), *KXX*, no 5, 1985, pp 11-12.

Anon 'The State Science and Technology Commission Issues a Circular on Right Lines of Distinction for Determining the Direction of Reform and Against Unhealthy Tendencies', *Jishu Shichang* (*Technology Market*), 25 June 1985, p 1, translated in *JPRS – CST – 85 – 034*, pp 9-11.

Awe B 'Development of an Indigenous Capacity for Science and Technology – Discussion Report' in M Goldsmith and A King (eds), *Issues of Development: Towards a New Role for Science and Technology* (Oxford: Pergamon Press, 1979).

Bastid M 'Chinese Educational Policies in the 1980s and Economic Development', *China Quarterly*, no 98, 1984, pp 189-219.

Beijing Review 'Why a Part of the Working Class?', *BR*, no 13, 31 March 1980, pp 23-25.
'Scientific Council of the Chinese Academy of Sciences', *BR*, no 22, 1 June 1981, pp 6-7.
'Science Fund Established', *BR*, no 1, 4 January 1982, p 9.
'Exchanges with Foreign Countries', *BR*, no 1, 4 January 1982, p 29.
'Transform Science and Technology into Productive Forces', *BR*, no 16, 19 April 1982, p 26.
'Transferring Technology', *BR*, no 39, 27 September 1982, p 7.
'Making Science Serve the Economy', *BR*, no 10, 5 March 1984, p 11.
'Communist Party Increases Members', *BR*, no 29, 16 July 1984, pp 7-8.
'China Launches Patent Agency', *BR*, no 32, 6 August 1984, p 5.
'China's Countryside Under Reform', *BR*, no 33, 13 August 1984, pp 16-20.
'CPC to Recruit More Intellectuals', *BR*, no 49, 3 December 1984, pp 10-11.
'Technology Fair Gets Results', *BR*, no 25, 24 June 1985, p 9.
'Price Reform: 6 Months Later', *BR*, no 49, 9 December 1985, pp 6-7.

Berliner J *The Innovation Decision in Soviet Industry* (Cambridge, Mass: MIT Press, 1976).

Bernstein T P 'China in 1984: The Year of Hong Kong', *Asian Survey*, vol XXV, no 1, 1985, pp 33-50.

Bhargave B M 'Penetration of Science and Technology into Society: The Role of Basic Research', in M Gibbons and B M Udgaonkar (eds), *Science and Technology in the 1980s and Beyond* (London: Longman, 1984), pp 51-66.

Bian Diping 'Making the Best Use of China's Limited Scientific Talent', *Jishu Jingji yu Guanli Yanjiu*, no 1, 1985, translated in *JPRS – CST – 84 – 022*, p 4.

Bian Gu 'Wenhua kaoshi henyou biyao' ('Educational Examinations are an Absolute Necessity'), *RMRB*, 23 October 1977, p 1.

Cao Zhi 'Cong Zhanlüe gaolu kandai youxiu zhishi fenzi rudang wenti' ('Assess from the High Plain of Strategy the Question of Recruiting Party Members from Among Outstanding Intellectuals'), *Hongqi*, no 23, 1984, pp 16-18.

Central Committee of the CCP
'Communist Party of China Central Committee Circular on Holding National Science Conference', *PR*, no 40, 30 September 1977, pp 6-11.
'Communiqué of the Third Plenary Session of the 11th Central Committee of the Communist Party of China', *PR*, no 52, 29 December 1978, pp 6-16.

'Decision of the Central Committee of the Communist Party of China on Reform of the Economic Structure', *BR*, no 44, 29 October 1984, pp i-xvi.

'Zhonggongzhongyang guanyu kexue jishu tizhi gaige de jueding' ('Decision of the Central Committee of the Communist Party of China on the Reform of the Science and Technology Management System'), *RMRB*, 20 March 1985, pp 1, 3.

'Proposal of the Central Committee of the Communist Party of China for the Seventh Five Year Plan for National Economic and Social Development, September 23, 1985', *BR*, no 40, 7 October 1985, pp vi-xxiv.

Chen Chuansheng and Ma Aiye 'Shilun woguo de kexue shengchan lianheti' ('A Preliminary Discussion of Our Nation's Scientific Production Body'), *KXX*, no 3, 1984, pp 2-5.

Chen Xianhua 'Zhuajin jianli hangye kaifa zhongxin' ('Pay Close Attention to the Establishment of Technology Development Centres'), *KYGL*, no 1, 1984, pp 35-36.

Chen Yong 'Fund System will Promote China's Basic Science Development', *KXX*, no 3, 1985; translated in *JPRS – CST – 85 – 020*, pp 48-51.

Chen Yun 'Zai zhongguo gongchandang quanguo daibiao huiyishang de jianghua' ('Speech at the National Conference of the Communist Party of China'), *RMRB*, 24 September 1985, p 2.

Chen Zujia and Chen Dong 'Kexueyuan jijin kaishi fahui zuoyong' ('The Science Fund of the Chinese Academy of Sciences Has Begun to Play a Role'), *RMRB*, 12 January 1984, p 3.

Chi Hsin *The Case of the Gang of Four* (Hong Kong: Cosmos Books, 1977).

China Daily 'Universities Contribute to Economy', CD, 6 February 1984, p 1. 'New Rules Help Students Go Abroad', CD, 14 January 1985, p 3.

Chinese Academy of Sciences *The Chinese Academy of Sciences: A Brief Introduction* (Beijing: Chinese Academy of Sciences, 1981).

Cocks P N *Science Policy in the Soviet Union* (Washington, DC: Government Printing Office, 1980). *Coupling Science with Production: The Architecture of Linkage*, mimeograph, n p, n d.

Conroy R 'Recent Issues and Trends in Chinese Policy Towards Science and Technology', *The Australian Journal of Chinese Affairs*, no 6, 1981, pp 171-183. 'Technological Innovation in China's Recent Industrialisation', *China Quarterly*, no 97, 1984, pp 1-23. 'Technological Change and Industrial Development', in G Young (ed), *China: Dilemmas of Modernisation* (London: Croom Helm, 1985).

Cooper C (ed), *Science, Technology and Development* (London: Frank Cass, 1973). 'Science, Technology and Production in the Underdeveloped Countries: an Introduction', in C Cooper (ed), Ibid, pp 1-18.

Dai Beihua 'China Will Send More Students Overseas', *CD*, 30 November 1984, p 1.

Dai Guanqian 'Lun keji duiwu de "bumen jiegou" ' ('On the "Department Structure" of Scientific and Technical Ranks'), *KXX*, no 5, 1981, pp 39-41.

Dean G and Fingar T *Developments in PRC Science and Technology Policy October-December 1977*, United States-China Relations S&T Summary no 5, (Stanford), pp 1-28.

Deng Ruizeng 'Yao "yang ji chan dan" bu yao 'sha ji qu luan" ' ('We Should "Raise a Chicken to Lay Eggs", not "Kill a Chicken to Get Eggs" '), *GMRB*, 21 May 1984, p 2.

Deng Xiaoping 'Talk Given by Deng Xiaoping on Industrial Development', in Chi Hsin, op cit, pp 273-276.

'Comments by Deng Xiaoping on the Presentation of Hu Yaobang's Report', 26 September 1975, in Chi Hsin, op cit, pp 287-295.

'Speech at the Opening Ceremony of National Science Conference', *PR*, no 12, 24 March 1978, pp 9-18.

'Sixteenth January Report on the Current Situation', Cheng Ming, no 29, 1980, translated in *SWB:FE* 6363.

Dongbei Technical College 'Daxue keyan de fangxiang' ('The Direction for University Scientific Research'), *KXX*, no 2, 1984, pp 9-10.

Du Shunxing 'Kexue yanjiu danwei de jingji guanli' ('The Economic Management of Scientific Research Units'), *KYGL*, no 4, 1984, pp 73-76.

Fang Yi 'Fang yi tongzhi zai sijie zhengxie quanguo weiyuanhui qici kuoda huiyishang zuo de guanyu kexue he jiaoyu shiye qingkuang de baogao (tiyao)' ('Report on the State of Science and Education Delivered by Comrade Fang Yi at the Seventh Enlarged Meeting of the Standing Committee of the Chinese People's Political Consultative Conference (Excerpts)'), *RMRB*, 30 December 1977.

'On the Situation in China's Science and Education', *PR*, no 2, 13 January 1978, pp 15-19.

'Zai quanguo kexue daihuishang de baogao' ('Report to the National Science Conference'), *RMRB*, 29 March 1978, pp 1, 4.

'Address to the Fifth Session of the Scientific Council of the Chinese Academy of Sciences', *Xinhua* in Chinese, 5 January 1984; translated in *SWB:FE* 7541.

'Zai quanguo kexue jishu gongzuo huiyishang de kaimuci' ('Opening Address to the National Science and Technology Work Conference'), 2 March 1985, n p, pp 1-9.

Fudan University Science Department Mass Criticism Group 'Yifen fangeming de xiuzheng zhuyi tigang ping "kexueyuan gongzuo huibao tigang" de "pipan" ' ('A Counterrevolutionary Revisionist Outline, Reviewing the "Outline Report on the Work of the Academy of Sciences" "Criticisms" '), *RMRB*, 19 July 1976, p 1.

Gao Lu and Zheng Ge (Kao Lu and Cheng Ke) 'Comments on Teng Hsiao-p'ing's Economic Ideas of the Compradore Bourgeoisie', *PR*, no 35, 27 August 1976, pp 6-9.

Gao Yulong 'Guanyu heli rencai liudong de jige wenti' ('Concerning Several Problems with the Rational Movement of Talent'), *KXX*, no 7, 1983.

Gibbons M and Udgaonkar B M (eds), *Science and Technology in the 1980s and Beyond* (London: Longman, 1984).

Goldman M 'Teng Hsiao-p'ing and the Debate over Science and Technology', *Contemporary China*, vol 2, no 4, 1978, pp 46-69.

Goldsmith M and King A (eds), *Issues of Development: Towards a New Role for Science and Technology* (Oxford: Pergamon Press, 1979).

Gu Wenxing 'Shanghai keji tizhi gaige de wuxiang cuoshi' ('Five Measures for Reforming Shanghai's Science and Technology System'), *KXX*, no 4, 1985, pp 16-17.

Guangming Daily Commentator 'Daxue gao keyan dayou kewei' ('There is Much to be Gained from Universities Engaging in Research'), *GMRB*, 23 March 1978, p 1.

'Yao jiji tuiguang zhuzhoushi dianzisuo de gaige jingyan' ('It is Necessary to Actively Popularise the Experience of the Zhuzhou Electronics Research Institute in Carrying out Reform'), *GMRB*, 24 May 1984, p 1.

Guangming Daily 'Woguo keji tizhi gaige chuangzaole jiaogao de jingji xiaoyi' ('The Reform of Our Nation's Science and Technology System has Produced Better Economic Results'), *GMRB*, 24 January 1984, p 1.

'Shanghai chengli keji rencai dkaifa yinhang' ('Shanghai Establishes a Scientific and Technical Talent Development Bank'), *GMRB*, 31 August 1984, p 1.

Hu Mingzheng 'Patent Law Encourages Chinese and Foreign Investors', *BR*, no 15, 9 April 1984, pp 23-25.

Hu Ping 'Education and Development of S&T Personnel', in Committee on Scholarly Communication with the People's Republic of China, *US-China Conference on Science Policy* (Washington, DC: National Academy Press, 1985), pp 282-291.

Hu Xian 'Jijinzhi de shixing shi dui keji tizhi de yixiang zhongyao gaige' ('Trial Implementation of Fund Systems is an Important Reform of S&T Systems'), *KXX*, no 5, 1985, pp 43-45.

Hu Yaobang 'Speech at the Second Congress of the Chinese Scientific and Technical Association (Excerpts)', *BR*, no 15, 14 April 1980, pp 13-16.

'Create a New Situation in all Fields of Socialist Modernisation', in *The Twelfth National Congress of the CPC* (Beijing: Foreign Languages Press, 1982), pp 7-86.

Hua Guofeng 'Unite and Strive to Build a Modern Powerful Socialist Country!', in *Documents of the First Session of the Fifth National People's Congress of the People's Republic of China* (Beijing: Foreign Languages Press, 1978), pp 1-118.

'Raise the Scientific and Culc and Cultural Level of the Entire Chinese Nation', *PR*, no 13, 31 March 1978, pp 6-14.

'Speech at the Third Session of the Fifth National People's Congress', in *Main Documents of the Third Session of the Fifth National People's Congress of the People's Republic of China* (Beijing: Foreign Languages Press, 1980), pp 143-201.

Huang Wei and Zhang Jiexu 'Woguo keji duiwu de jiegou ji dangqian de tiaozheng cuoshi' ('The Structure of Our Nation's Science and Technology Ranks and Current Measures for Readjustment'), *KXX*, no 4, 1982, pp 3-6.

Ishihara K 'The Price Problem and Economic Reform', China Newsletter, no 46, 1983, pp 2-7.

Ji Dong 'Keyan tizhi gaige de guanjian he tupo kou chuyi' ('My Humble Opinion on the Key to and Breakthrough in the Reform of the Scientific and Technological Research System'), *KXX*, no 3, 1985, pp 19-22.

Jin Baohua 'Scientific Research Given Tasks in Economy', *CD*, 6 January 1984, p 1.

Kang Li and Yan Feng ' "Huibao tigang" chulong de qianqian houhou' ('The Ins and Outs of the Appearance of the "Outline Report" '), *Xuexi yu Pipan*, no 4, 1976, pp 20-27.

Kautsky J *The Political Consequences of Modernisation* (New York: Wiley, 1971).

King A and Lemma A 'Science and Technology for Development', in M Goldsmith and A King (eds), op cit.

Kneen P *Soviet Scientists and the State* (Basingstoke: Macmillan Press, 1984).

Korzec M and Saich T *The Chinese Economy: New Light on Old Questions*, Working Paper no 28 (Amsterdam, University of Amsterdam, 1983), pp 1-20.

Kühner H 'Between Autonomy and Planning: The Chinese Academy of Sciences in Transition', *Minerva*, vol 22, no 1, 1984, pp 13-44.

Lederman L 'Science and Technology in Europe: a Survey', *Science and Public Policy*, vol 12, no 3, 1985, pp 131-143.

Li Guogang and Fan Qiongying 'Shixing youchang keyan hetongzhi dashi suoqu' ('Implementing Paid Contracts for Scientific Research is the Irresistible General Trend'), *RMRB*, 13 December 1984, p 5.

Li Minquan 'Shilun hangye yanjiusuo tiaozheng chongshi wei hangye jishu kaifa zhongxin' ('A Discussion on Transforming Research Institutes of Various Trades into Technology Development Centres Through Readjustment and Improvement'), *KYGL*, no 1, 1984, pp 42-46, 50.

Li Xing 'Science Research Funding Overhauled', *CD*, 7 January 1985, p 1.

'Tie Science to Nation's Needs, Says Hu Yaobang', *CD*, 14 January 1985, p 1.

Li Xue 'How Many PRC Students are Studying Abroad?', *Banyuetan*, 25 August 1985, p 39, translated in *JPRS – CST – 85 – 037*, p 4.

Li Yongzeng 'Research System Undergoing Reforms', *BR* no 12, 25 March 1985, pp 18-20.

Liang Xiao 'Yangwu yundong yu yangnu zhixue' ('The Yangwu Movement and Slavish Compradore Philosophy'), *Lishi Yanjiu*, no 5, 1975, pp 68-74.

Liu Ying 'Fazhan woguo kexue jishu gongzuo de jige wenti' ('Some Questions Concerning Developing Our Nation's Scientific and Technological Work'), *RMRB* 6 June 1982, p 3.

Lu Jiaxi 'Guanyu dangqian keyan guanli de jige wenti' ('Concerning Several Problems of Current Scientific Research Management'), *KYGL*, no 3, 1982, pp 1-6.

'Nuli kaichuang kexue gongzuo de xin jumian' ('Arduously Start the New Phase of Scientific Work'), *RMRB*, 23 September 1982, p 3.

Lu Jianming 'Shanghaishi jin yibu gaige keji tizhi' 'Shanghai Municipality Further Develops the Reform of the Science and Technology System'), *GMRB*, 4 September 1984, p 1.

Ma Hong and Sun Shangqing (eds), *Zhongguo jingji jiegou wenti yanjiu* (*Research on the Problems of China's Economic Structure*), vols 1 and 2 (Beijing: Renmin chubanshe, 1981).

Ma Lili 'The Concept of China's Scientific Research System – a Visit to Wu Mingyu, Vice-Minister of the SSTC', *Gaige Zhisheng* (*The Voice of Reform*), no 4, 1985, p 31; translated in *JPRS – CST – 85 – 028*, pp 1-3.

Ma Longxiang 'Ying shixing keyan he gaodeng jiaoyu tongyi de guanli tizhi' ('A Unified Management System Should be Adopted for Scientific Research and Higher Education'), *GMRB*, 21 June 1984, p 2.

Ma Xiliang 'Lun keji shichang de xingqi he fazhan' ('S&T Markets Play a Vital Role in Scientific Progress and Prosperity'), *KXX*, no 1, 1985, pp 2-5.

Marx K *Capital*, vol 1, (Harmondsworth: Penguin Books, 1976).

Mass Criticism Group of Beijing and Qinghua Universities 'A Confession of Attempts of Reversal of Verdicts and Restoration – Criticising an Article Concocted at Teng Hsiao-p'ing's Bidding', *PR*, no 28, 9 July 1976, pp 9-12.

Men Jinru 'Gaohao diqu jishu xiezuo, tuidong jishu yanjiu' ('Do a Good Job in Technical Co-operation Between Localities, Promote Technological Research'), *RMRB*, 15 October 1982, p 2.

Ministry of Education *Zhongguo jiaoyu chengjiu: tongji ziliao 1949-1983* (*Achievement of Education: Statistical Documentation 1949-1983*) (Beijing: Renmin jiaoyu chubanshe, 1985).

Mu Gongqian 'Gaige guojia dui yanjiusuo guanli de sanxiang cuoshi' ('Three Measures to Reform State Management of Research Institutes'), *GMRB*, 7 May 1984, p 1.

Na Baokui 'Guanyu keyan tizhi de jidian yijian' ('Some Opinions on the Scientific Research System'), *KYGL*, no 4, 1982, pp 50-52.

'Keyan danwei de zerenzhi wenti' ('The Question of a Responsibility System in Scientific Research Units'), *KYGL*, no 1, 1984, pp 69-71.

Nanhua Power Machinery Research Department 'Nuli zuohao "sange zhuanyi", dali cujin minpin keyan de fazhan' ('Strenuously Carry Out the "Three Transitions" Well and Promote the Development of Scientific Research on Civilian Products in a Big Way'), *KYGL*, no 3, 1982, pp 61-66.

National Defence Science, Technology and Industry Commission Comprehensive Planning Department 'Jungong jishu xiang minyong zhuanyi shi woguo jishu shichang de zhongyao zucheng bufen' ('The Transfer of Military Technology to Civilian Use is an Important Part of Organising Our Nation's Technology Market'), *National Science and Technology Work Conference Exchange Material* Number 6, pp 1-9.

Office of the Science and Technology Leading Group of the State Council 'Guanyu gaige keji bokuan guanli banfa de zanxing guiding' ('Temporary Regulations Concerning the Reform of the Administrative Method for Science and Technology Allocations'), *National Science and Technology Work Conference Consultation Document* Number 1, pp 1-4.

'Guanyu jiji kaizhan yinhang keji xindai de jueding' ('Decision Concerning Enthusiastically Developing Bank Science and Technology Credit'), *National Science and Technology Work Conference Consultation Document* Number 2, pp 1-4.

'Guanyu gaige keji renyuan guanli zhidu, cujin keji renyuan heli liudong de jixiang guiding' ('Several Regulations Concerning the Reform of the Scientific and Technical Personnel System and the Promotion of the Rational Flow of S&T Personnel'), *National Science and Technology Work Conference Consultation Document* Number 5, pp 1-6.

Office of the Scientific Fund Committee of the Chinese Academy of Sciences 'Jichuxing yanjiu shixing jijinzhi de qingkuang huibao' ('Report on the Conditions of Implementing a Fund System for Basic Research'), *National Science and Technology Work Conference Exchange Materials* Number 6, pp 1-11.

Organisation Department of the Central Committee, et al 'Guanyu jixu fahui tuilixiu zhishi fenzi zuoyong de guiding' ('Regulations Concerning Continuing to Give Play to the Role of Retired Intellectuals'), *National Science and Technology Work Conference Discussion Document* Number 6, pp 1-4.

Orleans L *The Training and Utilisation of Scientific and Engineering Manpower in the People's Republic of China* (Washington, DC: US Government Printing Office, 1983), pp 1-71.

People's Daily Editorial 'Tongxin tongde, zaijie zaili, wending wujia' ('With One Heart and Mind, Make Persistent Efforts, Stabilise Commodity Prices'), *RMRB*, 10 January 1981, p 1.

People's Daily 'Wei quanmin kaichuang shehui zhuyi xiandaihua jianshe xin jumian gongxian liliang, zhongguo kexie bufen quanguo weiyuan xuexi dang de shi'er da wenjian faxin zhaideng' ('Devote Strength to Creating a New Situation in the Construction of Socialist Modernisation, Excerpts from Speeches given by Members of the Chinese Association for Science and Technology on Studying the Documents of the Twelfth Party Congress'), *RMRB*, 5 October 1982, p 3.

'Zhongguo kexueyuan chengli keji zixun kaifa fuwubu' ('The Chinese Academy of Sciences Establishes a Scientific and Technological Consultancy and Development Service Department'), *RMRB*, 8 May 1983, p 3.

'Zhongguo kexueyuan bochu jingfei ze you fuchi zhongqingnian keji gugan' ('The Chinese Academy of Sciences Allocates Funds for Supporting Young and Middle Aged Scientific and Technical Personnel'), *RMRB*, 25 August 1983, p 3.

'Shanghai bumen danwei shixing keji renyuan pinyongzhi. Zunao rencai jiaoliao jiang shou xingzheng ganyu' ('Some Units in Shanghai Departments Try Out the System for Hiring S&T Personnel. Interference with the Flow of Personnel will be Dealt with Through Administrative Intervention'), *RMRB*, 31 July 1984, p 3.

Qinghua University 'Guangfan kaizhan keji xiezuo, wei zhenxing jingji duo zuo gongxian' ('Extensively Develop Scientific and Technical Co-operation, Make a Greater Contribution to Upgrading of the Economy'), *KXX*, no 2, 1984, pp 5-6.

Rubin K 'Spotlight on Chinese Students Returned from Abroad', *CEN*, no 2, 1985, pp 34-35.

Saich T *China: Politics and Government* (Houndsmill: Macmillan Press, 1981).

'New Directions in Politics and Government' in J Gray and G White (eds), *China's New Development Strategy* (London: Academic Press, 1982), pp 19-36.

'Constitution of the People's Republic of China', translation and annotation, *Review of Socialist Law*, vol 9, no 2, 1983, pp 183-208.

The Chinese Communist Party: The Search for a Suitable Form, Working Paper no 31 (Amsterdam: University of Amsterdam, 1983), pp 1-23.

'Party and State Reforms in the People's Republic of China', *Third World Quarterly*, vol 5, no 3, 1983, pp 627-640.

'The Constitution (Statutes) of the Communist Party of China', translation and introduction in W B Simon and S White (eds), The *Party Statutes of the Communist World* (The Hague: Martinus Nijhoff, 1984), pp 85-113.

'Party Consolidation and Spiritual Pollution in the People's Republic of China', *Communist Affairs: Documents and Analysis*, vol 3, no 3, 1984, pp 283-290.

The Evolution of Science and Technology Policy in the People's Republic of China, Amsterdam Asia Studies no 55 (Amsterdam, University of Amsterdam, 1985), pp 1-74.

'Linking Research to the Productive Sector: Reforms of the Civilian Science and Technology System in Post-Mao China', *Development and Change*, vol 17, no 1, 1986, pp 3-33.

Shanghai Branch of the Chinese Academy of Sciences 'Ruiyi gaige wenbu qianjin' ('Keenly Desire Reform, Steadily Advance'), *National Science and Technology Work Conference Exchange Materials* Number 9, pp 1-13.

Shanghai Jiaotong University Party Committee Office (Compilers) 'Shanghai jiaotong daxue quanli gaige chutan' ('First Explorations of Reform of Management at Shanghai's Jiaotong University') (Shanghai: Jiaotong daxue chubanshe, 1984).

Shen Xiaodan 'Cong fazhan jingjixue jiaodao yanjiu woguo zhili yinjin de fangzhen' ('A Study of Our Nation's Policy of Importing Brainpower Viewed from the Angle of Economic Development'), *KXX*, no 11, 1984, pp 23-26.

Sigurdson J *Technology and Science in the People's Republic of China* (Oxford: Pergamon Press, 1980).

Simon D F 'Rethinking R and D', *The China Business Review*, July-August 1983, pp 25-27.

'Chinese-Style S&T Modernisation: A Comparison of PRC and Taiwan Approaches', *Studies in Comparative Communism*, vol xvii, no 2, 1984, pp 87-109.

'Science and Technology Reforms', *The China Business Review*, March-April 1985, pp 32-35.

State Council *The Sixth Five Year Plan of the People's Republic of China for Economic and Social Development* (1981-1985) (Beijing: Foreign Languages Press, 1984).

'Zhonghua renmin gongheguo xuewei tiaoli' ('Regulations of the People's Republic of China for Academic Degrees'), *RMRB*, 14 February 1985, p 2.

'Temporary Regulations on Technology Transfers Issued by the State Council (10 January 1985)', *JPRS – CST* – 85-012, 23 April 1985, pp 11-13.

State Science and Technology Commission 'Outline Report on Policy Concerning the Development of Our National Science and Technology by the State Science and Technology Commission', *Issues and Studies*, vol xviii, no 5, May 1982, pp 88-101.

'Quanguo keji gongzuo huiyi jianbao' ('Bulletin of the National Science and Technology Work Conference'), 2 March 1985, n p, pp 1-4.

State Statistical Bureau *Zhongguo tongji nianjian 1983* (Statistical Yearbook of China 1983) (Beijing: Zhongguo tongji chubanshe, 1983).

Zhongguo tongji nianjian 1984 (*Statistical Yearbook of China 1984*) (Beijing: Zhongguo tongji chubanshe, 1984).

'Communiqué on Fulfilment of China's 1983 Economic Plan', *BR*, no 20, 14 May 1984, pp i-xi.

China: A Statistics Survey in 1985 (Beijing: New World Press, 1985).

'Communiqué on Fulfilment of China's 1984 Economic and Social Development Plan', *BR* no 12, 25 March 1985, pp i-viii.

Stewart F 'Arguments for the Generation of Technology by LDCs', The Annals, 458, pp 97-109.

Stewart F and James J (eds), *The Economics of New Technology in Developing Countries* (London: Frances Pinter, 1982).

Sun Guangyun 'Shitan danchun junyong jishu xiang junmin jianyong de zhuanyi' ('Preliminary Discussion of Transferring Military Technology to Both Military and Civilian Use'), *KYGL*, no 4, 1982, pp 14-19.

Sun Jian and Zhu Weiqun 'Dangqian luoshi zhishi fenzi zhengce qingkuang jiujing ruhe? Jiangsusheng de diaocha biaoming: "zuo" de yingxiang wangu, wenti yuanwei jiejue' ('What is the Current Situation in Implementing Policies on Intellectuals? An Investigation of Jiangsu Province Shows that "Leftist" Influences Stubbornly Persist and the Problem is Far from a Solution'), *RMRB*, 8 July. p 3.

Suttmeier R P 'Chinese Scientific Societies and Chinese Scientific Development', *Developing Economies*, vol 11, no 2, 1973, pp 146-163.

Science, Technology and China's Drive for Modernisation (Stanford: Hoover Institution Press, 1980).

Tan Wen 'Deng xiaoping xuanyang "bai zhuan" juxin hezai?' ('What is Deng Xiaoping up to in Propagating "White Expertise"?'), *RMRB*, 6 June 1976, p 1.

Tao Kai and Zeng Qing 'Guanyu keji rencai de dingxiang liudong wenti' ('Concerning the Problem of the Directional Flow of Scientific and Technical Personnel'), *GMRB*, 12 July 1982, p 4.

Tong Dalin and Hu Ping 'Science and Technology', in Yu Guangyuan (ed), *China's Socialist Modernisation* (Beijing: Foreign Languages Press, 1984), pp 601-652.

Tow W T 'Science and Technology in China's Defense', *Problems of Communism*, July-August 1985, pp 15-31.

Volti R 'Technology and Polity: The Dynamics of Managed Change', *Studies in Comparative Communism*, vol xv, nos 1 and 2, pp 71-94.

Wan Li 'Speech to the National Education Conference', 17 May 1985, translated in *SWB:FE* 7968.

Wang Bingqian 'Report on Financial Work', *BR*, no 39, 29 September 1980, pp 11-22.
'Report on the Final State Accounts for 1980 and Implementation of the Financial Estimates for 1981', *BR*, no 2, 11 January 1982, pp 14-22.
'Report on the Implementation of the State Budget for 1982 and the Draft State Budget for 1983', in *Fifth Session of the Fifth National People's Congress* (Beijing: Foreign Languages Press, 1983), pp 187-214.
'Report on the Final State Accounts of 1982', in *The First Session of the Sixth National People's Congress* (Beijing: Foreign Languages Press, 1983), pp 91-104.
'Report on the Final State Accounts for 1983 and the Draft State Budget for 1984', in *The Second Session of the Sixth National People's Congress* (Beijing: Foreign Languages Press, 1984), pp 81-102.

Wang Haijiong 'China's Prospects for the Year 2000', *BR*, no 44, 4 November 1985, pp 18-20.

Wang Huangong 'Woguo keyan tizhi shang de jige wenti' ('Some Problems Concerning Our Nation's Scientific Research System'), *GMRB*, 22 August 1980, p 4.

Wang Kang 'Shixing jihua zhidaocia de keji rencai hetong pinrenzhi' ('Implementing the Contractual System for Hiring Scientific and Technical Personnel Under Planned Guidance'), *RMRB*, 31 July 1984, p 3.

Wang Minxi 'Shilun zhongguo kexueyuan de gaige qianjing' ('The Prospects for Reforms in the Chinese Academy of Sciences'), *KYGL*, no 2, 1985, pp 1-4, 16.

Wang Sanhou 'Xiwang jianli keji kaifa yinhang' ('In Hope of the Establishment of Science and Technology Development Banks'), *GMRB*, 7 May 1984, p 1.

Wang Yibing 'Tasks Set for Economic Reform', *BR*, no 51, 23 December 1985, p 22.

Wang Yingluo 'Woguo keji tizhi gaige zhong de jige zhanlüe wenti' ('Some Strategic Questions in China's S&T Reforms'), *KXX*, no 6, 1985, pp 2-4.

White G 'Revolutionary Socialist Development in the Third World: An Overview', in G White, R Murray and C White (eds), Revolutionary Socialist Development in the Third World (Brighton: Wheatsheaf Books, 1983), pp 1-34.

Workers Theoretical Group of the Shanghai Watch Components Factory 'Yige fubi daotui de tiaoli – "guanyu jiakuai gongye fazhan de ruogan wenti" pipan' ('A Restorationist Retrogressive Regulation – Criticism of "Some Problems in Accelerating Industrial Development" '), *Hongqi*, no 7, 1976, pp 31-35.

World Bank *China's Socialist Economic Development, vol 3. The Social Sectors Population, Health, Nutrition and Education* (Washington, DC: The World Bank, 1983).
China: Long-Term Issues and Options, Annex A: Issues and Prospects in Education (Washington, DC: The World Bank, 1985).

Wu Shimin 'Lüelan hangye jishu kaifa zhongxin' ('A Brief Discussion of Technology Development Centres for Various Trades'), *KYGL*, no 1, 1984, pp 40-41, 39.

Wu Tingman and Jin Xiaoyin 'Jiehe bensuo tedian nuli wei difang de jingji jianshe fuwu' ('Serve Local Economic Construction by Linking up Our Institutes' Characteristics'), *KYGL*, no 3, 1982, pp 35-37, 55.

Wu Xinghua 'Hunan geji renmin yinhang jiji fafang keji daikuan' ('Hunan's People's Banks at Various Levels Positive About Granting Science and Technology Credits'), *RMRB*, 19 October 1984, p 3.

Xia Yulong and Liu Ji 'It is Necessary to Eliminate Erroneous "Leftist" Influence on the Science and Technlogy Front', *Jiefang Ribao*, 2 June 1981; translated in *FBIS-China-81-112*, 11 June 1981, pp K8-K12.

Xiang Qun 'Zhongshi kexue puji gongzuo' ('Attach Importance to Popularising Science'), *Hongqi*, no 11, 1975, pp 68-72.
'Dazhou fan fubi de qihao gao fubi – pipan "sirenbang" dui "lun zonggang" de "pipan" ' ('Flaunting the Banner of Opposing Restoration to Engage in Restoration – Criticise the "Gang of Four's" "Criticism" of "On the General Programme" '), *RMRB*, 7 July, p 1.

Xiao Guangen 'Shanghai chengli rencai yinhang dali cujin rencai liutong' ('Shanghai Establishes a Talent Bank to Vigorously Promote the Circulation of Personnel'), *RMRB*, 28 January 1985, p 1.
'Dui keji renyuan cizhi yao zuo fenxi' ('We Should Analyse the Resignation of Scientific and Technical Personnel'), *RMRB*, 25 May 1985, p 1.

Xiao Liang 'Lun jishu shangpinhua de jige lilun wenti' ('On Several Theoretical Problems Concerning the Commercialisation of Technology'), *GMRB*, 7 April 1984, p 4.

Xie Shaoming 'Shixing youchang hetongzhi' ('Implement the Paid Contract system'), *GMRB*, 22 October 1984, p 2.

Xie Ze 'Cujin jishu jinbu de yitiao zongyao tujing – guofang kegong wei yu tianjinshi jingji jishu hezuo de qishi' ('An Important Channel for Accelerating Technological Advance – Learn from the Economic and Technological Co-operation Between the National Defence Science, Technology and Industry Commission with Tianjin Municipality'), *KXX*, no 7, 1984, pp 14-17.

Xu Qianwei 'Shitan keyan tizhi gaige' ('A Preliminary Discussion of the Reform of the Scientific Research System'), *KYGL*, no 1, 1984, pp 30-34.
'Tan keyan jigou de zhengdun yu gaige' ('Discussion of the Adjustment and Reform of Scientific Research Organs'), *KXX*, no 7, 1984, pp 27-29.

Yan Zheng 'Daxue xinsheng wei shenmo bu shiying daxue jiaoyu' ('Why Don't New University Students Adapt to University Education?'), *GMRB*, 14 January 1983, p 2.

Yang Peiqing 'Jingji tizhi he keji jinbu' ('Economic Reform and Scientific and Technological Progress'), *KXX*, no 1, 1985, p 13.

Yang Peiqing and Liu Ji 'The Changing Understanding and Management of Science in China', Science and Public Policy, vol 12, no 5, pp 241-252.

Yang Weizhe 'Improving Science and Technology Capability: Some Chinese Impressions', in R Lalkaka and Wu Mingyu (eds) *Managing Science and Technology Acquisition: Strategies for China in a Changing World* (Dublin: Tycooly International Publishers Ltd, 1984).

Yang Weizhe and Gan Shijun 'Erlinglinglingnian zhongguo de kexue jishu' ('China's Science and Technology in the Year 2000'), *Jingji Ribao*, 11 November 1985, p 4.

Yellow Crane Centre *A Brief Introduction to China's Yellow Crane Associated Development Centre for Education, Science and Technology* (Wuhan, 1985), pp 1-10.

Young G (ed), *China: Dilemmas of Modernisation* (London: Croom Helm, 1985).

Yu Hongjun, Wang Zonglin and Cheng Hengmo 'Kexue jishu yu jingji jiegou' in Ma Hong and Sun Shangqing, (eds) *Zhongguo jingji jiegou wenti yanjiu* (*Research on the Problems of China's Economic Structure*), vol 1 (Beijing: Renmin chubanshe, 1981), pp 601-652.

Yu Ren 'Yitiao xinluzi' ('A New Approach'), *KXX*, no 2, 1984, pp 7-9.

Zeng Decong 'Gaodeng xuexiao keyan guanlizhong de jige lilun wenti' ('Some Theoretical Problems in the Management of Scientific Research in Institutions of Higher Learning'), *KYGL*, no 1, 1984, pp 56-60.

Zhang Binglu and Zhang Yifu 'Jiang xiaolu, qiu xiaoyi, yan zeren – shanghai jiaotong daxue keyan guanli gaige diaocha zhisan' ('Stress Efficiency, Seek Benefits, Pay Attention to Responsibilities – Part Three of a Survey of Reforms of Scientific Administration at Shanghai's Jiaotong University'), *GMRB*, 19 July 1984, p 2.

Zhang Jingfu 'Report on the Final State Accounts for 1978 and the Draft State Budget for 1979', *BR*, no 29, 20 July 1979, pp 17-23.

Zhang Penghui and Xiao Zuliang 'Shixing nongye shengchan zerenzhi hou keji gongzuo shang de jige wenti' ('Several Problems in Scientific and Technical Work After Implementation of the Responsibility System in Agricultural Production'), *KYGL*, no 4, 1982, pp 59-62.

Zhang Wen 'Social Sciences: A Hundred Schools of Thought Contend', *BR*, no 14, 6 April 1979, pp 9-10.

Zhao Ziyang 'A Strategic Question on Invigorating the Economy', *BR*, no 46, 15 November 1982, pp 13-20.

'Report on the Sixth Five Year Plan', *BR*, no 51, 20 December 1982, pp 10-20.

'Report on the Work of the Government (Delivered at the Second Session of the Sixth National People's Congress on May 15, 1984', *BR*, no 24, 11 June 1984, pp i-xvi.

'Gaige keji tizhi, tuidong keji he jingji, shehui xietiao' ('Reform the Science and Technology System, Promote the Co-ordination of Science and Technology with the Economy'), *RMRB*, 21 March 1985, pp 1, 3.

Zheng Haining 'Xueshu yanjiu "jinqin fanzhi" nianqing housheng nan yu "bajian" ' (' "Inbreeding" in Scholarly Research Hinders Young People "Excelling" ') *GMRB*, 21 December 1984, p.1.

'Woguo jiang shiban boshi hou keyan liudongzhan' ('Our Nation Will Experiment with the Setting-up of Mobile Scientific Research Centres'), *GMRB*, 11 July 1985, p 1.

Zhou Enlai 'Report on the Work of the Government, January 13, 1975', in *Documents of the First Session of the Fourth National People's Congress of the People's Republic of China* (Beijing: Foreign Languages Press, 1975), pp 45-66.

Zhou Jin 'Housing China's 900 Million People', *BR*, no 48, 30 November 1979, pp 17-27.

Zhou Peiyuan 'Make Concerted All-Out Efforts, Strive to Modernise China's Science and Technology', 15 March 1980; translated in *SWB:FE* 6387.

'Tantan "san ke" de fengong yu xiezuo' ('On the Division of Labour and Co-operation Between the "Three Scientific Organisations" '), *RMRB*, 28 January 1985, p 3.

Zhu Chuanbo 'Zenyang ba yanjiusuo gaohuo' ('How to Make Research Institutes Lively'), *KXX*, no 6, 1985, pp 17-18.

Zhu Shu 'Mobilise the "Remaining Enthusiasm" of Retired Scientific and Technical Personnel to Serve Construction of the Four Modernisations', *Yancheng Wanbao*, 25 January 1984; translated in *JPRS- CST – 84 – 031*, p 43.

Zhu Ximin 'Nongye keji renyuan guanli chutan' ('A Preliminary Study of the Management of Agricultural Scientific and Technical Personnel'), *KYGL*, no 1, 1982, pp 27-30.

INDEX

STUDIES ON EAST ASIA

Editorial Board

James Cotton, University of Newcastle
Gordon Daniels, University of Sheffield
John Gardner, University of Manchester
David S G Goodman, University of Newcastle
Ian Neary, University of Newcastle
Don Starr, University of Durham